PELICAN BOOKS

COMMUNITIES IN BRITAIN

Ronald Frankenberg was born in London and
attended Highgate School until 1947. After the
war he went to Caius College, Cambridge, in-
tending to go on to a London Medical School, but
was diverted into social anthropology. He later
obtained a Ph.D. at Manchester, working on
African states and Welsh villages, and spent two
years at Cardiff University where he studied the
impact of a new steel works on social life. After four
years as Education Officer to the South Wales
Miners' Union he returned in 1960 to Manchester,
where he lectured in sociology. From 1966 until
December 1968 he was first Professor of Sociology
and also Dean of Humanities at the New University
of Zambia in Central Africa. In January 1969 he
returned to England to become the first Professor
of Sociology at the University of Keele. Ronald
Frankenberg has also written *Village on the Border*,
a book about North Wales.

D1350413

RONALD FRANKENBERG

COMMUNITIES IN
BRITAIN

*Social Life in Town
and Country*

PENGUIN BOOKS

Penguin Books Ltd, Harmondsworth, Middlesex, England
Penguin Books Inc., 7110 Ambassador Road, Baltimore, Maryland 21207 U.S.A.
Penguin Books Australia Ltd, Ringwood, Victoria, Australia

—

First published 1966
Reprinted 1967
Reprinted with revisions 1969
Reprinted 1970

—

Copyright © Ronald Frankenberg, 1965, 1969

—

Made and printed in Great Britain
by Richard Clay (The Chaucer Press) Ltd,
Bungay, Suffolk
Set in Monotype Baskerville

CONTENTS

ACKNOWLEDGEMENTS

I wish to thank the following for their courtesy in allowing me to use material from their publications: The Clarendon Press and the authors for passages from *Small Town Politics* by A. H. Birch, and for passages and Figures 3–9 from *Tradition and Change: A Study of Banbury* by Margaret Stacey; Isaac Pitman & Sons Limited and the author for Figure 10 from *Intelligent Machines* by D. A. Bell; Eyre & Spottiswoode (Publishers) Ltd and the authors for passages from *Coal is Our Life* by M. Dennis, F. M. Henriques and C. Slaughter; Routledge & Kegan Paul Ltd and the authors for passages from *The Family Life of Old People* by Peter Townsend, *The Sociology of an English Village: Gosforth* by W. M. Williams, and *Family and Kinship in East London* by M. Young and P. Willmott; Chapman & Hall Ltd and the author for passages from *On Human Communication* by Colin Cherry; Tavistock Publications and the author for passages from *Family and Social Network* by Elizabeth Bott; University of Wales Press and the author for passages from *Life in a Welsh Countryside* by Alwyn D. Rees; Cohen & West for material and Figures 1–2 from my own *Village on the Border*; and Contact Books, P. S. King and the author for passages from *Britain between East and West* and *Watling* by Ruth Glass.

PREFACE

THIS book, like most social phenomena, has complex origins. It is partly in response to the challenge issued by a leading sociologist attending a conference of the Association of Social Anthropologists. Partly it was inspired by a reading of Maurice Stein's *Eclipse of Community*. Dr Jack Goody also provided stimulus at various points on the way.

I would like to thank Professor Max Gluckman whose influence on this book will be very apparent and who read the whole manuscript in long hand and made many helpful comments. I am also especially grateful to Mr Colin Lacey, Dr Joyce Leeson, and Dr V. G. Pons who read and commented on each chapter as it was written.

When it was nearly completed I presumed (without invitation) to send copies to Dr D. Allcorn, Professor C. M. Arensberg, Professor A. H. Birch, Professor J. A. Barnes, Dr Elisabeth Bott, Dr John Evans, Dr A. H. Halsey, Mr Angus Hone, Dr Albert Kushlick, Dr J. B. Loudon, Professor R. K. Merton, Professor D. M. Mackay, Dr Robin Mackenzie, Dr Ray Pahl, Dr Emrys Peters, Mr Alwyn D. Rees, Professor Aidan Southall, Mrs Margaret Stacey, Mr Mel Thomas, Dr C. Turner, Professor W. Watson, Professor W. M. Williams and Mr Peter Willmott. I am grateful for all their comments and apologize where I have failed to accept them. Their mention here is not intended even as a *nihil obstat* let alone an *imprimatur* but as a genuine expression of thanks.

I wish further to express appreciation to fellow members of the Manchester seminar in social anthropology and sociology for continuous and sustaining intellectual stimulation.

Finally the book would have been different and worse without the patient editing and forbearance of Mrs Venetia Pollock.

1965   RONALD FRANKENBERG

INTRODUCTION

THIS is a book about Britain and British communities. Four-fifths of the population of Britain live in towns with a population of over fifty thousand. A half of these live in the six great conurbations. This book is mainly about the social behaviour of the other fifth. Why is this minority worth focusing on?

Firstly, there is a practical reason. Writers and politicians from Feargus O'Connor, the Chartist, to Chesterton and Belloc have sought to lead us back to the countryside. The desire for a semi-detached in its own garden, and the summer weekend trek out of the towns are part of the national stereotype of ourselves as longing to get back to the country life. What has been lost by urbanization and what gained?

A second practical reason is that there exists a number of studies of British communities made mainly since 1945 which up to the present have been little used for the development of sociological theory (see, however, Plowman, 1962 and Klein, 1965).* For reasons of convenience, nearly all these units of study have had fewer than 50,000 inhabitants.

Thirdly, I believe that such community studies – as they are known – can be a most fruitful source of knowledge about our society. This, however, involves academic daring – it means generalizing grandly, sticking my neck out so that my academic colleagues can hack at it. This I propose to do.

The book is in two parts. In Part One I have arranged descriptions of communities that have been studied in a rough order of increasing economic complexity. Within each chapter I have arranged the order in which facts are presented to enable them to be used in illustration of Part Two. In Part Two I have drawn together some aspects o sociological theory which I believe illuminate and are illuminated by the empirical studies of Part One. I am concerned to illuminate the differences between truly rural

* For title and bibliographical details of works cited see page 297 ff.

and less rural areas of Britain that happen to have been studied by sociologists. I think this is interesting in itself. Together with other facts and interpretations, this knowledge helps to shape my views and the views of other people on what Britain is like. I hope also to illuminate what society in general is like and the processes of social change. My method here is to borrow ideas and concepts from other branches of sociology, social history, and even communication theory. This is dangerous ground. My generalizations are illustrated by the presentation of the contents of the community studies. This in some cases makes necessary reinterpretation of the studies though I have tried to keep this in line with their authors' evidence but my theoretical approach (cf. Stein, 1960).

Although I am concerned with the description of small-scale communities, I do not think my book is irrelevant for the student of towns and cities or for those who want to understand Britain as a whole. Towns and cities make more sense if they are seen as a part of an evolutionary process in which the progression from a simple to a diversified technology is accompanied by certain sociological changes. This does not mean that I shall describe an evolutionary process in any one town. Nor does it mean that I imagine that the communities described in this book can be arranged along a scale of unilineal evolution. In Part Two, however, I shall attempt to construct a morphological continuum as a model against which to measure the adequacy of our knowledge of real social life in different parts of Britain.

PART ONE
The Content of Community Studies

The areas that make up the subject matter of Chapter 1 are two townlands in the West of Ireland, Rynamona and Luogh in County Clare. They were studied by two American anthropologists, Arensberg and Kimball, before the Second World War and are included here because they are pioneer studies. The economy of Western Ireland is (or was at the time the books were written) almost entirely agricultural. The subjects of the study were small farmers employing virtually no hired labour and using relatively simple techniques. They are not, however, hoe-cultivators and certainly not pastoral nomads or hunters and collectors. The 'primitiveness' of their internal economy must not be over-emphasized. They are not even subsistence farmers since much of their produce is sold. Through this sale of produce they are part, if a marginal part, of a capitalist industrial economy. The chapter on Ireland appears first because the County Clare townlands have the simplest economy. By chance they were also the first to be studied.

The second chapter describes social life in the scattered farmsteads and tiny hamlets of the parish of Llanfihangel-yng-Ngwynfa in mid-Wales.

Here once again we are concerned with small farmers on marginal land employing little hired labour. They are, however, less isolated and more integrated into the main economy of Britain. Alwyn D. Rees who wrote the study stayed there from 1940 to 1948.

The remaining studies were all carried out in the early fifties and published in the late fifties. Chapter 3 is about Gosforth, a village and parish in West Cumberland. Here too there are near-subsistence farmers on marginal land and a predominance of agriculture. But there are also wage-earners in industry, an atomic power station, and businessmen and landowners. Gosforth is more like a microcosm of Britain than the Irish or Welsh areas. It is still distinctly rural and traditional, and on these aspects W. M. Williams, a pupil of Alwyn D. Rees, has concentrated.

Gosforth is followed by a chapter based on my own work in 1953 in the village of Glynceiriog in north-east Wales. Whereas Rees is concerned with the countryside, and Williams with the village and the countryside, I concentrated on the village. Glynceiriog is an industrial village, or rather an ex-industrial village, which I originally christened Pentrediwaith – the village of no work. Its men are nearly all wage-earners who used to be quarrymen. Its women are

housewives. Quarries in this region were developed late and
abandoned early. Although social life remains distinctive,
the economy of Glynceiriog is virtually fully integrated with
that of near-by towns and England as a whole. Chapter 5 is
also about a village based on one extractive industry. It is
in Yorkshire and has been given the fictitious name of
Ashton. In this case the industry is coal-mining and is still
carried on. Dennis, Henriques, and Slaughter studied it in
the years 1953–5. There is a big jump in size from Glynceiriog with 600 inhabitants to Ashton with nearly 14,000.
Ideally I would have liked a study or studies of capitalist
farming areas to put between Gosforth and Glynceiriog and
of several small towns/villages with different kinds of industry to put between Glynceiriog and Ashton, but such
studies have not yet been made.

All Ashton men, and many Ashton women, are wage-
earners. Its isolation (if it is isolated) is purely social. Geographically it is within easy reach of a conurbation.

The first part of Chapter 6 is devoted to Glossop, a small
manufacturing town in the High Peak area of Derbyshire,
which was studied in 1953 and 1954 by A. H. Birch, a
political scientist, and a team including a historian and
psychologists. It has a population of about 18,000. It was
not, however, studied as a whole but with a concentrated
specialist interest in 'grass-roots' politics. The second half
of this chapter is devoted to Banbury, the study of which was
the most ambitious of them all. Banbury is a market and
manufacturing town in Oxfordshire, with a population of
about 19,000. It was studied by a team of people from 1948
to 1952 and the results were written up by Margaret
Stacey and published in 1960.

Banbury is a microcosm in the fullest sense of any of the
communities studied. Stacey's book describes all social
classes and all status groups to be found in Britain as a
whole. There are many sorts of industry, trade, and commerce. There is a traditional pattern of life and immigrants
who disrupt it. The traditional pattern is also threatened
by internal change in economy and attitude.

From here we go on in the last chapters of Part One to the consideration of explicitly recognized segments of large towns – Bethnal Green, and housing estates in Watling, Liverpool, Sheffield, Oxford, and 'Greenleigh'. Bethnal Green is a borough in the East End of London with a total population of 54,000, which has been much studied, from Charles Booth onwards. The analysis in the Bethnal Green chapter (Chapter 7) is based mainly on the work done during the early fifties by Michael Young and his colleagues at the Institute of Community Studies in Bethnal Green.

The analysis in the chapter on housing estates (Chapter 8) is based, firstly, on Duncan Mitchell and Tom Lupton's studies of a Liverpool estate in 1950–1 and Mark Hodges and Cyril Smith's of a Sheffield estate in 1951–2, published together in *Neighbourhood and Community* in 1954. Next, I make use of what may be regarded as the classical British housing-estate study – Ruth Durant's *Watling*, published in 1939. Two Oxford studies of Barton, a housing estate three miles from the centre, and St Ebbe's in central Oxford were done by J. M. Mogey from 1950 onwards and published in 1956. The second part of Young and Willmott's book is about the housing estate, fictitiously called Greenleigh, to which some of the population of Bethnal Green were being moved, and I use this to conclude this last chapter of Part One.

Since I have confined myself in this book to the description of communities, I have left out of consideration the many other urban studies.

As an operational definition of community I have followed MacIver and Page, who write that a community is 'an area of social living marked by some degree of *social coherence*. The bases of community are *locality* and *community sentiment*' (MacIver and Page, 1961, p. 9). The concept, however, is discussed more fully in Part Two. Broadly, my dividing line is between those areas of social life which can best be studied by face-to-face methods – personal observation supplemented by questionnaire survey; and those which it is more economical to study, door-to-door, by questionnaire survey supplemented by personal observation.

When I went to Glynceiriog I was always conscious of my anthropological colleagues' anecdotes of how they sat in the centre of African villages while life went on around them and encompassed them. They could not avoid becoming part of the social processes they wished to observe. In my early days in the village I would often climb a hill and look sadly down upon the rows of houses of the housing estate and wonder what went on inside them. When I became involved in the affairs of the football club and other activities which concerned the village as a whole, I too was able to observe social process but never as intensely as my Africanist colleagues. Had I studied Bethnal Green or the Sheffield housing estate the observation of social process would have presented even greater difficulties. As we shall see, students of areas of this kind try to devise techniques to get over this problem. By and large, however, they can only deduce social process from the information they can collect by questioning people in their homes or elsewhere. For there are no activities which concern the estate as a whole.

Part Two
A Morphological Continuum

From this starting-point of the changing nature of community the second part of this book sets out to explore the social characteristics which are associated with economic diversification and increase in scale. To do this I make use of a few technical terms and hypotheses which it is as well to introduce in a preliminary way now. I do this without detailed references or discussion which will be provided in Part Two.

The first is the concept of *role*. We shall see the individual in society as occupying a number of social positions. These social positions bring him into relation with the incumbents of other social positions. People expect appropriate behaviour from the holder of a particular position. The sum of these expectations is the role.

Roles are not played in isolation. Each role has its appropriate audience. We can see this in terms of pairs of roles – teacher–pupil, father–son for example. Another way of seeing roles in relation to each other is to write of *role-sets*. Examples are *father* and wife, son, daughter, mother-in-law, or *teacher* and school governor, pupil, headmaster, parent. As soon as we look at roles in this way we see that expectations about father's behaviour may be different for his wife, for his son, or for his daughter. There is a built-in tension surrounding all roles which arises from this conflict of expectations. The tension is likely to break into open dispute in circumstances where a particular individual has to fulfil conflicting expectations simultaneously and in full view of all the members of his *role-set*. Such a 'transparent' state of affairs is particularly likely to arise in a face-to-face community.

In face-to-face communities each individual is related to every other individual in his total network in several different ways. In an extreme case a man's father is also his teacher, his religious leader, and his employer. A shopkeeper in the village is also a relative of many of his customers and a chapel deacon. Behaviour appropriate to the role, shopkeeper–customer, may be inappropriate to shopkeeper–employee in any part of our society. If the shopkeeper has also to behave appropriately in situations involving shopkeeper–shopkeeper's nephew and deacon–member of congregation we may say that his social life has a complexity which his urban counterpart's lacks. Alternatively we may say that he is bound to his customers by a multiplicity of ties. He has perhaps a smaller choice of roles than he would in the town, and he has to play them all to the same audience.

The town shopkeeper may have open to him roles in many different systems, but there is a degree of insulation between them that leads us to say that urban society is complicated rather than complex.

It is common usage in sociology to distinguish between groups and categories. The term *group* has been variously defined, but it generally carries the implication of social interaction between the individuals comprising it. Further, its members are often seen as having aims in common which impose a group boundary. In other words there are not only members but also individuals who are definitely and clearly not members. Examples of groups are the elementary family, the members of a particular congregation in a particular village church, a trade union branch, a village, a village football club, and so on. By *category* we mean a collection of people who share certain characteristics, but who do not necessarily interact with one another. People with red hair form a category which is, however, of little use in sociological analysis. Other categories to which reference will be made include: those who have in common the necessity to work for wages, employers of labour, men, women, Anglicans, trade unionists, and Nonconformists. Thus all groups are partial categories but not all categories are groups.

It is possible to see the individual in society as belonging to many categories and participating in many groups. But this twofold classification leaves us without a means of analysis of very important parts of social life. If I consider 'my friends' they are clearly a category who have in common the fact that I interact with them. But they do not necessarily interact with each other nor have common aims. Nor do they have other characteristics which make them a group. The same is true of those related to me by blood or marriage. Both sets of people are a little more than category but less than group. To deal with this gap in analytical terminology, the metaphor 'social network' has been introduced. In Barnes's words:

Each person is, as it were, in touch with a number of other people, some of whom are directly in touch with each other and some of whom are not. Similarly each person has a number of friends, and these friends have their own friends; some of any one person's friends know each other, others do not. I find it convenient to talk of a social field of this kind as a *network*. The image I have is of a set of points some of which are joined by lines. The points of the image are people, or sometimes groups, and the lines indicate which people interact with each other ... A network of this kind has no external boundary, nor has it any clear cut internal divisions, for each person sees himself at the centre of a collection of friends (Barnes, 1954).

I have made considerable use of the term 'network' in both parts of this book. I shall follow suggestions made by Barnes and Bott (Barnes, 1954 and Bott, 1957) that the nature of social networks changes as societies become less complex and more complicated. This is true whether the network is seen as one in which individuals, groups, or roles form the nodes (Nadel, 1957 and Lancaster, 1961).

Thus in truly rural society the network may be close-knit; everybody knows and interacts with everyone else. In urban society individuals may have few friends in common. In a study of urban families, Elizabeth Bott put forward a hypothesis that the nature of a family's network in these terms was related to the division of labour between husband and wife within the home. She distinguished three kinds of family organization. The first she called complementary, where husband and wife have different activities but fit together to form a whole, as in farming communities. The second she calls independent, where husband and wife act without reference to each other. The third she describes as joint organization, when husband and wife work closely together or their activities are covered by either one alternating. Where complementary and independent organization predominates, Bott speaks of segregated role relationships. It is then possible to arrange families on a continuum ranging from those having highly segregated role relationships to those having joint ones. She states that 'the degree of segregation in the role relationship of husband and wife varies directly with the connectedness of the family's social network'. I have used this hypothesis to illuminate differences in 'the segregation of sex-roles' in the areas of Britain I have described.

Generally speaking the pattern of change in roles from rural to urban is one of increasing role differentiation. That is to say that there is progressive specialization of roles and separation out of parts of a role to form new roles. This is another way of describing the division of labour, which involves the change from all members of a society being able to carry out all tasks to specialization. Interestingly, roles within the family are apparently inversely related to those outside it. As laundries, medical and welfare services, and schools take over roles formerly performed within the family, and as women achieve social position outside, so differentiation within the home breaks down and household sex-roles are regeneralized, so that in urban households husband and wife have more in common than their country counterparts.

In the last chapter of the book I summarize the continuum to which these theoretical discussions seem to lead. I do this in two ways; by drawing them together under twenty-five heads and by subsuming them all under the concept of a changing pattern of *social redundancy*.

The term 'redundancy' I have borrowed from communication theory where it has been defined as 'a property of languages, codes and sign systems which arises from a superfluity of rules, and which facilitates communication in spite of all the factors of uncertainty acting against it'. It is also used to describe the condition of communication networks when several channels are connected in parallel to overcome the chance of error which arises if one or more channels are faulty. I suggest that the successful organization of social life is also beset by uncertainty.

If people are to continue to live together and if food, clothing, shelter, and entertainment are to be continually produced and replaced, uncertainty must be overcome. In rural society one sort of redundancy ensures this, in urban society another. I am drawing an analogy between rural social redundancy and redundancy in spoken language, and urban social redundancy and redundancy in written language. In the last chapter I discuss the pitfalls and advantages of this analogy building. Here I state the analogy baldly by restating in terms of society a statement of Colin Cherry's about language:

Rural society is built out of a relatively small number of roles and role-relationships . . . but they may be arranged with great fluidity into varied patterns with repetitions, stressings, gestures, and a wealth of reinforcing 'redundancy'. Urban society must make up for the lack of gesture and stress, if it is to combat ambiguity, by introducing redundancy through a greater number of roles and a closer adherence to the formal relationships between them.

Note for the 1969 Reprint

In this reprint I have made a few changes, mainly to add clarity. I am grateful to my colleagues at the University of Zambia and especially to Dr J. Van Velsen for helping me in this task.

PART ONE

THE CONTENT OF
COMMUNITY STUDIES

CHAPTER I

Truly Rural: Ireland – The Pioneer Study

As early as 1932 the American anthropologist W. Lloyd
Warner, who had successfully studied Australian Abori-
gines and a town in New England, travelled with another
anthropologist, Conrad Arensberg from Harvard, to
County Clare in the West of Ireland. Warner went home
after a few months, but Arensberg, later joined by Solon T.
Kimball, stayed for two years. Later they wrote two books
about their studies which were the first of their kind, and so
I am including them here although this book is ostensibly
concerned with British communities (Arensberg, 1939 and
Arensberg and Kimball, 1940).

They set out to study as anthropologists the significance
of custom in County Clare, especially among the Gaelic-
speaking holders of small farms.

While especially in *Family and Community* they use statisti-
cal material covering the whole of County Clare and even
all the small farmers of Eire, they concentrated their detailed studies on two 'townlands' – the equivalent of civil
parishes in England and Wales – Luogh and Rynamona.

Luogh is a remote upland townland half a day's tramp
from the market town of Ennistymon. Ennistymon itself has
only 1,200 people. There was in 1932 no public transport
joining Luogh and Ennistymon – yet Luogh was not totally
isolated. A reminder of the outside world were the English
Atlantic liners anchored in Galway Bay.

More practically, some of the farms had horse-drawn
mowing machines made of English manufactured steel.
Arensberg lodged in a white-washed, two roomed stone
cottage, one of twenty-six scattered about the townland. It
stood on sixteen acres of upland, and eight more in the
valley – it was described locally as 'a place of four cows and
a horse' (Arensberg, pp. 21–3). Only one of these twenty-
six farms is over twenty-five acres. The land is officially

described as general purpose land. Each has some bog, some meadow, some grazing fields, and a small garden of less than an acre. The last grows potatoes, rye, cabbage, and oats. The biggest farm has six cows, two calves, or two bullocks. The smallest is owned by an old-age pensioner who works four acres and has only hens (Arensberg and Kimball, p. 72).* The farmers of Luogh, inhabiting 'the table land between mountain-top of bracken and black bog and the cliffs', are not socially isolated. They are nodes in overlapping networks of relationships stretching in different directions for different purposes.

Such a farmer cooperates with neighbours in Luogh townland, but he also has kinsmen four miles to the north at Mount Elva, three miles to the south at Liscannor. He attends the parish church at Killilagh two miles away, but his children attend school at Ballycotton one mile away. He sells his produce at Ennistymon (eight miles) or Lisdoonvarna (five miles). He votes in an electoral district which cuts across these boundaries. He is associated by tradition with Clare and Munster rather than Galway and Connaught (Arensberg and Kimball, p. 283).

As Arensberg and Kimball put it:

The small farmer of Luogh has allegiances to all these communities.† He is quite ready to find his emotions stirred in any one of them. He is ready to back the men of Luogh against the men of the neighbouring townland; to back those of the mountain region against those of the valley lands; those of his parish against the rest; those of the countryside against the towns of Lisdoonvarna and Ennistymon; those of North Clare against other sections of the county; those of Clare against all other counties; those of his class against all others; of his religion against all others; of his nation against all others. Each one of these allegiances has a geographical base, though in the last analysis each one of these is built up out of his personal experience of human relations (p. 283).

* There are minor inconsistencies in figures between the books.
† They use the word communities in a less restrictive sense than I have defined it.

The other townland is called Rynamona and seems to have a more nucleated settlement pattern. Again, it is difficult to reach, for it lies around a little upland lake. Eight of its houses stand in an irregular cluster on the shores. Another five are scattered through the townland. No one has more than nine cows, and only one fewer than two. As far as one can tell from Arensberg and Kimball there does not seem to be the positive aversion from living in nucleated settlement that Rees describes for upland Wales. Perhaps the fact that the need for defence in the Irish countryside continued until the recent past is the explanation.

Ireland at the time of this field study had a population of some three million of whom about 1,800,000, or 63 per cent, lived in rural areas. Over half the occupied population were engaged in agriculture, and the annual value of their produce was nearly twice that of industry. The Irish census of 1926, the common knowledge of the countryside, and the realities of Irish politics all demonstrated the existence of two distinct classes in the Irish countryside – large farmers and small farmers. This distinction is emphasized by being geographical as well as economic. There is a greater concentration of small farmers in the south and west of Ireland than in the north and east. By and large the smaller the holding, the more people it is likely to support. Thus the ranching country of Meath supports fifty persons per square mile and small-farming County Mayo seventy-five. Sociologically and economically County Clare occupies a middle place among the counties of Eire.

The main differences between small and large farmers is that the small farmer tends to be a subsistence farmer producing, mainly for his own consumption, milk, bacon, poultry, eggs, potatoes, and butter. He uses mainly hand tools and his fellow workers are his family and the co-operative group of his 'friends'. The large farmer is a beef stockman who keeps cattle to sell. He buys more of his own food than he produces and is more likely to use mechanized methods. Above all, he has hired labour and competes rather than cooperates with his peers. The two classes are complementary as well as antagonistic, for the small farmer sells his surplus calves to the large farmer and to the east. The ranchers fatten them and sell them farther east, and ultimately they are sold again across the sea to England. Already in 1932 the small farmer was selling some milk products to creameries but not in Luogh or Rynamona.

Luogh and Rynamona were inhabited mainly by small farmers as we have seen, and for the rest of the chapter we shall be entirely concerned with their social life. It is, however, as well to remember that this social life is always played out against a backcloth which includes the migration of cattle and people. One must remember also that the small farmers are tied to the large farmers by economic necessity and divided from them by antagonistic interests. Like the Welsh parish of the next chapter, the Irish townlands maintain their single-class appearance because their proletariat and their economic controllers are elsewhere.

This provides the basis for the political divisions of Southern Ireland. There are many more Irish wage-earners in the six counties of the North, in England, and in America than in Eire. The political division has been between two sorts of farmer rather than between employer and employee. In Arensberg and Kimball's words:

Consequently the small farmers are much less immediately affected by disturbances in the cattle trade with Great Britain. The fact has been evident throughout the years of the De Valera regime. It has blasted the prognostications of those who agreed that a restriction and interruption of the trade with England, such as grew up in the 'economic war' which followed De Valera's retention of the land annuity payments and the English retaliation in the form of import duties on cattle, would alienate the farmers' support of De Valera's government. It certainly alienated the larger farmers, who were immediately affected, but the 'farmer' of the politician is not always the whole population of that name. It left the small farmer relatively undisturbed. He was at one or two points removed from the actual trade with England and saw it only as a sale to big farmers. With the small farmers, the economic arguments of De Valera's opponents failed (p. 29).

Later we shall see how this touches townland life in the secret adherence of one richer farmer to De Valera's opponent, Cosgrave.

The Irish farmer makes little profit and has little chance of moving east to take over a farm. Some, as we shall see, may move into town which 'the country-people flock into' and 'the townspeople all die out of' (Arensberg, p. 152). A majority of each generation, however, moves out of agriculture and Ireland altogether. Nor is this a new phenomenon. Arensberg and Kimball date its major upsurge from the famine of 1845–7, but acknowledge that it had been going on even before that. Not far from where the university stands in Manchester was the district already known by Engels and his contemporaries in 1844 as 'Little Ireland' (Engels, 1845).

It was, however, only in 1846 that the population of Ireland began to decline as a result of this emigration. This is the period in which the number of farms declined through the disappearance of small farms and the growth of pasture as against tillage. Ireland, which up to the repeal of the Corn Laws had been the bread-basket of England, became its cattle ranch and sheep station.

The Irish small farmer's economy is a domestic economy in the most literal sense. He is born, lives out his life, receives much of his education in, as well as derives his livelihood from, a farm. The actual living quarters often consist of only two rooms. The kitchen–living-room where he spends his active life, and may even sleep, and the west room to which he will retire. The more prosperous may in addition have separate sleeping quarters in the loft. To describe what happens in his house and in his small fields is to give an account not only of his economy, and the division of labour, but also of his relations with his immediate family.

Arensberg's description in *The Irish Countryman* cannot easily be improved upon. I find it helps to give a clearer picture of the organization of economic life in this part of Ireland to think of three cycles of changes: the daily round which makes up the work of women – this revolves about the farmhouse; the yearly round which limits the work of men – this revolves about the farm; and finally, encompassing them all, the life cycle – birth, first communion, marriage, retirement, and death.

The woman's daily round is easy to describe. It is characteristic not only of her lot but also of the house and haggard in which she lives out her life. She is the first to rise, at 7.30 a.m. in winter, and earlier in summer; she rakes the ashes of the slaked turf fire, puts down new sods and re-kindles the blaze.

Then she hangs the kettle up to boil for tea. This she will keep going all day to provide tea for the family or for visitors. Now the men rise and eat their breakfast of bread, eggs, and milk. When they have had their fill and have departed to the fields or their jobs around the haggard, the women and children eat their meal. The schoolchildren are dressed and packed off, the cows milked, and preparations are made for churning butter. The women have also the responsibility of feeding the hens and younger animals. Full-grown cattle and horses (if there are any) are the men's responsibility. Soon after eleven o'clock the second kettle must be hung on its hooks for dinner – potatoes, white cabbage, when in season, and perhaps salt bacon. At 11.30 the men come home from the fields for their dinner, the main meal of the day. The family, save for schoolchildren, are reunited, and gossip and news picked up in the course of the morning is relayed. For the women the afternoon is much the same except that they must fit in washing, mending, knitting, other household tasks, and getting ready the schoolchildren's tea at four o'clock. The men in winter come home to supper at five, and a pipe afterwards ends their working day. The women, however, work on – for 'tradition and proverb demand that "one woman in the home be always working" ' (Arensberg, p. 47).

This is the daily round of the women and it varies little through the week, except on Sundays. Ireland is strictly sabbatarian when it comes to work. Even on Sundays cows must be milked and fed. The women's daily round varies as little through the seasons as it does through the weeks. In some periods of intense agricultural activity it is true women are drawn in as auxiliaries. The timing also may vary with the seasons and the hours of daylight.

The men's lives are geared much more to the seasons than to hours or days. Around Christmas the weather is cold and wet; the days seem bitter and short. This is a period of festivity with only odd jobs to do. At Epiphany, 6 January, the weather does not suddenly change, but the country-man's attitude does. The year's work begins in earnest. All must be planned and made ready for the feast of St Bridget, 1 February, the beginning of spring. Gardens are prepared and potatoes planted; in the February spring fair the last of last year's calves are sold. In March and April the new calves are born, bringing an intensification of dairy acti-vities for the women too. In a dry season, May marks the beginning of turf-cutting and stacking for next year's fuel. June and July see cabbage ready for cutting. Old women in 1932 called these the hungry months, for often cabbage was all there was. Potatoes do not have a harvest but are lifted as required, so the first harvest is the hay. This, known appropriately as 'saving' the hay, is a battle with the ele-ments and a race with time. In a good year it starts in late July or early August. Late in the summer is the corn harvest of oats and rye. Rootcrops follow in September, October, and November. In November too the turf is brought down to the haggards, the gardens ploughed, and attendance at the Autumn Fair brings the farmer's year full circle.

All these tasks are mainly the work of the men, but for potato planting, turf-cutting, and haymaking all the family are involved. Women and children come into the fields as well. Their roles there, however, are strictly limited. The plough, the harrow, and the mower, the scythe, the spade, and the turf-cutting *slan* are essentially masculine tools. Country people say wielding them is no more natural for women than milking or selling butter would be for men. To the Irish countrymen the segregated and complementary nature of sex roles in the Irish countryside is sanctioned by custom, legend, fairy myth, and natural law.

All this activity is directed and controlled by the head of the farm family – 'The father and husband is normally owner and director of the enterprise. The farm and its income are vested in him' (Arensberg, pp. 54–5).

The yearly cycle of farm activities is also the means of initiation of the child into the life of the adult. At first no distinction is made between boys and girls; confined to the house, they revolve silently in the mother's daily round. They have little contact with their father. For girls this continues until they wed, but for boys there is a turning point at about the age of seven when they take their first communion. Now they move from the mother's side to their father's. Indeed, the old Irish custom is to dress boys and girls in similar clothes until this age to deceive the fairies who might otherwise substitute a boy child with a changeling.

At first the boys run errands, but they are gradually initiated into men's work, 'the boy learns work as he learns manhood' (Arensberg, p. 57).

But although the boy learns to do men's work and to do it like a man, socially he remains a boy. As one old man put it, 'you can be a boy forever as long as the old fellow is alive'. Nearly all the boy's social relations are mediated through his father. This is especially true of economic matters. Boys may attend fairs from the age of eleven or twelve, and yet still at forty-five have to say to a shopkeeper, 'the old fellow will pay later'. When the land commissioner employed farmers' sons, it was the fathers who came to collect the wages.

The life of the Irish small farmer's son is like the story of Sleeping Beauty in reverse. At the age of eight his social status is changed and remains frozen until marriage releases him into social adulthood.

However, the analogy is not exact, for marriages do not just happen in Ireland. Matches are made. In Arensberg's words:

Life in organized society is a drama. In the match, even though the marriage of one principal is the theme, the action includes the whole cast. Internally, the action forcibly and finally changes the interrelations of all the characters; externally the parts they play to the audience alter and grow. The changes must run their course till the action resolves itself in the crystallization of a new situation; and the act is over (p. 80).

The process begins when a farmer who feels ready to retire starts looking around for a suitable wife for his son. Not that this is regarded as an affair for the father alone; the whole of his kindred is involved. When a likely girl is in prospect a friend of the young man's family known as 'the speaker' will sound out her father and family and see if they will consider the match. If the signs seem favourable the young man and his father will set out with the 'speaker' to a pub to meet the girl's father. The occasion is a delicate one and friction must be avoided by a little lubrication. It will be the young man's task to call the first drink. The young lady's father calls the second. Then the round moves backwards and forwards between the members of the two kindreds as the negotiation proceeds. The 'speaker' does well out of this.

'The young lady's father asks the speaker what fortune do he want. He asks him the place, of how many cows, sheep, and horses is it? He asks what makings of a garden are in it; is there plenty of water or spring wells? Is it far from the road, or on it? What kind of house is it, in slate or thatch?' (p. 74).

And so it will go on. The girl's father wants to know where the nearest school and church are, and what sort of paths there are to them. This is all a necessary preliminary to the discussion on how much 'fortune' the girl must bring with her. Hard bargaining follows on this and in 1932 a place of eight cows might finally command about three hundred pounds. By the time this stage is reached, all the parties may be quite drunk and ready enough to call it a day.

The next stage is for the couple, duly chaperoned by their

kin, to meet and see if they suit each other. If they do not it is too bad. No reasons are given. There are no hard feelings. Nothing is lost and both have to try again. If they seem to suit, a day is arranged for the prospective bride's people to walk the land. Geese are killed the day before, a stock of whiskey and porter got in, and the house white-washed. Occasionally, it is said, the odd extra cow is borrowed to make up the numbers.

If all is well, it is now time to get in the lawyers and make out the writings ready for the wedding the following shrove-tide.

To the outsider, unaccustomed to this process, it seems bad enough perhaps to have an arranged marriage. The process of bargaining which leads up to it may seem to add insult to injury. To the Irish countryman, however, the bargaining is a ceremonial necessary to establish the equality between the parties. Dignity is maintained on both sides. The daughter who is marrying is reasonably provided for. Her fortune is made over to her groom's father. He cannot alas usually keep it for himself. He may have a daughter of his own for whom he must provide a fortune in order that she in turn may marry. He may have other sons, who, now the farm is disposed of, will have to 'travel', to seek a living elsewhere, in the towns of Ireland or even in England or America. The old man himself with his wife will now retire, for the farm is made over to the son. But the 'writings' will stipulate that the west room will remain for the use of the old couple, who will also have the right to some grazing, their keep, and perhaps some pocket money.

The old couple will still be there, but dramatically the roles of father and son have been reversed. As father used to collect the son's wages from the land commission, now son collects the father's old age pension from the post office. A wise son, however, will not presume too quickly and drastically on his position as head of the household. One such told Arensberg that each morning he asked his father what to do on the farm, then he went off to do what he himself thought ought to be done.

Mother similarly must watch the new mistress of the household feed the calves and make the butter, and usurp all her other authority. At first again there is tension which, if the daughter-in-law does not soon become pregnant, will mount and may even end in the wife being sent home and the farm passing to another of the husband's family who *can* make a fertile match. If, however, signs of a baby appear, tension tends to go and the Irish bride is glad of her husband's mother's help with the baby. This leaves her free for her many tasks in the farm economy. The birth of sons to keep the name on the land will be greeted with especial joy.

Obviously, only if all Irish families had at least one son and one daughter would things go as neatly and smoothly as this. There will be many variations on this basic theme. The theme, however, of a re-ordering of the internal arrangements of both family and farmhouse will remain.

Nor is the re-ordering created by the Irish match confined to the family's internal organization. Farms have become linked affinally and kindreds brought into alliance. This will reinforce the patterns of cooperation, 'friendliness', or 'cooring' which are one of the networks uniting the small farmers of the countryside. This is a point to which we must return shortly. Before that, however, let us note that even the ones who travel do not travel right outside the family system of Ireland.

They continue to correspond and especially at Christmas to send money home. The links in this network provide paths along which future emigrants can travel, their fares often sent for them. Thus Boston has its districts of relatives and friends which reflect districts of Ireland. Four cases are recorded where Luogh boys and girls had married one another in Boston. Two more couples married in Luogh and travelled out (Arensberg and Kimball, p. 149). It is said that the district of Cross at the mouth of the Shannon was supported by remittances from the Shanghai police force commanded by a man from the place.

But cooperation and contact with relatives and affines as

far off as Boston, Melbourne, or Shanghai, must at best be spasmodic and intermittent. Cooperation in Luogh, in Rynamona, and elsewhere in rural Co. Clare is continuous and intimate. It is the process of matchmaking which to some extent provides the scaffolding. Despite the patrilineal emphasis on the inheritance of land which demands male children to keep the name on the land, Irish kinship is not exclusive. That is, there is no elaborate terminology to distinguish one sort of kin from another, and to define the different sorts of behaviour expected towards each category. The cognatic kin of the farmer and his wife are all described as 'friends'. A man distinguishes grades of relatives only on the basis of generation and speaks of 'my friends' and 'my father's friends'.

Between a man and his 'friends' there grows up an elaborate system of reciprocal cooperation. Although for reasons already put forward this is declining, it is one of the fundamental social customs which makes the cleavage between small and large farmers in Ireland. The rancher with three hundred acres in Luogh for example took no part in cooperation.

Men lend one another tools and machinery. Women club together to make up a tub or firkin of butter or lend a girl when a family is shorthanded for the work of dairying.

There is communal work at turf-cutting, the oat harvest and threshing – usually in the form of lending a boy.

Arensberg observed the process most closely in the 1933 hay harvest in Luogh. Only about half the farmers had horse-drawn mowing machines. They started to bring in their hay working throughout the hours of daylight from dawn to dusk. At every stage they had the assistance of boys from their neighbours who had no machines. The boys ate all their meals with the farmers they were helping. When the farmers with machines finished their own land they took the machines over to the meadows of the fathers of the boys who had helped them.

One farmer was helped by the sons of three others, his second cousins, and in due course, he mowed their meadows.

Another was helped by the son of his cousin and his nephew. In due course he took his mowing machine to do the fields of their fathers. In Luogh, as in the song, when one man goes to mow he is rarely accompanied merely by his dog. There were, however, five cases who although obviously short-handed had no help. Two of these were bachelors who could not reciprocate, and two 'strangers' who would not be expected to.

'So it went over the townland. No man had mowed for all his relatives, that was not necessary. One man had mowed not for a relative, but for a boon companion. Furthermore, the bachelors, whom no one had helped, had been able to help no one. The two "strangers", who had moved into the town land, in one case fifty years before, in the other thirty, had no relatives "on this side"' (Arensberg, p. 66).

Luogh people themselves treat cooperation among farmers in economic tasks in the same way as the obligations of kin to help at weddings and at funerals, or to give stock and services to mitigate disaster. When some one dies you expect relatives who may also be neighbours to help dig the grave, carry the coffin, and serve at the wake. One 'has right to help one's friends'. But this custom is more than just an expression of community norms. It has severe, if informal, sanctions. These are both negative and positive.

The man who refuses to help, or for that matter to be helped, is opting out of society and condemning himself to social isolation. The man who helps his neighbour and kinsmen and is helped in his turn is, with each exchange of services, cementing and reinforcing the ties which bind him to the community. He strengthens the strands of the network, the existence of which enables us to write of the Irish townlands as communities.

This network not only spans seas and continents; it is also the means by which town and country are linked reciprocally in the rural economy of Ireland.

The demonstration that debt relations may be a cohesive rather than a disruptive force is one of the achievements of Arensberg's Irish study. But it is important to emphasize that it is only debt relations between equals that are cohesive.

The Irish towns were built by the Norsemen and the English to dominate the countryside, but with the departure of the invaders they have become themselves dominated. They are centres of distribution rather than production and exist as islands of commerce in a sea of small farmers. Like other islands they depend for their livelihood on the products of the sea around them. And like other islands they take their character from the sea. For if we can speak of Irish small farmers as subsistence peasants, we can describe the small town shopkeeper too as a peasant in his way of life. Like the farm, the two-storey small shop is more than a mere place of business: 'It is first of all a household, of which one section and one only is devoted to the world of affairs' (Arensberg, p. 151).

Its workers, again like those of the farm, are often unpaid members of the family – young unmarried men and women. The young man shop-assistant, however, may not be a son – he may be an apprentice whose father has paid a premium for him. He will have wages and most likely be saving to marry and buy a shop of his own. It is very likely too that he will not be the son of another shopkeeper but of a farmer. The small farmer sees the town as a step up in the world and may, when the family is dispersed, spend some of the fortune he received buying an apprenticeship for one of his sons in the town. The shopkeeper in his turn would rather have a country-bred apprentice, who, he feels, will be more honest, and more hardworking. Above all, the apprentice's kin will become customers, since there is a cooperation in trade between 'friends' parallel to that between farmers in the countryside: 'trade follows friendship'.

The link between shopkeeper and customer is not merely the cash nexus – like other economic institutions of the countryside it makes possible (and is made possible by) a complex network of social relationships.

Young men are not the only ones to come from the countryside into the towns. The socially ambitious farmer may try to make a match for his daughter to a shopkeeper instead of to another farmer. The mechanism will be the same except for points of detail. The kin will 'walk the shop' as in the country they 'walk the land'. A 'fortune' will come in with the girl which will ensure that the 'name' is kept on the shop. For shops in Ireland are often labelled merely with the name of the family who owns them. If finances are low an incoming farmer's daughter will bring the means which preserves the ownership of the patrilineal line just as late nineteenth- and early twentieth-century dukes and earls paid the mortgages on their estates by judicious marriages to the daughters of American million-aires. She will bring with her too the loyalty of her kin who will become customers. As in the rural match, the old shop-keeping couple will retire and the other members of the family will have to 'travel'.

'Money buys the shop, credit may stock its shelves, but it is the social alliance, contracted in a country marriage, which supplies the trade upon which business rests' (Arensberg, p. 161).

This economic and social link with the countryside has another effect on the lives of the shopkeepers. The small farmer does not have a regular income once a week, once a fortnight, or even once a month. Although he may get some money at the weekly produce market, his main sources of actual cash will be the spring and autumn fairs. Most of the time he must live on credit and be in debt to the shopkeeper.

This is an additional bond which ties the shopkeeper to the customer. It is not one to be lightly broken. The farmer who pays his debts in full is indicating clearly that he is going to shop elsewhere, just as an Arab who pays off his bride-wealth debts announces his intention to seek a di-vorce.* Similarly the shopkeeper who is too keen to collect may find he has lost not merely a single customer, and a small amount of money, but also a whole group of the customer's kinsmen whose enmity may persist through generations.

---

* Emrys Peters, personal communication.

If despite this danger the trader feels strong enough to insist, the countryman believes that one so grasping stands in danger of supernatural punishment. Too much emphasis on money will dissolve the social ties. This is perhaps the reason why the character in Irish folklore most likely to suffer misfortune is the finder of a 'crock of gold'.

The small farmer and shopkeeper are not ashamed to carry a burden of debt to their equals; it is a measure of their status in the countryside, a sign of their 'ability to support that network of social obligation which gives one's self and one's family a place in social life' (Arensberg, p. 175). Debts to one's equals are debts of honour; they are carried on from generation to generation and never fully paid off. Debts to large farmers and to landlords are quite different. They are a matter of business and are regarded in a different light. The debts of the shopkeeper to wholesaler and banker also lie in a different system. The general problem of rural indebtedness to capitalist outsiders is not affected by Arensberg's analysis of internal debt between equals.

In the days of British rule, the tenants did not regard the rent as a debt of honour, although the landlord did. A British Royal Commission insensitive to the interests of other social groups than their own thought this a facet of the unaccountable contradictoriness of the Irish character!

Considerations of social class do affect the behaviour of the Irish small farmer within the townlands, but other social classes play their roles as it were off stage. Political leadership, for example, in the country as a whole has been taken by the shopkeeper–publicans. Not only are their economic interests most closely affected by major policy, but they have the time to devote to bring their influence to bear on the authorities. They also have social networks in both directions, back into the countryside through the institutions we have just described, and outwards into Dublin, Cork, and Limerick through their sons who travelled and their peers who prospered and bought shops in the cities.

It is interesting to speculate how much the operation of the city political boss in the United States owes to the political training of the small town in rural Ireland (see Merton, 1957a, pp. 71–82).

Although the Irish townlands are almost homogeneous in terms of social 'class' (in the sense in which I use the word), this does not mean that they are innocent of considerations of prestige.

In Rynamona, for instance, there is what might almost be regarded as an informal group of leaders. Its three characteristics are that it includes the main farm owners, that it includes the old (but still active) men, and that it includes the fathers of complete farm families. Thus, as we would expect, prestige derived from occupation, age grade, and leading position in kinship units are inextricably mixed.

That it is informally recognized as a leading group is perhaps revealed by its village nickname of the 'Dail' – the name of the Irish Parliament. The nicknames given to the participants are also significant. It meets in the house of O'Donoghue, known as 'the judge'. He is an old man who lives with his nephew and his nephew's wife who work his land under his direction. O'Halloran, known as the 'drawer-down' because it is his role to choose the subjects of discussion, farms with his wife and six children on a prosperous farm near by. He has travelled a bit in Southern Ireland and is thought to have a 'head on him'. He was probably a secret supporter of Cosgrave rather than De Valera in national politics. This group of old men after discussion, however, decided the village should vote for 'Dev', and O'Halloran anxiously impressed on the authors that they should keep his real views to themselves. Somewhat of an anomaly in the group is O'Loughlin, a bachelor in his late fifties. He speaks seldom and has no nickname. Roche, the 'public-prosecutor', a man of sixty, farms with the help of his wife and a grown-up son and daughter. It is his role to extract precise opinions on the themes that O'Halloran has introduced. His cross-examinations serve to clarify the issues discussed and are not resented. Cullinan, the 'senator', delivers weighty opinions as befits a man of fifty with five children including sons over twenty-five. Ruin (called Noonan in *Family and Community*) is not taken very seriously by the others; he is voluble, very voluble, and tactless. He is a near neighbour of O'Donoghue and sixty years old with two sons in their twenties and a daughter. He probably serves a useful purpose in the group despite his tactlessness, for when fools rush in, subjects may be raised which need discussing. Hostility, which the raising of controversy may engender, can be better resisted by a fool, or a stranger.

The Dail is completed by Quinn who only moved into it while the authors were in Rynamona. Quinn was a man who had married into the farm of a widow by marrying her sister. They had not yet any children. He was the youngest of the Dail and arriving rather than arrived.

This group takes on its full significance in the light of those who did not attend. Two houses sent no representatives – one was too poor, the other too rich. Moroney, a man of sixty with a son and daughter in their thirties, was perhaps disliked for personal reasons, but he was also rich by comparison with the others. The public prosecutor's elder brother, Roche, was, at seventy-five, old and had retired from active life. O'Brien, a mere sprig at forty, had only two children under fifteen. While he might have moved into the group, his bad temper limited his popularity. Mackey, an orphan, had only recently married and sent his brother to the town.

Mackey, Moroney, and sometimes Quinn spent their evenings at the home of the carpenter, nicknamed Oscair, after a folk hero, because of his great strength. There they met O'Sullivan, the vet, and one or two others, bachelors and the like who would never – because of their landlessness – be able to reach full status in the community. These last, however, were grown too old to meet and play cards with the young men at Roche's house. Nor did they accompany the young men to dances or hurling matches.

The Dail, which met nightly, concerned themselves

mainly with serious matters. Requests from the County Council were discussed and agreement informally recommended, or otherwise. They decided which way the townland ought to vote and how village disputes should be settled. They had of course no sanctions they could apply to make villagers do as they wished, but out of respect for the old and established, and for fear of adverse gossip, they got their way. Representing the village to the official external world and in a sense to itself, they are one of the major factors in maintaining the unity of Rynamona.

The young men also represent the village to the outside world but in a different way. Their prowess at dancing and at gambling and hurling bring glory, albeit transitory, to the townland. They too represent a unity, at once narrower, in that it is confined to the young, and wider in its geographical spread.

As Arensberg and Kimball put it: 'The activities of young men unite them across family and clique lines even from one community to the next. But those of the old men do more; they unite young and old as well' (p. 197).

I have now tried to give some picture of the sort of society Arensberg and Kimball found in Southern Ireland in 1932. I have done this mainly because this was a pioneer study. For the *first* time, in the British Isles, anthropologists looked at a community, and tried to describe and analyse its life as others had done in the South Seas or in Africa. They showed, in what seemed then great detail, but would now be regarded as thin, the part played by custom and the apparently irrational in the maintenance of rational order. They showed how in a community of economic identity of interest such as exists among the small farmers, economic and social life, politics and kinship are inseparably linked together.

They showed too how, under the impact of the town and industrialism, things were beginning to change. Ireland revisited in 1962, thirty years later, has changed in more than just the name. Even in 1932, cooperation was declining, farmers were beginning to keep accounts, craftsmen were being replaced by town-made factory goods. I hope that someone will go back to Rynamona and Luogh and see what they are like now. Meanwhile in the chapters that follow we shall look at communities which have already moved to successively further stages along the path away from the style of life we have illustrated in rural Ireland.

CHAPTER 2

Truly Rural: Wales

AFTER Arensberg and Kimball's pioneer study described in Chapter 1, no further major study of a British community was undertaken for some time. The next book was about Wales. Just before the Second World War, Professor Daryll Forde, then head of the Geography Department at Aberystwyth, and the Principal of the University College of Wales, Ifor L. Evans, encouraged Alwyn D. Rees to study the parish of Llanfihangel-yng-Ngwynfa in mid-Wales. This was part of a plan for many studies in Wales which, for obvious reasons, was delayed for many years. Rees himself then encouraged others to follow him (Rees, 1950 and Davies, 1960) both in Wales and elsewhere.

The predominance of Welsh studies is partly therefore historical accident, if the appointment of three such remarkable professors of geography as H. J. Fleure, Daryll Forde, and E. G. Bowen may be so regarded. It is partly also due to the success of Rees's study.

An additional consideration, however, is the fact that those wishing to do research of this kind will tend to look for places where they can study a community as a whole. They seek a place that can be seen as a more or less self-contained, self-sufficient system. Areas of this kind in Britain are only found in relative isolation from the main stream of agricultural and industrial development. Such areas have marginal land which is also too far from markets to be worthwhile buying or developing by other than local inhabitants. Thus for various reasons, would-be rural researchers have either selected 'tassels from the Celtic Fringe' in Scotland, Wales, or Ireland, or they have gone to highland areas of England like Gosforth in Cumberland, or the Derbyshire and Devonshire moors (for the latter see Williams, 1958 and 1963). These latter areas would themselves be Celtic but for the power of bygone Saxon kings, a power itself based on trade, manufacture, or more advanced agriculture.

Another factor which drives researchers to such places is that they are strange – they have customs and practices not shared by the majority of *urbane* town dwellers even in Wales. They are therefore interesting to the English as quaint reminders of the past; to the Welsh and Scots they sometimes nurture a romantic view of what might have been, had English industry and its camp followers not invaded or depopulated their homelands.

LLANFIHANGEL-YNG-NGWYNFA

Excluding Ireland, Llanfihangel will be at one extreme of our continuum – truly, truly rural.

Llanfihangel society is not really based on village life at all. It is a parish of three hamlets and scattered farmsteads occupying 15½ square miles of rolling uplands in Montgomeryshire, north central Wales. The population in 1940 was about 500 people. In 1840 it had more than 1,000 but since then its numbers have on the whole steadily declined. About 450 of its inhabitants live in scattered farms and cottages around the countryside, embedded in the land from which they derive their livelihood.

There are, however, three small hamlets, Llanfihangel, Dolanog, and Pontllogel. Each of them has a little church and a few buildings. The largest of them, Llanfihangel, known as the Llan, has only eight dwellings – the rectory, the schoolhouse, two shops, the post office, an inn, and two other cottages. The church, a village hall and a school make up this miniature town. For, as Rees says, the hamlets in upland Wales are 'towns' serving the agricultural people of the hills, rather than homes housing them. Even Llanfyllin, six miles to the east, the traditional market town of the parish, has only 1,000 inhabitants.

Llanfihangel adjoins eight other parishes all within eleven miles radius of its centre. In all they cover 177 square miles and within this area were born 85 per cent of the householders of the parish and their wives as were 75 per cent of their parents. They were not all born in the parish, however. In the course of the family cycle and as part of the trickle from west uplands to better eastern land and eventually the Shropshire plain, farmers frequently change farms. Only a half of the household heads were born in the parish itself, a third of their wives, and a quarter of their mothers and mothers-in-law.

So here is our area of social interaction, the social field in which the inhabitants pass most of their lives. It has a distinctive culture of its own, overwhelmingly Welsh-speaking, but cut off from the main stream of Welsh culture by the Berwyn Mountains. Despite trips across the border to Oswestry for shopping, it is cut off from English culture by the barriers of class and language.

Finally, it is a culture impoverished by depopulation (and also enriched perhaps by the struggle to retain its identity); in Rees's words, 'on every hand there are cottages in decay, fields reverting to rough pasture and churches and chapels which are too numerous and too large for the present community' (Rees, 1950, p. 14).

The Economy of Llanfihangel

Life in Llanfihangel is firmly based on the land and on agriculture. Within this economic base the most common activity is stock rearing rather than dairying or tilling the soil. In 1939 four-fifths of the land was permanently under grass. Of the other fifth more than half was clover and temporary grasses. Even the residue of arable was mainly under oats.

Nearly all the dwellings in the parish had land attached to them. Sixteen houses without land included two vicarages, two school houses, and one country house. The remaining eleven were occupied by widows and retired farm workers living on their own.

Some plots of course were very small. Thirty-two (out of 114) had less than twenty acres. Of these, twenty-three tenants had other occupations – and the remainder like the landless were old and retired. At the other end of the scale sixty-one farms of more than fifty acres accounted for nine-tenths of the total area of the parish. Some of these had several hundred acres but most of them were between 100 and 150 acres.

At one time they were mainly subsistence farmers who bought their few outside necessities by the sale of surplus stock. Now they can be described as specialized pastoralists. Llanfihangel has become an 'importing' area for finished goods. The wheelwright and the smith repair the products of the factory. Shops on wheels visit the outlying farmers and the three hamlets contain general stores selling groceries, patent medicines, and smaller hardware. Household goods may be fetched in from Llanfyllin, Oswestry, or even Liverpool. This then is very much of a money economy but 'pre-industrial conditions and values have partially survived and these account for much that is distinctive in the culture ... it must be realized that unlike a modern factory, the farm remains a home and a means of subsistence as well as an instrument for making money' (Rees, p. 29).

In Llan families, the father has the multiple roles of husband, father, manager, and workman. Once he provided family entertainment and conducted prayers as well, but this has now passed.

In Wales in 1931 farmers and their relatives made up 80 per cent of all persons engaged in agriculture. On farms of over twenty acres in the parish, farmers and their relatives do 80 per cent of the men's work; 90 per cent of the women's work is done by farmers' wives and other kin. Larger farms at some stages in the family cycle, when the children are too young or have married and left, are obliged to hire labour. Only a third of the farms over fifty acres in 1940 had hired hands, and two thirds of those over a hundred acres. Even then hired hands were often nephews or cousins of the farm family. Such hired labourers usually live on the farm as members of the family – only on one or two of the largest farms were there separate dining tables for family and labourers. This is not surprising since many of the labourers are themselves sons of farmers who will eventually have farms of their own. The lack of a real free market in farm labourers is, I think, a sharp distinguishing feature of this kind of economy. When labourers live out and travel daily to work as they do in lowland Britain and in some large farms in Wales, we have a real industrial agricultural economy. The farm *is* like a factory, and the farmer has an office where he calculates his profits and his losses. Farmers in such a system compete rather than cooperate, sons feel demeaned by working for wages, and labourers eat in the kitchen. Unfortunately there is no full-length study published of such an area.

Ascriptive Roles – family, kindred and neighbours

In a society like Llanfihangel where formal specialized links are rare, the family, both in the sense of mother, father, and children and in the sense of uncles, aunts, and cousins, is of great social importance. Most people in any society are born into a family. Each has a mother and father, who themselves have mothers and fathers. Mothers and fathers have brothers and sisters. Children have children. Brothers and sisters have children. So each individual has a set of people, different from every other individual who is related to him (or her) by 'blood'. These are his cognatic kin. But, as Rees points out, consanguinity is one thing, social relationships another. Different societies select different groups of kin as the most important. In some societies and situations one's mother's mother's line may be emphasized, in others one's father's father's. Sometimes the former may be important in one aspect of life and the latter in another. In rural Wales all kin reckoned through both mother and father are recognized as 'belonging', as being 'my people' or 'my blood'. In any situation most people in Llanfihangel have plenty of kin to choose from. Thus two thirds of the households have members whose father, mother, brother, sister, son, or daughter lives in another household in the parish.

A third of the households are linked to two other households in this way. One of Rees's parish friends criticized the son of his mother's second cousin 'although he is belonging to me'. Second cousins in general are usually known and acknowledged as kin. Llan people compare the complicated blood relationships between households to 'pig's entrails'. Nor, of course, do the links in this network stop short at the parish boundary. They extend eastwards into England, and westwards into Wales 'tying up many of the isolated households in Llanfihangel with relatives in the wider neighbourhood' (Rees, p. 75). These distant kin renew their bonds ritually at times of crisis – weddings and especially funerals.

Indeed, funerals are a time of ritual renewing of unity even within the parish. A representative of each family attends and 'the bond between an individual and the general body of neighbours is perhaps never so fully manifested' (Rees, p. 96).

At shearing times, too, when neighbours cooperate, distant kin are called in to help and to maintain their ties with the household and the community.

It is from his kindred that a man acquires the beginnings of his reputation. The key question in placing a man is not here 'what does he do for his living?', or even 'where does he come from?' – but 'to whom does he belong?', 'what is his family background?'; 'for', as the Welsh proverb says, 'the nature of the chick is in the broth'.

Each household then, and each individual within it, lives enmeshed in a kindred. Some he knows of, but never sees; others he sees and greets; others he cooperates with and befriends. But all belong to him and he belongs to them – they do not like to see him poor or ill and uncared for, for they share the disgrace. Nor for the same reasons will they tolerate his departure from moral rules without comment and informal pressure. A kindred, says Rees, provides both security and social control.

If a man gets involved in a quarrel or dispute, his kin should support him. But his wife also has a set of kin who may be committed by the same ties to another party. If cooperation in economic matters is to continue, and above all if a family event such as a wedding or funeral occurs, this may be a powerful incentive to make it up and resume friendship.

The demands of cooperation and the settlement of disputes make it an advantage as well as a matter of prestige to 'belong' to the people in as many households as possible. So it is not surprising to the sociologist that in such a society, first-cousin marriage should be rare.

Although there are other reasons for this which are discussed in another chapter, to marry first cousins would be to miss an opportunity of spreading the scale of cooperation and very special 'friendship' based on kinship.

Nor is it surprising that outside second cousins the precise nature of kinship links should not be emphasized. The ideology of all belonging together would be damaged if degrees of belongingness were stressed. The kindred which recognizes kinship in all lines is, unlike the unilineal corporate kin group of tribal society, mainly a mechanism of inclusion rather than exclusion.

'Strangers' remain strangers until they have been in Llan a long time, and do not become integrated fully until their children and grandchildren have married and had children who by marriage earn themselves places in 'the pig's entrails'.

Nevertheless, the networks of which every Llan farm household is a part, in agricultural cooperation, for visiting, and in recreational and religious activities, are not confined to kin. Neighbours too are important. Just as consanguinity does not necessarily lead to social relationships neither does physical proximity. 'Each farm is the centre of a circle of cooperators which differs slightly from those of its neighbours while overlapping with them, and in this way the whole countryside is covered by a continuous network of reciprocities' (Rees, p. 94).

The farms with which a farmer cooperates are to some extent traditional and linked not so much to him personally

as to the farm. When a new tenant moves in, the traditional neighbour will call with offers to help. These offers
are accepted and in due course returned; and so the relationship is renewed.

'Neither a borrower nor a lender be' would be poor advice to a Welsh upland farmer, for both his economy and
his social life are sustained by exchange of loans. No
farmer would buy a collar to fit his horse, if he knew a
neighbour had the right-sized collar and no horse to fit it.
All sorts of veterinary and agricultural implements are lent
and borrowed, sometimes going through a whole chain of
temporary users before returning to the owner. With this
cooperation goes also companionship. People in Llan do not
go into their neighbours' houses and bluntly ask a loan or
favour, nor do they even go to purchase something. They
pass the time of day first and only as an apparent after-
thought do they state the real reason for their coming.

'Even a business transaction is a social event,' says Rees
(p. 96). Perhaps he should have said a business transaction
especially is a social event, for the courtesies and apparent
irrelevancies surrounding exchange in a society based on
reciprocity provide an instance of what I will later describe
as social redundancy, without which it would be a different
sort of society. Thus payments for services are nearly always
in kind rather than in cash. It is not only roles which are
multiple in this kind of society, but social processes and
practices also appear to the superficial observer to be un-
necessarily complex.

Sheep-shearing in Llan provides an excellent example.
On the larger farms this is an important event calling for
the 'assistance of from half a dozen to a dozen neighbours'.
As I have already said kinship is also involved and may
bring kinsmen from a distance.

This is particularly true of shearing-days at the moorland farms,
which are held on the same day from year to year, and bring together relatives for miles around. Shearing-day is essentially a
'farmers' day'. Labourers are not usually good shearers, and even
if they were, it would be an insult to send one to assist a neighbour

or a relative. The farmer must go himself if possible, and, if he cannot, he must be represented by a grown-up son or some other near relative. In the same way, the farmer who is helped will have to spend a week or two going from farm to farm in return.

In addition to their practical value, these days of cooperative activity are important social events. Elaborate meals are prepared, the best rooms in the house are used, the best cutlery and china are brought out and every effort is made to give the guests a handsome welcome. The prestige of the family is involved in the lavishness of this hospitality, which is a concomitant of voluntary work the world over, and any indication of niggardliness will be criticized among neighbours and ridiculed by the young men. All the cooperative tasks are ones where men work in groups, but shearing has the additional social advantage of being a relatively quiet task performed indoors. It is usually done on the barn floor, the shearers being seated on stools. They take great pride in the speed and skill with which they work and the opportunity for display and competition is not missed. When the evening feast is over they will gather round the hearth and there will be long discussions on the events which have occurred in the district 'since we were here a year ago', reminiscences of shearing-day at this particular farm in days gone by, with allusions to departed friends, and speculation as to 'how many of us will be here a year tonight'. And when these time-honoured topics have been reviewed, the discussion may be turned to a theological or a political subject (p. 95).

We have seen that the individual in Llanfihangel is a node in many overlapping networks, some based on kinship, some on proximity, some on both and some on neither. Not only, in Barnes's terminology (Barnes, 1954), is the distance round each hole in the network small, but the mesh at one level also overlaps and cuts across the mesh at another. A is linked to B in many ways. Even if they are not encapsulated in village groups Llan householders have a highly-connected, close-knit network; and, as Elizabeth Bott has suggested for all such cases, household roles are segregated between husband and wife (Bott, 1957). They are also segregated between parents and children, and between girls and boys. Between the individual and the network stands the elementary family. Being born gives the individual a social position in the family, getting married a social position in the network of community relationships. There is little ambiguity about this division in the individual life cycle since there are few three-generation households in the parish. Only thirteen of eighty-one farm families had three generations, and of these six were makeshift. Two were married daughters with children for whose households farms were yet to be found, two were widows, and two were unmarried daughters with illegitimate children. Four were married sons living with aged fathers and three married daughters living with aged parents.

The members of a farm family have each their allotted tasks. The men work in the fields under the direction of their father. The women are for the most part confined to jobs in house and yard. This includes the care of poultry and the preparation of butter. The butter and eggs are the mother's to dispose of, and the profits made on them serve to buy household necessities, groceries, and clothes for the younger children. Farmer husbands know little of the amount and fate of such money; while in all but the smallest farms there is usually work for more than one man, most farm wives work alone, and unmarried daughters have to seek work outside the parish.

The sons (and the daughters) are entirely subordinate to their fathers while they stay on the farm. They receive no wages, only their keep and occasional pocket money. The sons are even, by local custom, so engrained as not to be conscious, denied a surname and referred to by their Christian name together with the name of the farm.

On marriage all this changes, for to marry you must usually have a farm of your own which the groom's father provides and stocks. The girl's parents too will give some help with the stock. There is no official marriage bargain, but considerations of family prestige usually ensure generosity.

With the farm, the son acquires independence, a surname, and a place in the network of cooperating kin and neighbours. The cycle begins again. While in theory the youngest son remains at home until the father dies and then marries and takes over the 'home' farm, in practice what happens depends on other factors, like the stage in the family cycle at which a parent dies. There are never two mistresses in one farm, and in those three-generation cases where sons and their widowed fathers lived on the same farm it was the father who had moved in on the son, not the son who had stayed at home.

The need to provide a farm at marriage means that men marry later than elsewhere in Britain and that there are more bachelors. Even so there were six marriages where husband and wife remained separately in their own parents' homes awaiting the availability of a farm. Three of these couples already had children.

The norm that each married man is head of a farm household should act to prevent three-generation households from arising. In point of fact it creates them. Two women do care for children and do housework in the same house. Two men, both fully adult, do work from the same farmstead. So the very mechanism which set out to avoid three-generation households, with the role-conflict that might be involved, creates them. The certainty of rules in Llanfihangel is typical of small-scale societies in containing an uncertainty of operation which makes it possible for society to function.

The Welsh farmer is born a potential farmer, serves a long apprenticeship to his father, and is transformed by marriage into the incumbent of a cluster of roles: father, husband, controller of productive unit, node in the network of friendship, kinship, and cooperation. Even if for the individual there are variations in this pattern, for the society it has inevitability. Llanfihangel, however, is also part of an industrial society. For example, farmers receive letters and telephone calls and there is a post office to mediate these. Although children may miss some school to help on the farm (and learn in the process), there is a school and they spend most of their days there. It is convenient to have groceries near at hand and there are general stores to provide them. Religious beliefs require the specialized services of vicar, minister, church cleaner, sexton, and organist. The state is represented by the police; and so on. It is evident that Llanfihangel is not only made up of farmers and their wives and families. There is a postman, a school-teacher, ministers of religion, and shopkeepers. Rees assumes either that we all know how they are selected and trained or that this process is largely external to the system of Llanfihangel which he is describing. And so, of course, it is.

It is worth noting, however, that their social life takes on its colour from the surrounding countryside. The three hamlets are the countryside writ small. Here too there is borrowing and lending of household equipment, books, and newspapers. But their physical proximity makes the network so close-knit as to be a group: 'if a member does not turn up during the course of a day his absence is noticed and questions are asked' (Rees, p. 99).

The doors of the houses are always open and even the shops never close. Indeed, they seem to be at their busiest between ten and eleven o'clock at night. Here again the multiplicity of roles operates. 'A shopkeeper interests himself in cures and his advice is sought in case of illness. He also takes a lead in the organization of sports and coaches the local teams, while his wife plays the piano and has now succeeded her father as church organist. The latter, a retired blacksmith and part-time postmaster, was very well read, and good use was made of his literacy not only by his immediate neighbours, but also by the inhabitants of the surrounding district. The postman makes walking-sticks in return for which farmers give him presents of tobacco, and he is also the church bellringer and organ blower' (Rees, p. 99).

So in the hamlets as in the countryside we can accept Rees's judgement that the community has many of the attributes of a large family. But we must remember that the family joke and the family quarrel also have their importance.

If parishioners in Llanfihangel are united by a relatively

inclusive kinship system and patterns of cooperation and neighbourliness, they also have their divisions both of class and of religion. Even here, however, dominant cleavages are few and the edges of groups are blurred.

Among the farmers themselves class distinction is weak. Until recently nearly all, large and small, were tenants of the Llwydiarth Estate. All of them are involved in actual manual work side by side with their labourers. Many farms are small, as are the profits derived from them. Farms can now be bought and are relatively cheap to buy. It is not uncommon for a thrifty farm labourer who marries an equally thrifty girl to acquire his own farm. Sixteen per cent of the farmers of over twenty-five acres were the sons of wage-earners. As we have seen, the sons of all but the most prosperous farmers often work as labourers at one period of their lives. Kindreds also cut across lines of class division. There are few so poor as not to have some rich relations; and few so rich as to have no poor. Most Llan people share the same elementary education and even where farmers' sons before the 1944 Act went to secondary school, they are often recalled at fourteen to play their part in the work of the farm. Girls were sometimes encouraged to stay on and even sent to private schools in Oswestry. An accomplished daughter, especially for farmers with ambitions to move into the high-status and profitable farms of the Shropshire plain, is a marriageable asset. The larger farmers also are inclined to marry their daughters upwards if possible, or at least to another farmer's son. There were thirty-eight farmers of farms over fifty acres who were themselves farmers' sons. Thirty-two of them were married to farmers' daughters. Status symbols apart from the ownership of a horse were in 1940 little valued. Clothes, and expensive household equipment were little sought. Money as such is, it is true, valued highly more for itself than what it can buy. The leaders in the Nonconformist chapels, always short of funds, were men of means. But although money is valued, life is not completely subordinated to its pursuit, nor are careful accounts kept on farms. Only the income-tax regulations of the Second World War persuaded the farmers to keep accounts at all. Farmers take days off to attend sales where they do not intend to buy, for the sake of the gossip and conversation. An extensive network is a source of prestige and long-term economic advantage for which the sacrifice of short-term gains is well worth while. The larger farmers are not only endogamous but self-perpetuating since 78 per cent of farmers' sons become farmers themselves. Only just over half of smallholders' sons remain on the land, the rest go to mining, quarrying, industrial work in the towns, or emigrate to the U.S. or Dominions. This in fact is the mechanism by which Llanfihangel maintains its class homogeneity. At the bottom it exports its wage-earning class to England; at the top during the course of the centuries it has 'exported' the gentry into Anglicized culture.

In the past the squires, the Vaughans and the Watkins Williams-Wynns, collected their rent, but they spoke little Welsh and played little part in Welsh culture as Llanfihangel farmers understand it. Today there is an industrialist living in the parish, but despite his generosity he barely touches its life. There only remain teachers, preachers and the like who while speaking Welsh have their kin elsewhere and are kept at a social distance by being addressed as 'Mr'. The parish remains almost one class, the medium farmers. They all have the same relation to the land. They derive prestige from the size of their holdings, their reputed wealth, the number of people they know, their contribution to religion and to Welsh bardic culture, but as Rees says: 'there is little scope for pretentiousness in a community where the past history of every individual and his relatives is known to everyone else' (p. 147).

Religion and politics in the past have also both reflected and complicated this situation. The religious revivals of the eighteenth and nineteenth centuries in Wales provided the ideology of an opposition which had already developed between Anglicized landlords and Welsh tenants. Howell Harris, a great eighteenth-century Welsh preacher and

founder of the Calvinistic Methodists in Wales, regarded
Sir Watkins William Wynn as one of his greatest enemies.
It is said that the first Sir Watkin died of a fall while
returning from the hunt, and that at the same time at a
Methodist prayer meeting they were appealing, ' O Lord,
cast down the great Devil of Wynnstay'.

Again, Sir Watkin was a Conservative who upheld the privileges
of his class and a representative of English culture in Wales. His
tenants were predominantly Nonconformist, radical and Welsh.
The political history of Wales from the early decades of the nineteenth century until a generation ago consisted primarily of the
intensification of the struggle between these two groups of interests,
a struggle which, after passing through the bitter days of political
evictions following the elections of 1859 and 1868 and the tithe war
of 1880s and 1890s culminated in a victory for Nonconformity and
Liberalism (p. 155).

The bitterness of these struggles lies now in the past, but
'the politico-religious cleavage bears some relation to
economic status. In 1940, the Nonconformist group com-
prised four-fifths of the farmers of holdings over 20 acres,
and half the smallholders and cottages, leaving the church
with half the smallholders and only a fifth of the farmers'
(Rees, p. 157).

As we shall see later I found a similar situation in the
village of Glynceiriog.

In 1940, most parishioners, like many in Glossop, voted
Liberal if they were Nonconformist and Conservative if they
were Church. Labour votes were few and far between and
the main class consciousness was not felt by the few wage-
earners but by the farmers. These feel themselves to be
threatened by the large farmers of England on the one hand
and industrialism on the other. In some parts of Wales this,
in my view, and not nationalism, was the driving force
which led to the setting up of the Farmers Union of Wales
as a breakaway from the National Farmers Union.

While the social and economic split between gentry and
their tenants goes some way to account for the growth of
Nonconformity, it is neither an explanation nor an

adequate analysis of the existence of differing Nonconformist sects.

There are four such groups in Llanfihangel: Indepen-
dents, Baptists, Calvinistic Methodists, and Wesleyan
Methodists. I will make no attempt to explain their origin
or the doctrinal differences between them. In present-day
Llanfihangel, however, 'sectarianism remains an established
part of the social structure'. It has important effects on
social life in that it provides yet another series of overlapping
networks of cross-cutting ties. Although the Episcopal
Church is the largest single denomination, there are twice
as many Nonconformists as Anglicans.

A member of one of these Nonconformist denominations
by virtue of his chapel membership finds, at a very early
age, that he has a slightly different life experience from a
member of one of the others. The sects differ in their organization, in the hymns they sing and the arrangement of the
tunes they sing them to. The well-known personalities of
one group are scarcely known in another. Even the child's
view of world geography will differ. The Methodist will hear
missionary descriptions of the Khasi Hills in Assam whereas
the Independent will learn more of mission life in the South
Sea islands.

A Wesleyan, for example, goes to chapel each Sunday and
meets the same people, selected from among his kin and
neighbours. Through joint singing festivals and preaching
meetings, the chapel member meets others in his denomination from outside the parish. Religious organization unites
the people of Llanfihangel with a wider area while it
creates further cross-cutting subdivisions within the parish.

The Nonconformist conscience with its emphasis on conformity to moral norms (if not to the Anglican prayer book)
pervades the society. The chapels frown on drinking and
above all on sexual immorality. In practice this moral disapproval is selective and without sanctions.

It is selective in that 'illegitimacy', while not approved,
is nevertheless not strongly condemned or sanctioned. It
would be difficult to find the kin-group without sin to cast

the first stone. Adultery between people who are already married, however, is more strongly disapproved.

The courtship pattern perhaps makes illegitimacy and 'shotgun' marriage inevitable. The young men enjoy considerable licence and thirty to forty of them gather each evening for horse-play, joking, and perhaps drinks. The girls, however, are more closely surveyed and are only allowed to wander abroad for specific reasons. Thus, when a branch of the Welsh League of Youth was set up and met once a week in winter, the girls asked if it could meet in summer too. It was their only excuse to get out. Paradoxically, youth clubs, seen as a means of keeping young people off the streets in towns, provide an excuse to get on the street in Llanfihangel.

Courtship, then, at least before the Welsh League of Youth, could not be a public affair. A young man, after the male 'peer group' gathering had broken up, went to the house of the girl of his choice and attracted her attention by tapping on her window. If she liked him, she would invite him into the house (her parents by this time sleeping). At first, she would entertain him to light refreshments in the kitchen, and sometimes later, if the affair went well, to courting in bed. This interesting custom, with or without benefit of bolster, known as 'bundling' and described elsewhere both in Rhys Davies's novel *Black Venus* and in the folklore literature, does not need detailed discussion here. It is enough to point out that its secrecy makes possible trial and error, and it ensures a choice of partner to the girl and boy concerned at the same time as giving the community and the parents some control over who marries whom. While village gossip knows early what's what, a public and hence relatively irrevocable announcement comes late in the process.

This is only one example of the rather special position of youth, or at least of young men, in Llanfihangel. It must be remembered that youth is roughly equivalent to unmarried, and the peer groups of boys have an age range from sixteen to thirty-five. This group is known as 'the lads', and behaves boisterously at home and away, especially on visits to other areas. The boys play pranks and fight the groups of other areas. I would suggest that their behaviour away from home is an informal representation of Llan unity, just as the village choir's performance in Eisteddfodau is a formal one. In a later chapter I shall discuss the way the football team performs this role for Glynceiriog. When Rees says that parishioners have practically no interest in horse-racing and football (p. 138), but that every one cares about Eisteddfod winners, he is demonstrating that Llanfihangel looks to a different external environment of reference groups from Glynceiriog in 1953.

As the young men represent the community as a whole outside the Llan, so they do in some senses within it. For, oddly enough, through their own irresponsibility they can curb the irresponsibility of others. They exercise social control by ridicule and in extreme cases almost sadistic practical jokes. Rees gives two striking examples:

Not far from Llanfihangel a middle-aged widow was being visited repeatedly at night by a young lad, and the youth group blamed the widow for enticing him. To break up the association they congregated around the house of the widow every time the lad was there, stopping up the chimney and throwing dead vermin and other obnoxious objects in through the doors and windows. In another district I was told of a married man, who was associating with another woman, being met by the youth group one night on his way home. They plastered him with cowdung and dragged him through the river (p. 83).

Peters has given a fascinating analysis of why this is possible. He points out that the lads are at once outside and inside the community. Through their families they receive information and statements of values. They can apply sanctions in a way which is not possible for their elders, in an egalitarian society. Since they are always playing pranks out of mischief, an extra one which is purposive can be excused by the communities without offence to the victim. Nor can the victim complain, to do so would only draw attention to his misdemeanour. Again, since they are a group, individual responsibility is hard to attribute.

This is a special case of a joking-relationship which, as I will suggest in Part Two, is especially common in the sort of community where there are multiple roles. It is in this sort of society that Professor Radcliffe-Brown's statements become relevant, although they were originally based on African anthropological material (Radcliffe-Brown, 1952).

The joking relationship is a peculiar combination of friendliness and antagonism. The behaviour is such that in any other social context it would express and arouse hostility; but it is not meant seriously and must not be taken seriously. There is a pretence of hostility and real friendliness. To put it another way, the relationship is one of permitted disrespect.

and again:

The relation can be described as involving both attachment and separation, both social conjunction and disjunction.

Rees in fact points out that 'jokes' of this kind are confined to victims considered to 'belong' in Llan and would not be employed against outsiders. He points out too that oblique comment of this kind occurs elsewhere in this society. He describes the custom of 'striking the post for the wall to hear' – teasing someone by criticizing his behaviour in a jocular way in his presence, but in the third person as if it concerned someone else.

These cases and the discussion on the stranger in Glynceiriog are examples of the social actor (individual or group) taking on the role of a maintainer of social order, or a keeper of the norms, while dissociating himself from it. It is made possible in the case of Llan young men because they play two roles simultaneously. As sons of their farmer fathers, they must be upright, moral, virtuous, obedient, and hard working in the serious affairs of Llan as a community. As young men they must be jocular, irresponsible, and aggressive in the recreational affairs of the young men's peer group. In the interests of the maintenance of orderly behaviour in others who are already adult, they are permitted, even encouraged, to use disorderly behaviour in the normal context of the former. The community, by exploiting the uncertainty of context, can avoid the imposition of sanctions. Hence I suggest this definition of the circumstances in which joking relationships can occur.

A joking relationship occurs when one actor who is performing two or more roles simultaneously uses behaviour appropriate to one role in the role-system of another role. It may be used to enforce moral norms in the second system. This is a means by which role conflict becomes functional. It is possible because the uncertainty of context makes the sanctions against such behaviour in the second system ineffective in the first.

The behaviour of the youth group, although as we have seen it may have a serious purpose, introduces the subject of recreation in Llanfihangel. I consider that this is a subject which is always of major importance. Recreation is at once the most sensitive index of social change and the most resistant to it. It seems to be the first social activity to show signs of the effect of economic change and yet the last to change fundamentally. Thus, although Rees says of Wales in general and Llanfihangel in particular that 'its material culture is far less "Welsh" than its non-material culture' (p. 166), which implies stability, he shows at the same time how the general social and economic changes have changed the pattern of recreation:

Thus three stages may be distinguished in the history of organized recreation in the parish. Like religion it was centred at first at the Llan and its main occasion was a religious feast day. Later it was carried with religion into the neighbourhoods and revivified. Now, with the self-contained life of the neighbourhoods and the chapels waning, it is returning again to the hamlet where it is supported largely by organizations, the foundations of which, like those of the church, lie outside the parish (Rees, p. 141).

He also shows how these 'outside fountainheads' do not all come from the same source or aim to refresh the same people. Outside authorities do not see Llan as a unity but as a place which happens to contain groups of farmers, of youth, and of women. They see people with different roles and different interests, requiring different organizations. Whereas the old chapel, as Ty Cŵrdd, the meeting-house, was for all, the new societies are exclusive and sectional. Here, I consider, outside authority is both recognizing and creating a trend. Roles are becoming more and more segregated.

The farmer tends to become a specialist in his own line, leaving the preaching to the preacher and the educating to the school-master (Rees, p. 168).

Elsewhere:

Generally speaking, when men come together, they come together to do things, and when the things they do together become fewer, social intercourse also declines.

The social significance of a meeting or a visit often outweighs its practical purpose, but without such a purpose, it would rarely occur at all (Rees, p. 166).

In the terms which I shall elaborate in Part Two social redundancy is decreasing and, as it becomes integrated in industrial society Llanfihangel is moving, albeit slowly, towards the other end of our continuum.

CHAPTER 3

Truly Rural: England

IN this chapter, thanks to the painstaking work of Professor W. M. Williams, trained by Alwyn D. Rees at Aberystwyth, we can consider the social life of an English civil parish – Gosforth in West Cumberland.

It makes no claim to be a *typical* English rural area, for such a place does not exist. It was in fact chosen to some extent for its unusual features. It is a remote area, difficult to reach from urban centres and correspondingly far removed from the ultimate markets for its produce. The civil parish covers eleven square miles on the western fringe of the Lakeland fells of Cumberland. Two miles to the west lies the sea. To the north it merges with uninhabited moorland. It had in 1951, when Williams lived there and studied it, 723 inhabitants. Two-thirds of them lived in a village and the other third in scattered farms and cottages over the parish. Most of its inhabitants were Cumbrian by birth, four-fifths of the male householders and three-quarters of their wives. Nearly three-quarters of their parents also were Cumberland folk. The inhabitants, although local, are not all tied to one specific spot. It is true that some yeomen farmers' families have inhabited the same farm for four centuries, but tenant farms change hands often. Two-thirds of the household heads were born within a ten mile radius of the parish, but only a third within the parish itself. As in other agricultural areas of Britain, the population of Gosforth has been declining since 1870. The population figures for Cumberland as a whole conceal the trend because of migration to towns within the county. Similarly, within the rural district of which Gosforth forms a part there has been migration to the industrial parishes. In Gosforth itself the village has grown at the expense of the surrounding countryside. Some formerly inhabited farms, called fire-houses because of the association of hearth and home, now serve as byres and barns.

Gosforth as a parish is not entirely agricultural, but farmers, farm ways, and the farm calendar still dominate it. Out of an employed population of 318, ninety-six were farmers, their sons, and labourers. Forty-five were un-skilled and semi-skilled labourers, some at the near-by works of the Atomic Energy Authority. Clerical workers accounted for twelve and retail trade for twenty-eight. In the village itself only 6·7 per cent of the working population were agricultural labourers while 20·3 per cent worked in more recently developed industry. Providing different sorts of job is not the only effect that the Seascale Nuclear Power Station has had and will have on Gosforth. Villagers who work there meet fellow workers from all over Britain; they earn more money, and come to think in terms of shift payments, overtime, and payments for results. This is not necessarily bad, but is certainly different from employer–employee relationships on the farms where Williams tells us 'the urban idea of exact payment in money for all com-modities and services is absent'.

The village is mainly inhabited by persons not engaged in agriculture, but it also houses some farm labourers, ex-farm-labourers, and ex-farmers. There are kinship and friendship links extending from village into the countryside. Fell farmers with their emphasis on sheep affect a hostility to lowland farmers for their 'lazy' reliance on machinery and motor cars. Lowland farmers and fell farmers regard themselves as superior to villagers and hold themselves a little aloof from village associations. One end of the village affects to look down on the other. But in all these cases the relations of almost mock hostility bind the parish together as a community. 'Gosfer folk' remain 'Gosfer folk' to out-siders. Their special knowledge and enjoyment of these internal feuds adds to their solidarity against ignorant and excluded folk from elsewhere. Through the agency of gossip mediated by milkmen, postmen, and newspaper deliverers, or direct in 't'gossip shop' as the blacksmith's is known, news is spread over the parish. 'Parochial matters are still passed on from neighbour to neighbour, brother to brother, and uncle to nephew, and the occupiers of out of the way farmsteads are as well informed of recent events in the locality as the villagers living around the square' (Williams, 1956, p. 163).

Gosforth, then, provides us with a useful transitional study to bridge the gap between the totally agricultural areas we have been discussing and the small towns in the countryside which are to come.

The agricultural economy which gives the parish most of its character is based on sixty-seven holdings whose owners or tenants reside in the parish. Of these one is over 300 acres and five are over 200 acres. Twenty-eight are between 50 and 150 acres. There are twenty-eight holdings under 50 acres of which only four are worked by full-time farmers. Farms just big enough to support a family would be about 15 acres, known locally as 'wheelbarrow farms', but most of these disappeared during the 'gay hard times' between the First and Second World Wars. In 1951 the farms over 50 acres were about equally divided between tenants and freeholders. There would have been more free-holders if the landlords could have persuaded some tenants to buy. Less than a third of the farms employ hired labour and eight out of twenty-eight labourers are either relatives of the farmers or work on one of the three farms run by agents.

Highly specialized fell sheep farming, as well as arable and dairy farming, occur in Gosforth. Farms specializing in dairying and stock-raising exist side by side. Farm prices and rents vary greatly for a variety of reasons, and despite an emphasis on keeping land in the family, farms *are* bought and sold. Local farmers see the ideal farm as one that can be worked without hired labour, but this is no subsistence economy. The bank that stands in the village square keeps urban hours, and monthly cheques from the Milk Marketing Board have, since the thirties, supplemented the half-yearly income from spring and autumn fairs. Williams classifies four types of farm:

(a) there are ten dairy-farms with subsidiary stock rearing;

(b) there are twenty 'mixed' farms with a slight bias towards dairying;

(c) there are seven cattle-rearing farms;

(d) there are three sheep-farms with subsidiary cattle-rearing.

Pigs, except for home-consumed bacon, are not of great importance. Poultry is an important sideline on many farms, and there are two herds of fell and Shetland ponies destined to supply the pits of the Durham coalfield. For comparison with our other rural areas we may note that two-fifths of the cultivated land is under permanent grass, less than one-third under temporary grass, one-fifth is under oats, and one-twelfth is under rootcrops.

The yearly cycle of the farmers remains geared to the seasons and largely determines the pattern of recreational life for their fellow parishioners. The year begins with short days and a slow tempo with the odd jobs of trimming hedges and repairing walls. February the 2nd, the feast of Candlemas, is traditionally the first day for ploughing and the beginning of the farmers' financial year. Between then and Lady Day, 25 March, the fields must be ploughed and a half-year's rent paid. February also includes the horse fair and the spring sales. From then until April the farmer's life is very busy and recreation at a minimum. The potato land must be prepared, the cereal fields harrowed, oats planted, lambs cared for, and the ewes put back on the fells.

May, June, and July, despite the hay harvest at the end of June and beginning of July, are lighter months. Many farm workers take a week's holiday at Whitsun and there is time to organize the school outing to Morecambe or Blackpool in July. The first of the villagers' two main annual events, the British Legion sports day on August Bank Holiday, ushers in the farmers' next busy period, that of the cereal harvest. The Gosforth Show takes place on the first Friday in September. While the sheep must be fetched from the fells and the cattle brought in from the fields, autumn is again a season of shows and fairs. The week's holiday after Martinmas on 11 November may celebrate the payment of the second half-year's rent and refresh the farmers and their wives ready for the efforts of preparing the Christmas poultry for sale.

The farmer's yearly round determines also his contacts with the outside world. There are times to go to White-haven and Penrith to sell and buy stock, and to Egremont for seed. Small domestic items can be bought daily in Gosforth. An expedition to Whitehaven is organized for bigger items and smart clothes. Special requirements may even take the farmer or his wife to Carlisle. Bread is de-livered once a week from Egremont, but otherwise little food is imported. Nearly all other goods are imported, for the mason and the wheelwright are the only surviving tra-ditional craftsmen. The smith spends much of his time re-pairing machinery.

Here, then, is a community with a more differentiated economy and a more highly developed division of labour than County Clare or Llanfihangel. Correspondingly, the homogeneity of small farm Ireland and Wales in terms of class and status are not found here. We shall find networks which exist side by side but do not overlap. This is, how-ever, by no means yet a city, and kinship and neighbourli-ness still cut across status and class divisions except at the very top of the class hierarchy.

There are three main economic classes who participate in the social life of Gosforth:

(a) those who live either on capital or on rent;
(b) farmers who own or rent land;
(c) the rest who work for wages.

The situation is complicated, however, by two other factors which to some extent either cut across or blur these objec-tive divisions. These are prestige in the community and considerations of family. A farmer's son who works for wages for another farmer while he is waiting for a farm of his own, at once modifies the rigidity of the definition I have suggested and reveals that social distance between farmers and labourers in Gosforth is not great. One does not find the son of one of the local gentry working for wages in Gosforth, though one might, of course, find him as an undergraduate working in a farm camp elsewhere.

Williams tells us that Gosforth people recognize two main status divisions – the upper and lower classes – and he himself divides these into seven categories. Following and adapting the rather clumsy nomenclature of Lloyd Warner, he called them upper-upper, lower-upper, intermediate, upper-medial, medial, lower-medial, and lower. We will roughly follow his division but not his names. We can, I think, get a clearer comparative picture by using other terms.

Nevertheless, the first category, which I shall call the gentry, as Gosforth people do, is quite precisely defined both by its members and by Gosforth people at large. While its twenty-three members* may be on speaking terms with many people, they do not invite all to their houses or encourage their children to associate with all. Thus when Mr A's daughter attempted friendship with an ordinary villager, it was regarded as both surprising and wrong. All but three of the gentry come from outside Gosforth and all had been to public or boarding schools. Those who had been to University had been to Oxford or Cambridge. In fact two of them shocked Williams somewhat when they told him they had not heard of the University College of Wales, Aberystwyth! Not all were obviously wealthy but none of them appeared to work for their living. They were all, in their own eyes, of good family, a subject which, like money, they regarded as poor taste as a subject of conversation with other than their peers. Unlike a genuine feudal aristocracy, they did not do more than touch the social and

* Williams's figures are not always easy to interpret since he felt unable to use the convention of measuring social class either by household, or by taking a woman's to be that of her father or husband. This was because he felt that some households were internally divided by class.

recreational life of Gosforth. They are in demand as presidents and patrons in village associations, where they make suggestions for others to carry out. I would suggest in fact that they make the suggestions that the majority of the villagers favour. In a situation where there is a minority of villagers in opposition, the isolation of the gentry from ordinary village social life makes them immune from the sanction of informal unpopularity which might be applied by this minority. Thus they have a position in two systems of social relationships similar to the young men of Llanfihangel already described, and the strangers of Glynceiriog in the next chapter. They are the group which we shall meet again in Banbury where Margaret Stacey says of them:

'The basis of the upper class social circle is national, with the West End of London as its town centre, *The Times* as its local paper, and certain national events, e.g. Ascot, as its focal points' (Stacey, 1960, p. 154).

It is possible that I have here promoted this group. Its local newspaper may be the *Daily Telegraph* and its focal event the Southport Flower Show.

Williams calls the status group below the gentry lower-upper and interprets much of their behaviour in terms of their aspirations to be accepted as upper class. The examples he gives are of two families, both Cumbrian born, and both rich as a result of their business activities. Although both couples were educated at state rather than public schools, their accents vary with the people to whom they talk. To the gentry they talk 'posh', to the villagers Cumbrian.

Another man in this group was said to boast too much of the money he made, and a fourth to lack appropriate education. Williams suggests that the altering of accents means that 'such people are aware (consciously or otherwise) of their position in relation to the "upper ten" and that they are attempting to "make the best of both worlds". In other words, they know that the majority of people class them as socially superior and at the same time as inferior to certain men and women; they therefore modify their mode of speech (unlike the "upper ten") to make themselves more acceptable to everyone – or so they believe' (Williams, pp. 93–4).

This, I think, puts too teleological an interpretation on their behaviour. This is in fact the group of small capitalists (ten out of twenty-two born locally) who are found in most English country towns. When one meets them in the town environment they no longer appear uncertain as to which social category they belong. Watson has called them 'burgesses', a term which I will borrow. Watson uses the term to distinguish them from another important category which Williams here calls intermediates and Watson calls spiralists (Watson, 1964). The emergence of this category is an important by-product of the processes of bureaucratization and the elimination of social redundancy which I shall describe below. It is significant that in Gosforth the spiralists, with only ten members, are the very smallest group.

Class and status-group are intimately related concepts, but synthesizing them into one complex phenomenon is only possible after they have first been treated as analytically separate. I am standardizing the description of status-groups in the various areas of social life of Britain of which there are studies by adopting a terminology introduced by Watson. He has suggested the term 'spiralist' for the socially, economically, and geographically mobile *national* category who move upwards through bureaucratic hierarchies and outwards through the communities to which their organizations send them. While spiralists form a category nationally, in a small community they may form a group. Spiralists for whom promotion has ceased, and with it perhaps geographical movement also, are called blocked spiralists. I also use his term 'burgesses' to indicate locally-born and oriented business men. In Gosforth such people are referred to as 'educated people' in a way that the gentry, despite their Oxbridge degrees, are not. The only example Williams gives is a schoolteacher, a West countryman educated at a training college. No doubt since 1951 Seascale has brought others to the parish.* We shall meet the group again in later chapters.

The 'spiralist' group is indeed an intermediate one, in Gosforth and elsewhere, not only between status groups but also between economic classes. Top spiralists can and do achieve independence through ownership of property. Lower spiralists like teachers may be as tied to the daily round of earning as much as are the small farmers and wage earners of Gosforth.

Williams's next category he calls upper-medial. They are, in fact, the 'respectables' or 'aspirants' of other writers about other places. They are distinguished from their neighbours not necessarily in wealth or by occupation but in their expressed desire to get on, or to better themselves. All thirty are villagers and some farmers. They live in thirteen houses in the village and keep themselves to themselves as individuals.

The two largest categories are those Williams calls medial and lower-medial. The first comprises 215 people of whom 113 are farmers and their women folk. Of the fifty-two houses they occupy, forty-two are outside the village. It would seem therefore that this category broadly corresponds to the farmers' class and their 'potential affines'. The division between it as a status group and the labourers, craftsmen, apprentices, and residual categories who make up the thirty-three lower-medial is exiguous and difficult to define. The economic classes of wage-earner and farmer-employer in Gosforth tend, as we would expect, to merge. The distinction between village and parish, fell and low-land, cuts across the division, and all 578 are likely to describe themselves or be described as just 'ordinary Gosfer folk'. We also will use this term for them. They form the main body of the parish and the village, their social life is

* Professor Williams confirms that this is in fact the case. There was by 1966, he told me, a new housing estate and a large permanent caravan park which is filled entirely with professional people from the Atomic Energy station.

contained within the geographical area and gives it its distinctive character.

There only remains what some have called the 'submerged tenth', the roughs of Gosforth as compared with the 'respectables'. In Gosforth they all live in the village in only six households of thirty-one people.

The significance of the status-group divisions described by Williams lies first of all in the fact that the seven groups have seven more or less distinctive 'styles of life'. Secondly, the networks of friends which radiate from each individual are influenced by considerations of social status. No doubt also, like marries like. In technical terms, they tend towards endogamy (see Rosser, 1961 and Loudon, 1961).

Another important function of a stratification system of this kind is only evident in a parish like Gosforth when there are newcomers to be placed. This was shown as much by the questions asked of Williams as by the questions he asked. The gentry were anxious to know what his university was (Oxford or Cambridge – to them, as one sometimes used to suspect of a Tory Cabinet, there were no others). The burgesses and spiralists asked if he had a car and what sort. The wage-earners asked how he managed to get paid for just 'messing around'.

Similarly, any incoming stranger is soon placed, and expected to behave appropriately. If he does not do so he will be forced to live in a social vacuum without a local network of effective relationships. This does not mean he will be denied milk or newspapers. Williams gives the example of the stranger who, arriving in a large car and bidding casually £3,200 for a house without fuss or agitation, was accepted as gentry by all except the gentry themselves who reserved judgement. At the level at which gentry are incorporated anyway, 'off comers' of high social rank can be accepted by those of lower. Acceptance lower down the scale, which requires more intimate contact, is more slowly granted. 'They've got to summer you and winter you and summer you and winter you afore you mak' friends in Gosforth.' This process may take twenty to forty years!

Behaviour considered appropriate by one's peers is not necessarily universally approved. The gentry family which raised only a small headstone to its deceased member was becomingly modest to its peers, stingy to the general. The businessman who owned four cars was considered extravagant by all save other businessmen. These conflicts in expected behaviour themselves may function as negative reference points to determine behaviour. Working-class children are threatened with sending to the 'roughs' if they fail to behave. Roughs who behave too respectably, or respectables who aspire to better themselves, are put in their place by accusations of snobbery.

In the discussion of the general social life of the parish, the gentry, burgesses, spiralists, aspirants, and roughs will play little part. Status group interaction only appears as affecting social behaviour directly in the formal associations centred on the village and to these we must now turn.

Gosforth is regarded in West Cumberland as having a particularly rich recreational life and Williams counted no less than thirty-one formal organizations. If we leave aside the Church with 689 members in communion, the largest association is the Agricultural Society which has 342 members who have all paid their ten shillings subscription. Of these, 105 are described as officers. The three smallest associations are the twelve Girl Guides, seven Beagles, and six Charity trustees. In between lie the others, large ones like the British Legion, Wrestling Academy, Oddfellows, and Conservative Association, and small ones like the Parish Council, and Reading Room Committee. There are men's and ladies' cricket clubs, a football club, a School outings committee, and several more. All have officers and in most the upper classes and especially the gentry are over-represented for their numbers in the population. It is for this reason that Williams regards the formal organizations as determinants of class position, maintainers of social prestige and providers of opportunities for social advancement. He gives no individualized examples of social advancement through them. The burgesses (like the roughs but for different reasons), whom he regards as hungry for social advancement, hardly participate at all. This is partly because their interests lie elsewhere, in the towns, and partly because those positions to which they might advance are already filled by the gentry. Notable exceptions to this dominance by the gentry are the Football Club, since the Association code is regarded as inferior to the Rugby Union of the near-by towns, and the School outings committee which has to do menial jobs of no appeal to the gentry or burgesses. In fact in all the organizations in which the gentry do take part, their function is to suggest rather than to do. Williams tells the story of how at a church meeting a lady of the gentry proposed that the parish should be canvassed to find people to clean the church in preparation for the harvest festival. Another lady seconded the motion, but it was a working class woman who was asked to find volunteers. The eight villagers who carried out the task were all working class, while two single ladies from the gentry simultaneously decorated the pulpit with flowers.

The presidents of all associations save the Dramatic Society are drawn from the gentry. The gentry, who form about six per cent of the total population, also fill over half of the posts of chairman, vice-chairman, and vice-president. Some of the gentry hold positions in many organizations and a political analysis would show that power in the village is concentrated in very few hands.

One of the gentry is chairman of the Angling Club, the services committee of the British Legion, and the Further Education Committee. He is also vice-chairman of the Parish Council and vice-president of the Agricultural Society, the Wrestling Academy, and the Dramatic Society, as well as being on the committee of the Conservative Association.

It happens, therefore, that the fate of the social amenities of Gosforth falls into the power of those who use them least. Cases in point are the Playing-field Committee, the Trustees of the six village charities, and the Parish Council. The examples taken from the accounts of the Wrestling Academy and the British Legion illustrate the social structuring of Gosforth recreational organizations. The Wrestling Academy draws its president and five of its vice-presidents from the gentry. One vice-president is from the burgess-group, and two are from the spiralists and farmers. The chairman is also a burgess, but its secretary, treasurer, and committee of eighteen are all drawn from those groups Williams calls lower-class. Neither burgesses nor gentry participate as ordinary members, the great bulk of whom, eighty-four, are 'ordinary Gosfer folk'.

The British Legion has gentry for its president, one of its vice-presidents, and its chairman. The other vice-president is a spiralist. The treasurer is also a spiralist. Fourteen other officers and committee are 'ordinary Gosfer folk' and once again burgesses, gentry, and spiralists are not found among the rank-and-file members.

The formal organizations of Gosforth, however, do not exist *just* to enhance and confirm the status of the gentry. Cumberland wrestling is popular as a sport, brings prestige to all its successful practitioners, and to the village. Village teams entertain and are entertained by other teams from all over Cumberland. The Women's Institute also visits and is visited by groups from other parts of the county.

The football team plays matches in all parts of West Cumberland and receives other village teams in its turn. These kinds of village organizations serve to represent the village as a unit against other village units and emphasize its values as a community in a way which will be discussed in greater detail in the next chapter. West Cumberland people as a whole express their unity against authority in another way. This is through the illegal sport of cock fighting. Unfortunately however, the secrecy necessary, and the hostility to outsiders, excluded Williams also, so he is unable to tell us the details about it which he has for other formal recreational activities.

Social status, also modified by age, sex, and marital status, helps to determine in which of Gosforth's four 'locals' men participate in the informal pastimes of darts, dominoes, singing, and drinking.

The daily round of work and the relations of kin, friends, and neighbours are not influenced, though they are de-limited, by membership in status-groups. To describe this situation within the boundaries of the parish, we turn our undivided attention to 'ordinary Gosfer folk' both in the village and the rural parish around it.

For underlying this pattern of dominance by class, status, and prestige in both village and parish at large is a system of family, kinship and neighbourliness which still shows some of the features we have described for more truly rural Ireland and Wales. Even here there is a gradation between rural area and village. In the village, individual prestige is at least partly determined by quality and quantity of possessions, while on the farms ability, success as a farmer, and willing-ness to cooperate are what counts. In the village, patterns of friendliness and cooperation follow lines of physical proximity; in the countryside, new neighbours may be by-passed for more distant kin and traditional partners. In the countryside, sons marry late out of loyalty to parents; in the village this tendency is less marked. Finally, in the village, the web of community woven by gossip is in the hands of the women who meet each other face to face, cooperate in household tasks, and meet in the shops. The farm wife is confined to the house and yard and relies on her husband and sons to bring her news of neighbours and kinsmen whom she may, in some cases, never have met.

Despite these differences there is no fundamental cleav-age between village and parish and many ties, both econo-mic and kinship, link 'ordinary Gosfer folk' across the two.

As we have seen, hired labour is rare on Gosforth farms especially those on the fells. This may in some cases be a new development arising out of a shortage of rural labour occasioned by industrial development. Although agricul-tural experts say much land is under-used, a lack of capital may make it difficult for farmers to pay a hired hand's wages while they wait for the extra profit his work should bring. Even where hired labour is employed, the idea of a family farm persists. Farmers seek other farmers' sons as

labourers and treat them as part of the family. This may
raise another difficulty in finding volunteers, for a member
of the family is not expected to worry about the hours he
works or the wages he receives. Although there are formal
contracts and recommended wages, farmers and their hands
informally agree to higher wages but unregulated hours –
'they tak' things as they come'. While few young men seem
to be attracted by this, still fewer will work on a farm on an
industrial basis, as one farmer in Gosforth who tried it found
out. So it remains the case that land is underworked and
'family labour operates at a maximum solely from the time
the sons and daughters leave school until they marry and
leave home' (Williams, p. 38). Seventy-five per cent of male
labour on farms is done by farmers and their kin, and 95
per cent of female labour by farmers' wives and their kin.

Over half the occupiers of farms who were themselves
farmers' sons had worked as farm labourers at some time in
their lives. The sons of farmers are dependent on their
fathers whose instructions they take about their work and to
whom they must go for pocket money. There is even a local
story that one committed suicide because of his shame at
being unable to live up to the expenditure of the farm
labourers and other workers with whom he mixed. The
division of farm tasks between a farmer's sons, and the
coming of the tractor, seem to be changing the pattern.
Farms with a tractor, which only the son can understand
and use, derive their work pattern from the instructions of
the mechanically minded son. A son does not usually know
the financial details of his father's farm, although his
mother, and through her the daughters, may well be in
charge of all the accounts. As in Ireland and Wales, the
wife is responsible for poultry and eggs, and she keeps the
money so raised for household goods and younger children's
clothes. But she is also often 'Chancellor of the Exchequer'
for her husband's accounts, and at times of stress may help
the men in the fields. The division of labour between the
sexes is less rigid than in Ireland or Wales, as is shown by
the survival in 1950 of three 'land girls', members of the

war-time Women's Land Army, as hired hands. Local religious and fairy beliefs would have soon put a stop to that in County Clare. The young men's group in Llanfihangel would also have had something to say.

The dependence of boys and girls ends, at least partially, at marriage. There is none of the wholesale re-ordering of roles in Gosforth that there is in Ireland and none of the accompanying dramatic ritual. Williams considers even the marriage ceremony is somewhat perfunctorily regarded when compared with baptism or burial. Courtship is similarly casual and personal although subject to the informal pressures of social status. It is usual for one son to stay unmarried at home until his parents die or retire, but others may marry and move into a cottage in the village. Some farms have two or three sons living elsewhere with wives and children but travelling daily to them to work for their fathers or elder brothers.

When the time comes to retire, the farmer and his wife move off to a house bought in the district and the inheriting son marries and takes over the farm. There is no rigid pattern as to which son should inherit, but in twenty-seven out of forty-five cases known to Williams it was the eldest or only son. Among present occupiers the expected heir was an eldest son in nine out of thirteen possible cases.

Arrangements made to redistribute land after retirement or death aim to maintain an economic family unit and to retain the land in the family. As a farmer told Williams, 'When you're born to a spot you're married to it.' Widows inherit from their husbands and frequently remarry, but three-generation households are rare. In forty-three cases there were only seven such households, and of these four contained widowed parents, and two had unmarried daughters with illegitimate children.

In the village, the traditional craftsmen that survive treat their craft and their tools as the farmers treat their land. Those villagers who are neither craftsmen nor farmers have little property to dispose of. Movables are shared out or auctioned off and the money divided. The house, as in

working-class districts elsewhere, tends to go to the unmarried child who stayed at home to look after the ageing
parents. Three-generation households are the exception
here too; there are only twenty of these. There are altogether a hundred and fifteen elementary families, while
forty-eight households consist of persons living alone, the
widowed, or groups of unmarried siblings.

In the village, as on the farms, the relationships of the
elementary family are enmeshed in a network of relationships based on consanguinity and proximity. To a great
extent kin and neighbours are overlapping categories in
Gosforth, for centuries of isolation and relative stability have
given the parish an endogamous quality which results in
relatives living near by and those who live near by being
relatives. Thus, just under half the house occupiers and
their wives in the parish have relatives as close as grandparents, parents, children, or siblings in at least one other
household. Some families extend at this level over as many as
six households within the parish. Eighty per cent of occupiers
and their wives have first cousins, uncles, aunts, or nephews
and nieces in one other household and 65 per cent have such
relatives in two or more other households. 'Claiming kin' is
regarded as an important pastime especially for women who
often know their own and their husbands' genealogies in
some detail. Men may confine themselves to remarking that
someone they know as distantly related is some 'mak' of
forty-second cousin'. Kinship also has dimensions in space
and time. Like birds in the hand, a father's first cousin in
Gosforth may be regarded as closer, in more ways than the
merely geographical, than an own first cousin in Australia.

Kinship in Gosforth also links the community with its
past. One family with no living relatives was not regarded
as a family of 'offcomers' since, as villagers pointed out,
there were plenty of headstones bearing the surname in the
churchyard. As in Ireland and Wales common possession
of a surname is seen (sometimes erroneously) as implying
not only common ancestry but also common characteristics
and family traits. The 'Xs' are 'gay queer' and the 'Ys'

'gay dishonest', while the 'Zs' are good solid industrious farmers – always have been and always will. This sense of family continuity and solidarity is further maintained by attaching ancestral farm names to surnames, by referring to married women by their maiden names, and by the use of family christian names passing from father to son and mother to daughter through generations. Williams found in his study of parish registers that, from the middle of the nineteenth century until the 1930s, maternal surnames were adopted as christian names and then retained until names combined three surnames like Sharpe Dixon Hindle and Noble Wilson Tyson. Some villagers today with no land to attach their own or their mother's name to, have abandoned the custom of family christian names and choose where fad and fashion suggest.

Williams gives two examples of the kinship networks in which Gosforth people live:

(a) Mrs —, a housewife, has three sisters and one brother, all married, living in the village. She has two first cousins in the parish and thirteen other 'close relatives' there also. Her husband has a widowed mother, a brother and two sisters in Gosforth, and four other 'close relatives' in different households. This couple also has a married daughter living in a house of her own, and the household is therefore 'closely related' by blood to twenty-seven other households in the parish.

(b) Mr —, a farmer, has three brothers in the parish who are farmers and a sister who is married to a farmer. He has one first cousin who farms in Gosforth and an aunt and first cousin living in the village. His wife's mother also lives in the village, and his wife has three aunts, two first cousins and three nieces living in different parts of the parish. This household therefore has sixteen 'close relatives' living in separate households in the parish, and there are also a further nine distant relatives.

The families of these two people and of their 'close relatives' total sixty-five and forty-two persons respectively. If the ties by marriage and blood of the two households are traced out fully they are found to embrace sixty-nine homes with a membership of two hundred and forty-seven people – over a third of the population of the parish (pp. 74–5).

It is one thing, however, to live in an environment of consanguinity, another to make use of these relationships as channels for social communication and control. In this, the village and the countryside differ, although they are linked to one another and to the world outside by kinship ties crossing boundaries of class and geography.

Villagers constantly borrow from their neighbours and lend to them. Irrespective of kin they look after each other's children, fetch items from Whitehaven for each other and 'pop' in and out of the ever open doors of each other's houses. Little thought seems to be given to exact reciprocities. The blacksmith, for instance, has many more oppotunities to lend than to borrow. Nevertheless someone who always borrows and never returns soon faces the gossiping disapproval of her neighbourhood group. Williams does not tell us much about it, but he hints that the long straggling nature of most of the village splits it up into little groups of neighbours which have the same sense of solidarity as kin-groups in the open country. An insult to one is an insult to all, and behaviour within each group is controlled by the informal sanctions it can apply. These groups are nevertheless joined by friendships and blood relationships which link individuals in different parts of the village.

In the farms of the countryside, cooperation between neighbours and kin is both economically more important and in a sense more formalized. There is not the daily face-to-face interaction of the village but lending and borrowing of farm implements and equipment is continual and reciprocal. Farmers who hold themselves aloof from such exchange are looked down on and described as 'cunning laal jokers', 'gay queer' or 'poor maks o' farmers'. Visits to neighbours or kin for the purpose of borrowing take on some of the attributes of a social occasion, with the farmer's wife at home eager for the gossip collected.

The full-scale social occasions connected with farm cooperation seem to be disappearing in Gosforth. Only one farm still has a 'sheep clippin' gathering of kinsmen for sheep-shearing and only threshing remains a universal excuse for getting together, bringing out the best Cumberland hams and rum butter. Threshing may bring together twenty-five or thirty farmers of a neighbourhood, some of whom otherwise scarcely meet. As in the other societies we have discussed there are traditional partners. One farmer asked a complete stranger from a mile away in preference to people nearer home he had known all his life. He explained to Williams:

'Folks have been coming to our threshings from that spot yonder all me life and in me father's time afore me, and I'll not be starting to change it now' (p. 149).

Even farmers who have their own threshers and no need for help take part in threshings, which have an atmosphere of boisterous good will. The unease which accompanies co-operation in an economy which is partly competitive and partly not perhaps helps to explain the boisterous humour of these occasions and the fact reported by Williams that 'the work is accompanied by good-natured chaffing and endless stories, most of which would be thought indecent or at least vulgar in polite society'.

In the past such boon-days seem to have been more common. Now they are disappearing, because of changes in technology and attitude. Williams, perhaps categorizing too simply, ascribes this to a modern 'premium on individual mobility [which] implies a more atomistic conception of society, and to a lesser degree to the introduction of a pseudo-materialistic philosophy, by which actions are judged by ultimate profit'.

Despite this, the Gosforth farmers – like the villagers – live in an atmosphere of neighbourliness in which resolvable conflict is dominant over irreconcilable antagonism. There are still, as Williams discovered when he sought to pay for a gift of eggs, things that must be returned in kind rather than cash. All are to some extent united by long experience of each other and each other's families, and by a common struggle to get an adequate subsistence from a beautiful but often inhospitable countryside.

CHAPTER 4

The Village in the Country: Glynceiriog

SHORTLY after Williams left Gosforth and set to work writing up his material, and during the period of his second visit there in the summer of 1953, I went to live in, and make a social-anthropological study of, the civil parish of Llansaintffraid Glynceiriog in Denbighshire on the border of Wales. I have since published a book on this, *Village on the Border* (1957), in which I disguised the village in the parish under the name of Pentrediwaith. Ten years later such disguises are no longer necessary although the name which means in Welsh 'village of no work' is still appropriate.

While Williams concentrated on the rural farming community around the village, as the name of my book implies, I concentrated on the village itself. This village had in 1953 a population of about 600. There was another village called Pandy with a population of about 200 partly within the parish, and another 400 people lived in the hamlets of Nantyr and Coed-y-glyn or in the scattered farmsteads and cottages of the open countryside.

The oldest route into the village is also the most spectacular and can only be tackled with comfort on foot. Starting from Llangollen in the valley of the Dee one climbs to a height of 1,250 feet and descends past the church, set on a ridge near the top, down a hill the gradient of which is in places 1 in $3\frac{1}{4}$, into the village High Street. If one pauses at the church, as I did on my first visit in 1953, and as George Borrow had done in 1854, one can look down on the village. It looks compact and isolated, a self-contained community in the elbow of a steep-sided valley. There are hills of slate refuse giving the impression that it is a quarrying village. Two disused and partly ruined mills show that once quarrying was not its only industry.

The oldest part of the village is in fact the few houses round the church on this ridge. This was the agricultural village. It is known as the Garth and there has been at least a church there for over five hundred years.

There are three terraces of rural cottages following the contour of the hill. One house is an old inn, empty and ramshackle, and half of the other fourteen cottages are falling in ruins. Others are weekend or permanent residences for outsiders from Liverpool and elsewhere. In 1953 four remained occupied by elderly villagers.

The road continues into the main street of the village, built for the most part between 1840 and 1890 to house the increasing population brought in by the slate industry. Thereafter it continues to the market town of Oswestry, sixteen miles away across the English border. This road crosses the hundred-year-old new road along the valley bottom from Llanarmon Dyffryn Ceiriog at its head to the coal-mining village of Chirk on the A5 road at the foot of the valley. Houses line all branches of the crossroads for a short distance. In the central part of the village there are four chapels, three public houses, the Ceiriog Memorial Institute and Hall, and all the shops. There are four main grocers including a Co-op, a draper, two cobblers, two butchers (one combined with a greengrocer's), a fishmonger and greengrocer combined, a baker, an electrician, two newsagents, tobacconists and confectioners, a chemist, a wool shop, and a number of other small shops that defy precise classification. It is no wonder then that Glyn people sometimes like to think of themselves as living in a town.

Another miniature town-like feature is the fact that although most of the formal social activity takes place in the part of the village I have just described, most villagers do not live there. There are nearly two hundred men, women, and children that do and of these only twenty-five are in fact children under sixteen.

About three hundred people with nearly seventy children live in ninety-two households on the council housing estate. This is in the angle between the Llangollen and Chirk roads. In the pre-war houses on the estate live the women who informally lead and direct the life of the village, several of whom moved there from the Garth. The post-war houses accommodate younger married couples whose growing families still attend the village council school.

In 1953 there was still a council house waiting-list of thirteen families. Some couples had been housed in the near-by village of Pontfadog but still came up the valley to see their families and to take part in Glyn village life. Nor were these the only ones to participate in the village but live outside it. There are, for example, the near-by farmers who have close kin in the village, employ village boys as labourers and come in daily to the public houses or shops. Sometimes they bring their families with them to social events like dances and whist drives, plays, lectures, and concerts. The Annual Sheepdog Trials and the sheep sales bring in farmers from farther afield.

I have said that the village seems isolated and villagers feel that it is. In reality this isolation is far from absolute. Geographically, Glyn is part of a valley that has its own organic unity. Socially, a network of kinship and friendship ties spreads from one end of the valley to the other and beyond. Local people say that if you tread on a dog's tail in Chirk it barks in Llanarmon. Historically and sociologically it is part of Wales as Wales is part of Britain, and the class divisions and economic social upheavals of the nations interpenetrate those of the village.

The Ceiriog valley is a microcosm, if not of Wales as a whole, at least of the north. If you add to it the manufacturing and commercial towns of Ruabon and Wrexham, our whole morphological continuum could be studied in one small area.

Llanarmon Dyffryn Ceiriog at the head of the valley is separated by the Berwyn Hills from the main small farming areas of central Wales. It is not far removed in culture or geography from the Llanfihangel of Chapter 2. Welsh is the only language of its people, despite the fact that it contains a fashionable hotel and some hill farms have been bought by the English. The year 1953 was the first during which a regular daily bus service ran from Llanarmon to Oswestry, although market-day buses had been operating for some time. Tregeiriog and Pandy sent men both to the quarries of Glyn and the sheep farms of Llanarmon. Glynceiriog was until recently a quarrying village, although now its men travel to work in the industries of Ruabon and Wrexham. Chirk stands astride the English border and the London–Holyhead road and is an entirely English-speaking mining village with a mainline railway station.

The valley as a whole is famous in Welsh history for its poets, the 'Cavalier' Huw Morus (1622–1709), Cynddelw (1812–75) and Ceiriog (1832–87), and more recently in 1923 for one of the early struggles on the question of water supplies for northern industrial towns. Warrington proposed to flood part of it for a reservoir, but this was defeated in Parliament after an eloquent intervention by Lloyd George.

The road through the valley peters out into a track at Llanarmon and it is to all intents and purposes a cul-de-sac. I could recognize nearly all the cars that passed by the windows of the bungalow where I lodged, except on high-summer weekends when tourists from the industrial north-west visit the valley and pass through Glyn.

Five or six buses a day leave the village for Llangollen, which they reach by way of Chirk and the A5 main road. These carry men to work and the children to the grammar school. Workers and shoppers bound for Oswestry or Wrexham can get other buses and trains from Chirk. In 1953 the local garage started a bus service of three or four buses daily to Oswestry sixteen miles away. Two of these started from and returned to Llanarmon. A bus for visits to hospital patients went to Wrexham on Sundays.

The distances covered by these buses are small, but the social distance between Glyn and neighbouring towns is great. Villagers find it a real hardship to have to travel to work on them. Their infrequency and the fact that they ceased during heavy snow sometimes gave both visitors and villagers the feeling that they really did live on an island.

This feeling is enhanced by the fact that food and provisions are not locally produced but fetched in from Oswestry.

On Mondays, foodshops are either closed or have very little stock. Before Bank Holiday, one has to do enough shopping on Thursday to last until the following Wednesday, for fresh food shops sell out early on Friday, are closed on Sunday and Monday, and need Tuesday to replenish their stocks from Oswestry. Certain foods can only be had on certain days – fish on Tuesdays and meat on Wednesday, Thursday, and Friday. Fresh foods cost a penny or twopence more in Glyn than in Oswestry and prices there were usually a penny or twopence more than current prices given in the *Liverpool Daily Post.* (No doubt deep-freeze has changed this picture since 1953.)

This physical isolation has least effect on farmers and tradesmen who have cars and vans, and workers who have motor-bikes or who travel regularly on the buses. The social as well as the economic consequences are greatest for the women. They may go weekly to Oswestry on market day and once a year to Wrexham or Chester for Christmas presents. In the summer, day trips go to the National Eisteddfod in its North Wales year, the coast, Shrewsbury Floral Fête, or even a Liverpool theatre. Generally speaking, however, the women of Glyn live, work, and amuse themselves in the village and have little occasion or opportunity to leave it.

To explore the way in which Glyn, despite its isolation, remains an integral part of England and Wales, I must briefly trace the history of its economy.

The valley lies on the borders of three great estates, those of the Wynnstay, Ruthin Castle, and Chirk Castle. Most of its farms that were not held by yeomen were on the Nantyr estate which from 1842 until 1952 belonged to the Storeys, Northern industrialists. There were quarries and fulling mills as early as the fifteenth century, but Glynceiriog became a slate-mining centre in the late nineteenth century as Bethesda and Ffestiniog had done in the early part of the century. Difficulties of transport made its rise later than the Caernarvonshire quarrying villages and its decline was earlier and more rapid. Nevertheless in the 1870s a narrow gauge tramway was built from Chirk to Glyn and lasted until 1935. Unlike the other communities we have discussed, the population rose from 1870 until the mid twenties and only then began to decline. From 1935 onwards the majority of men were forced to leave the village to seek work elsewhere. At that time the unmarried women and girls still went into domestic service in Manchester and Liverpool.

The Second World War temporarily solved economic difficulties but between 1946 and 1952 locally-based industry died. The large estates were sold up and one by one the stone and slate quarries and the little factories closed down.

Glynceiriog is not only located in Wales, but it is also very Welsh, since it is largely Nonconformist in religion and Welsh in language. The industrial and agricultural experience of the past confronted Welsh-speaking, Nonconformist, Liberal wage-earners and tenant-farmers with Anglicized, Anglican, Tory landlords and employers, as were Welsh workers elsewhere in Wales. English and Welsh were almost synonymous with landlord and tenant or capital and labour. As has often been pointed out, Disraeli's description of employers and employed as two nations applied literally to Wales. This class division remains important in village life although the gentry as squires have disappeared. As recently as 1926 when an heir was born to the Storey family, the whole village was invited and taken by bus to a party at the Hall. The coming-of-age party then promised for 1947 never materialized. During 1953 the last Storey to live in the Hall was brought back for burial. Not all villagers were enthusiastic about this. Some argued that he didn't think the place worth while staying in alive, why come there when he was dead? The Home Guard seems to have provided a last fling for the squirearchy under the command of the then tenant of Chirk Castle and the vicar.

In the past, the quarries brought Glynceiriog men into daily contact with men from other villages in the valley. Now in industry, the mines, or on building sites outside the valley, they work side by side not only with others from the valley but also with Englishmen, Irishmen, and even émigré Poles from a wide area of Denbighshire, Flintshire, and Shropshire.

This as we shall see tends to intensify the segregation of roles between men and women outside the home. Since we are still dealing with a community where individuals have highly connected or close-knit networks, as we would expect on Bott's hypothesis (see pp. 19 above and 245–8 below) role-segregation within the home is also the rule. This led me to suggest, with some exaggeration but much truth, that 'except for a brief period of courtship and early marriage, there seem to be two villages, one of men and one of women which rarely mingle'.

We shall again find a sex division of this kind in the coal-mining village which is the subject of the next chapter, but it is less marked in towns based on mixed industry and trade.

Although the sexes do not mingle in public, they do meet; and the occasions of their meetings give rise to conflict which adds to the interest, and paradoxically to the unity, of village life. Women in fact form a corporate group in Glynceiriog which determines the pattern of much of social life. Unlike the men, they share common work problems and spend nearly all their time actually in the village. They meet each other in the shops and constantly visit each other informally for cups of tea. They discuss village affairs while sewing and preparing equipment for social functions. When in the few mixed committees there is a conflict of interest, the committee often splits into groups of the two sexes. The Coronation Committee consisted of the parish council, a few other notables, and a number of women nominated by the British Legion, Women's Institute, and the chapels. The committee decided to hold a tea for the village, but the women engaged on other preparations discussed it among themselves, organized opposition, called an emergency meeting and had the tea cancelled.

The women of the Garden Produce Association Committee attended only one meeting – the last. Because they were offended by the attitude to women members of the male secretary, they had a special committee called two days before the show and forced its abandonment. A more detailed account of the women's group role in the organization of football and the carnival is given below.

Council and church schools are both mixed, but the children separate themselves into one-sex play groups. The double-decker bus which takes the fortunate ones to co-educational Llangollen Grammar School has boys upstairs and girls downstairs. In the billiard room, in the café, and in summer by the bridge where teenagers gather, there are groups of seven or eight or more boys and smaller groups of girls. Teasing and jokes pass between groups but serious courtship cuts off the boy or girl from his or her peers of the same sex. Evenings not spent actually courting are often spent at home alone. All this, of course, is very different from courtship in Llanfihangel or County Clare but not very different from the pattern of working-class youth in towns all over Britain.

Most villagers have little property to dispose of, so that the function of marriage in the redistribution of property does not arise. Marriage, however, still creates 'political' alliances; and this is perhaps part of the reason that marriages between first cousins do not occur.

Unmarried boys and girls who are seen together once or twice are soon assumed to be courting and gossip starts asking when the engagement will be announced and the date of the wedding fixed. This does not apply to first cousins, especially the children of two sisters who will probably have spent their early childhood in and out of one another's houses. First cousins can develop the intimacy of siblings without the strain which arises from actually living in the same house and competing for the attention of the same father and mother. In fact ordinary Glyn people live in almost the same environment of kinship as the 'pig's entrails' described by Rees and Williams. This enmeshes the housing estate and draws into social relationships the surrounding farms and even to some extent, as we shall see, cuts across social class.

Thus, there are two farmer brothers, Jack and James,

living on neighbouring farms on the parish outskirts. James's sister's daughter is married to a local tradesman on the estate. His son plays for the village football team. James's sister is married to one of his wife's brothers. One of James's wife's sisters has a married daughter on the housing estate. James's wife has other brothers and sisters in the village and on near-by farms. The menfolk meet regularly in the village pubs and their wives and sisters at church and

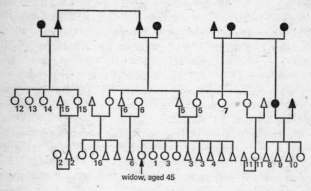

widow, aged 45

Fig. 1. Relationships of a widow on Glynceiriog housing estate. The numbers represent households.   O = Woman,   △ = Man,   ● ▲ = deceased.

at the Church Ladies Sewing Guild. Similarly, a widow aged forty-five living on the housing estate could claim relationship with sixteen other households. All the households on the estate had at least one spouse who had relatives in other households. I discovered only one couple who had no relatives at all in the village. The Glynceiriog view of kinship is at once exclusive in that it distinguishes Glyn people from outsiders, and inclusive in that details of relationships within the village are not too carefully explored. In a situation seen to be one of change, the fact that 'all villagers are related' cannot be taken for granted. I found villagers willing to detail their own siblings, and those of their father and mother. First cousins were also listed, but after that they became vague. Villagers whom I got to know well and who had many relatives in the village told me that they hesitated to list them for two reasons. Firstly, they feared to insult distant relatives inadvertently omitted; secondly, they hesitated to reveal to outsiders, and to have written down, illegitimacy in their kin-group. They might have added that an inclusive system of this kind benefits from imprecision.

Glyn villagers do not take such an interest in kindred out of idle curiosity. Membership of a kindred gives social standing, one way or the other. Characteristics like dishonesty, lack of balance, singing ability or business acumen are believed to run in families. Vagueness in genealogical detail enables an individual to choose at any time and in any situation with whom he will be associated and with whom he will associate others. Thus a headmaster in another village was eagerly claimed as kin. A man convicted of theft was disowned by those kin distant enough to do so. Their neighbours, however, especially those who were hostile to them, reminded them and mutual acquaintances of the connexion. Nevertheless an individual has responsibility for his kindred as they have for him and, as in the other societies so far discussed, this acts as a means of social control. People in Glynceiriog act as groups in formal situations. It is groups not individuals who resign from and join committees. As we have seen, one basis of such a group may be sex. We shall see occupation may also influence alignments as well as blood relationships.

Kin links also tie into the village one category which does not live in it but on the outskirts. These are the tradesmen or their children who are slightly more prosperous than the ordinary wage-earning villagers. An example is Seth. He is a builder employing about six of the village men. A Rural District Councillor, a J.P., and a devout Baptist, he has a married son whom he has established on a smallholding in the parish. Other single sons work for him and live at home. One daughter is married and lives on the housing estate. Another is a nurse outside Wales but engaged to a village boy. Seth's wife's sisters live in the village and are cousins of

James, the farmer already mentioned. Two of their father's brother's sons and two of his daughters live in the village and through this uncle they are related to at least seven households on the housing estate.

The people of the village and housing estate, the farmers and the householders like the one I have just described, are all Glyn people. They are linked together by ties of kinship and affinity, by the fact that they all speak Welsh, and by their tendency to be chapel members. These, especially the last, are not absolute criteria, for even on the housing estate 30 per cent professed to be church members.

Outside this nucleus of Glyn people, and usually outside the village too, there are a category of people I shall call 'outsiders'. They were in former times land and quarry owners. But now economic class and social status groups have diverged a little. In 1953 they were mainly small traders or retired and active professional men, usually monoglot English and Anglican. The patrons and vice-presidents of Glyn societies and judges for local events come mainly from this category. Their incomes tend to be derived from outside the valley and to be greater than those commanded by Glyn people. Their relationships with Glyn people tend to be formal and they are not usually related to villagers as kin. They cannot, as villagers do, drop in unheralded for a cup of tea or a gossip, and they are addressed formally and treated with polite respect.

Some people with those characteristics remain nameless English visitors to all but the shops and the post office. There are others who, while their main social life may be outside the village, are drawn into its formal social life.

Thus the president of the Garden Produce Association and director of the Sheep Dog Society was the former squire. The post of president of the football club was successively filled by a publican and an English immigrant shopkeeper. The latter took his duties too seriously and turned up to preside at a committee meeting. This led to dismay which was accentuated because his interest was rugby and the club played soccer. The Carnival Queen was crowned by this man's wife, and the carnival presided over by an Oswestry landowner. Another local landowner was President of the British Legion. All these were professed Anglicans, the publican was the only one able to speak Welsh, and the Oswestry landowner the only one who had kin in the village.

The football club had seven vice-presidents and twelve named large-scale subscribers. This in fact involved thirteen individuals and two brewery companies. Three of them spoke Welsh, twelve were Anglicans and one a Roman Catholic. Only two had relatives in the village. This club received nine pounds in anonymous donations. There was a similar pattern in other village associations. There are always anonymous donations from villagers who would consider it presumptuous to give openly in their own name.

In these particular cases, money and status in the county are exchanged for status and role in the village. Only outsiders by social class could play these roles.

There were other activities in the village from which such people were excluded by their very status. For these the 'intellectuals', a group overlapping at its lower levels with Watson's blocked spiralist category referred to in Chapter 3, might be called on. This group included the heads of the two village schools, the doctor, the chemist, the bank manager, the ministers of religion, and the assistant teachers. All of them were likely to be involved in village activities especially as secretaries.

Village intellectuals, three of whom had already graduated while two were still students at universities while I was there, work elsewhere and have neither opportunity nor desire to return.

Villagers themselves, although homogeneous in social status, are not entirely homogeneous in other respects, as we have seen. I found that in nearly every group activity it was possible to recognize some participant who had only that activity in common with other members of the group or who differed in some important social characteristic from the others. I suggest that, like the youth group in Llanfihangel

and the old men in County Clare, their simultaneous
position in two systems of relationships to some extent re-
moves them from the conflicts and informal social pressures
of full members of the group. This makes them, as I shall
show, of central importance in the precipitation and resolution of such conflicts. I shall call them 'strangers', with the
warning that a person may be a stranger only in a limited
context and not in other contexts. As we shall see, all outsiders in Glynceiriog are strangers, but to be a stranger one
does not have to be an outsider.

Glyn people are strongly egalitarian in outlook. Among
themselves they consider every man is every bit as good as
the next. This creates a problem when activities have to be
directed. The apparent reason for the brass band not playing
even though the village owned instruments and had sufficient players, was partly because it was invidious to choose
between the two conductors available, and partly because
the villagers would not take orders from either. Similarly,
one of the major problems of the football committee was to
persuade the playing captain to give orders to his fellows.
The role of leader who must contrive to achieve the aims of
his organization, and at the same time avoid splitting it and
village opinion, was not eagerly sought for by ordinary
villagers. They usually thrust it upon the stranger. Even
within committees, however deep the division of opinion,
villagers often held back their views until a stranger was
forced by the course of the discussion, or even by specific
request, to move a motion which revealed a split. These
considerations applied especially to the internal committees
which organized recreation and social life within the village,
although it must be recognized that it was by the success of
these internal activities that village prestige externally was
measured. The football teams and the carnival, like wrestling
in Gosforth and hurling in County Clare, are cases in point.

Considerations of this kind play their part also in the
official external relations of the village through local government, but here they are sometimes masked by straightforward factors of economic class and social status.

Thus it seems that the village and valley were in fact not unanimous in 1923 when the upper reaches were threatened with flooding by the Warrington Water Bill. The public protagonists on both sides were two stranger publicans in favour of the bill and Sir Alfred T. Davies against it.

In general, Williams's statement about Gosforth that the decisions on village amenities are taken by those who use them least holds good. Although in my view such people appear to take the decision for which they take responsibility. In internal committees my view is nearer the truth, but in local government the various councils show a familiar picture of economic class division and antagonism.

Economic classes are not mingled at random on local government bodies although in sharp contrast to Gosforth the parish council is made up of wage-earners. The county councillors and magistrates as might be expected are salaried or self-employed.

The self-employed parish councillors are the junior partner in the village drapers and a small-scale jobbing builder who himself works side by side with his men. The salaried parish councillor is a schoolteacher in another village. The salaried members of the Bench and Rural District Council are two doctors and the manager of the local Co-op. This last is the only one from among the County and Rural District councillors and magistrates who takes an active part in village life outside local government. He lives on the village high street but speaks no Welsh and belongs to the church. Five out of the six parish councillors are otherwise involved in the village, one as unpaid minister of the Scots Baptists and others as chapel deacons and society secretaries.

The activities of these groups show the differences as well. The magistrates meet six times a year to try petty offences and (with one exception) their remoteness from the lives of ordinary villagers is made abundantly clear. Their powers are of course considerable but they have little occasion to use these. Villagers take most interest in the parish council which is virtually devoid of any power except to offer advice about village affairs to more powerful organs of local government.

It meets every three weeks in private although in theory any member of the public can attend. It conducts its proceedings entirely in Welsh. This all-Welsh rule was the means by which it maintained its independence from the English squire and gentry. Welsh still serves to protect the parish

FIGURES IN THE POLITICAL LIFE OF 'PENTREDIWAITH'

	Salaried	Self-employed	Wage-earning	Church	Chapel	W	A
M.P. for County (1)	—	1	—	1	—	—	—
County Councillor for Rural District (1)	—	1	—	1	—	1	—
Rural District Councillors for Village (3)	2	1	—	2	1	1	1
Magistrates for Valley Petty Sessions (8)	2	6	—	6	2	2	—
Parish Councillors (6)	1	2	3	1	5	6	5

W indicates Welsh-speaking.

A indicates persons active in village life in other spheres than politics.

council from later English immigrants. The parish council reports annually to the village at public meetings conducted mainly in English. The poor attendance at these meetings does not mean that villagers are apathetic towards the parish council and its works, for the councillors are themselves villagers and very actively engaged in village social life. Their decisions are known and informally discussed with and without them. They are not long allowed to remain in ignorance of village opinion. The fact that their village critics do not come into the open at public meetings only makes them more annoying and their criticisms more effective. Parish councillors, as Glyn people, are unable to abdicate power to outsiders and put their worries and disagreements on to strange shoulders as do other committees. They have partly solved this problem by an attempted retreat into secrecy. They meet in private and no longer send reports into the local newspapers. I could not attend their meetings (any more than Williams could go to cock-fights), so I have no first-hand knowledge of how they reached decisions. That conflict threatened to break into open dispute which might spread to their supporters in the village is suggested by the fact that they had three chairmen during 1953. All were, in some sense, strangers to the rest of the council. One lived outside the village at the hamlet of Pandy, and of the other two, one was the Scots Baptist minister and the other a Wesleyan deacon. I think it is significant that no member of the Baptist majority of both council and village had this post, and that unlike other Glyn committees, there were no close relatives on it. When a husband and wife stood, the wife was rejected mainly because the parish council is a male preserve. But villagers also said about this: 'It isn't fair to have two from the same family.' I think this confirms that the parish council is seen as representing Glyn people as a whole and not merely a section of them. The subjects with which they are concerned, and the parish council's efforts to get other councils to take an interest in these subjects, reflect their position. Telephone kiosk siting, the whereabouts of government offices, work for the village, street lighting, a children's playground, were among the things considered during the year. Although they had the power to deal with none of these matters, villagers nevertheless held them responsible for their failures. They are in an intercalary position in a non-existent hierarchy.

The parish council represents the village to government and to those bodies like the county council and the rural district council on which villagers are represented by those whom they may consider economic, if not social, superiors.

Glyn people derive prestige among peers in other villages not from any political activity but from their prowess at football and the success of such symbols of their ability at organization and their skill at the flower show, sheep dog trials, coronation celebrations, and carnival. All these fit into systems of activity which are wider than the village, all are reported in the *Oswestry and Border Counties Advertiser*, and even the *Liverpool Daily Post*. A village where the men work among men from other villages is likely to be particularly sensitive about its showing in such activities. The politics of recreation in Glyn should not therefore be underestimated by those who live in towns and support Oxford against Cambridge, Manchester United against Arsenal, or Celtic against Rangers. There is more than fun in games.

In 1953, association football was the main village interest of this kind, although by 1954 organizing a carnival was taking its paramount place.

Football brought visitors into the village every fortnight during autumn, winter, and spring. A bus-load of villagers left every other Saturday to visit other villages and small towns round about. Football has many advantages as such a social mechanism. It has more than specialist interest, and the equipment required is relatively inexpensive and easy to prepare. There is a long season, but the summer is left free and football can be played in all weathers. The game fits into the national and local framework of an organization which deals with the mechanics of arranging fixtures and places to play. Finally, the professional sport provides an outlet for social mobility which gives an added spur, if one were needed, for the young men to take part. Billy Mere-dith, a former Wales and Manchester City and United player is from near-by Chirk, and many players of English teams in the Football League are from Wales.

The fact that matches were reported and the results dis-cussed elsewhere than in Glynceiriog created a depth of interest among both men and women in the village, which intensified the divergence of opinion inevitable in a small closely-knit community of this kind. But, although men and women shared an interest in football, their interests were not identical. The actual football committee consisted of men, mainly ex-players, mainly Glyn people and mainly wage-earners. This last is ensured by the fact that, as well as picking the team, the committee is responsible for preparing the ground before home matches. At the beginning of the 1953/4 season the committee was dominated by five coal-miners including the secretary. It is part of the group participation already remarked upon that when this secretary resigned most of this group soon followed, to be replaced by the brothers and father of the new secretary.

A village as small as Glynceiriog does not have enough talent to field an entirely local team that is capable of meeting and defeating those of larger or less scrupulous villages. The committee therefore had to decide whether it wanted a local team which would provide active recreation for village youth, or a team including mainly outsiders which would maintain village prestige externally by its successes in the league. This was the chronic dilemma which also underlines the division between the interests of men and of women in this situation. The women were organized into a supporters' club whose functions were to organize fund-raising whist drives, dances, and other entertainments which the division of sex roles in Glyn precludes men from doing. Their interest was partly in doing these things for their own sake, and partly in seeing that the men did their reciprocal part in attending the social occasions organized. As far as the football itself was concerned, although they wanted the team to win, they also wanted to see and applaud their own sons and husbands in the action of winning.

These difficulties had remained under control until the end of the season 1951/2 when the team stood third in the local league and played in a field between the council estate and the village on the Chirk road. This field had the advantage of being *in* the village, so that housewives passed it on their way to the shops, and one did not have to deliberately set out to watch a game. Its disadvantage lay in this very ease of access, so that no one paid to go in; but this was overcome by the village policeman's habit of making a collection in his helmet from the roadside spectators.

In 1953 the site was moved to a field outside the village. This change coincided with the advent of a new secretary, a miner whom I shall call Charley, and with a change of policy towards making use of more outside players.

The combination of a 'foreign' team and a distant field turned the already existing conflict between the men of the football committee and the women of the supporters' club into open dispute. It also changed the position of the secretary within the committee.

Previously the committee had chosen the team all of whom they knew personally and the secretary had then notified the players of committee decisions in which he took no part. The secretary was a buffer between the decisions of the committee and the discontents of the players. Now, with an outside team and competition with other clubs for the few good players of the region, the players took the decisions which were communicated through the secretary to an often discontented committee. But, however discontented the committee became, they remained in the power of the secretary since the players tended to be his workmates or workmates of his friends. Thus, one player from outside whom the committee wished to play half-back was said by the secretary to have refused to play except at inside forward. Only a temporary illness of the secretary enabled direct contact to be made with him by post and his position changed. This reversal in power relations between secretary and committee was another factor in bringing chronic but latent conflict into acute overt crisis. It is not surprising therefore that the season 1953/4 began, as it was to continue, in disputes. The first dispute arose out of the proceeds of a special series of matches which was held to mark the Coronation. The football committee at first decided on the motion of an English miner not to give the money to the Coronation Committee fund. After the Coronation Committee (which was run by the active women of the village) had protested, the footballers reversed their decision on the motion of the same stranger.

It is interesting to note that one incident united Coronation and football committees even during this dispute. That was their disapproval of the action of the parish council chairman in taking the matter outside the village by writing to the Welsh Football Association.

The second incident was the organization of a Sunday Sacred Concert by secretary Charley in aid of a fictitious 'Football Players Equipment Fund' and the spending of the proceeds on a dinner for players and committee in one of the local pubs. This led to the resignation of Charley from his position as secretary of the football club and his replacement by a young white-collar worker and ex-player, Biggs. The dinner, in fact, took place the night before the opening of the season, and both blasphemy and over-indulgence were blamed for the team's subsequent loss by nine goals to one.

Disputes within the committee and outside it continued through the season, gates fell and matches were lost, until at the end only three committee members survived and the main interest of the village had shifted from football to the carnival. This shift of interest which has been reported formally and informally from many villages seems to me significant in a wider context.

Disputes do not for long remain unresolved in such a formal association. Their common interest is not sufficiently strong. Committees split and groups of members resign. While the dispute within the committee is thus settled, the argument continues in the village. Eventually an opposition to the activity itself builds up. Thus in Glynceiriog by 1954 there were a large number of men who not only would not help the football committee but who actively opposed it. The club's notices were even torn from trees and players persuaded to leave the club and play elsewhere. There was a move, as we shall see, to cut off the club's financial support. When efforts to avoid conflict ripening into dispute have failed, the open breach spreads through the village. The 'face-to-face' nature of social contacts and the multiplicity of ties which close residence in an 'isolated' unit brings about, makes this spread inevitable. The village becomes so divided that the particular activity can no longer continue. This was already happening to the new carnival in 1954, and there was evidence that it had happened to choirs, dramatic groups, and the brass band in the past.

Once this process of losing support begins, and it is inherent in the beginning of any activity which replaces an old one, it is cumulative. Those who remained loyal to football for example provided a nucleus of resentment to the carnival. As opposition grows within the village, so the activity is less likely to succeed. This diminishes its value in maintaining the prestige of the village externally, which in turn adds to its organizers' internal difficulties. Where a village is no longer bound together by strong economic interests, when in fact villagers do not work or pray together, and do only some of their playing together, I suspect that quarrels which were contained within the pressure of an overall communal cohesion change first to disruptive antagonism and then to apathetic indifference. It is for this reason that I suggested that each successive failure might decrease the cross-cutting ties of sentiment, positive and negative, which bind Glyn villagers into a community. If they were to find it no longer interesting to talk about each other, and if they were to have nothing left to quarrel about, the village would cease to be a community and become a collection of dwellings housing, in chance proximity, some of the industrial workers of Britain. Whether in such circumstances new social ties would develop to restore lost social redundancy is one of the major questions of modern Britain.

The genesis and development of the carnival which replaced football as the external symbol of village unity in Glynceiriog throws further light on the nature of social processes within the village.

The idea of a carnival was conceived after the football club supporters' dance which formed part of the Coronation festivities. A Coronation Football Queen was chosen and after the success of the Coronation of Queen Elizabeth II at Westminster, and the locally important carnival at Pontfadog, Glyn villagers decided to hold a carnival and Coronation in Glynceiriog too. The decorating of lorries for tableaux and the making of fancy dress was already a popular pastime.

The supporters' club committee, consisting with the exception of the chairman entirely of women, devoted its time to making preparations. The women concerned met together several times a week as a sewing group preparing dresses for the queen and her retinue. These work meetings gave an opportunity for informal discussion which enabled them to reach a unanimous 'party line' before and outside the formal meetings of the joint carnival committee which included men. They also drew in women who, while hostile to the football club for family reasons connected with the disputed prowess of sons and husbands, were fond of sewing and making things. The main dispute which surrounded the carnival was the fate of the profits: should they or should they not go to the football club? I have already described the details in my book. Here I state only the sociological conclusions which I draw from the course of events. There were in fact three crucial formal meetings, and numberless informal discussions in shop, pub, and private house. Description of one of the formal meetings, the first, will give a picture of the multiplicity of ties, processes and functions involved in such an aspect of village life.

In the afternoon of this first meeting the sewing group had met as usual and discussed the disposal of the funds. They had decided that they did not want the money to be given to the football club. My landlady, Jane (15),* told me that she was determined to raise the matter in the committee. Jane in particular was to suffer from a multiplicity of roles. The least worrying of these (I think) was that of ethnographer's landlady, although I was in fact a member of the football committee. She was also treasurer of the supporters' club and the carnival committee, wife of a former football chairman and mother of a footballer (27) who played for the University of Wales, and made rare but very

* Numbers refer to Fig. 2 (p. 108).

welcome appearances for the village team. She was also active in the Baptist Chapel and British Legion (Women's Section). The treasurer of the football club was courting her daughter and was therefore a frequent visitor to her house.

Seating Plan of
FIRST CARNIVAL COMMITTEE

Secretary	Chairman	Treasurer
(14) Betty	(2) Percy	(15) Jane
O	△	O

△ (8) William

△ (11) Edgar

O (16) Mrs Morgan

△ (10) Adam

  O (17) Mrs Chairman

    O (18) Mrs Price   △ (27) Ian

      O (19) Mrs Morgan   △ (3) Timothy

(20) Mair   (21) Rhys   (12) Charley   (4) Myself
O   △   △   △

O (22)   △ (26) Mr Higgins

O (23)   △ (25) Edward

  O (24)

Not present but active
O (28) Mrs Green

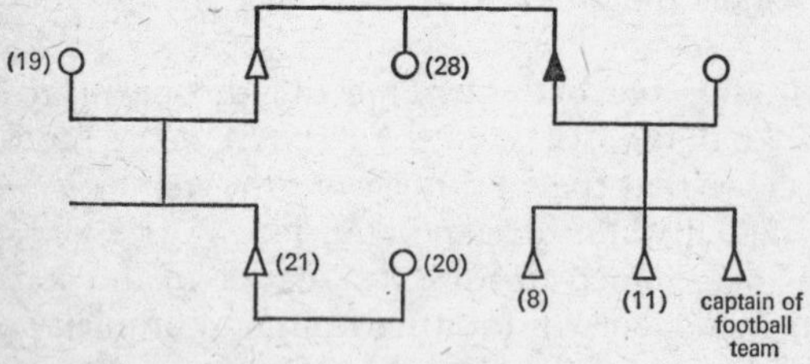

FIG. 2. Carnival Committee members' interrelationship.

When the committee met in the hall, it numbered 21 people who arranged themselves around the chairman. They did not sit at random but grouped as kin, as cliques, and as voting blocs of men against women (see diagram above). The one man (21) who voted with the women

sat nearest to them and Charley (12) and Edward (25), the
other dissidents, sat near by. The two outsiders who were to
play some part as strangers in the debates were Mr Higgins
(26) and myself (4). We too sat in a position consistent with
our marginality.

Although they did not all act in this situation as kin, many
members were closely related: (2) and (17) were husband and
wife, (27) was the son of (15) and (3) was courting (15)'s daughter;
I lived at (15)'s house; the largest group linked by kinship were
(19), (20), (21) and (28) and they acted and voted as a group; (8)
and (11) were also related to these but acted independently (their
relationship is shown below the main diagram); (19), (20) and
(21) lived together on the main street of the village, and it was in a
room of theirs that the sewing group met. In addition (28) was the
next-door neighbour, collaborator in handicrafts and friend of
(18); (23) was actually the daughter of (18), but they had quarrelled very seriously and were not on speaking terms; (22), (23)
and (24) were close friends and attended football matches together; they did not share the sewing interests of the other women
and were, in fact, very much younger than many of the others;
(23) was also brother's daughter to (10). All the women except
(22) were married; the three men who were not were either engaged or 'courting strong'; (12) and (25) were both miners in
1953, having been friends previously and having entered the mines
when a baking business in which they were partners failed. (10),
(11) and (18) were members of the miners' group of the football
committee (Frankenberg, 1957, p. 137).

When the discussion on the disposal of the funds got under
way, started by a motion first put and then withdrawn by a
member of the sewing group, most of the men supported the
football club. Two exceptions were Rhys Morgan (21), a
former but dropped player and Charley (12) who had already relinquished the secretaryship of the football club. A
clear split was inevitable. But it was a vigorous intervention
on grounds of equity and natural justice by Mr Higgins
(26), an immigrant from Lancashire, which led to a vote.
The result was 11 to 9 in favour of football. All the men except Rhys (21) voted in favour. Two women voted against

the motion – the chairman's wife (17) and one of the Mrs Morgans (16) who had not been attending the sewing group. The secretary (14) and treasurer (15) of the (football) supporters' club voted against their organization receiving the money. The decision was not accepted outside the committee and discussion continued with less unanimity among the women of the sewing group. But all the dissidents were united in support of Mrs Green's (28) view that the whole business was the fault of 'that Mr Higgins' (26), a stranger who had interfered in Glyn affairs. 'All strangers,' she said, 'ought to be shot.'

When the committee next sat, the carnival had been held and had made a handsome profit. At this meeting I found myself in the chair for most of the time, and it fell to Mr Higgins again to move the motion which split the committee. This time it was in the opposite sense to his motion at the first meeting. Once again the decision was not accepted outside the committee but this time I shared the blame with Mr Higgins.

At a final meeting involving mainly the same people (except for Mr Higgins retired hurt), but officially the annual general meeting of the supporters' club, a compromise was reached. The same person was elected secretary of both clubs and another was made treasurer of both. By duplication of roles in this way the two groups were made to coincide. The manoeuvres designed to make this possible were in the event wasted, for the football club, as had been feared, did not operate at all in the following season.

At all these meetings, the protagonists of different points of view were spokesmen for groups of villagers with differing viewpoints. They were affected by many factors apparently unconnected with the aims of the committees or with the proceedings. The side that people took at any stage was determined not by an impartial, objective judgement on the issues involved but by their own social position in the community, as individuals and as members of particular groups. The division between men and women cut across and complicated the discussions.

Charley (12) was concerned with his relations to the football club of which he had been secretary. But he had to reconcile these with his social position as a man and as a member of the sectional group of miners. He voted with the men and against his own expressed views at the first meeting. Jane (15), the supporters' treasurer, had to balance her position as a woman among other women of the sewing group against her responsibilities as treasurer and as wife and mother. The men wanted football to continue, the women wanted to go on sewing. Each group resented the alleged failure of the other to fulfil the obligations of reciprocity.

A whole history of previous disagreements was carried into a new situation. It is true that at crucial points in the public discussion villagers made suggestions which brought hidden conflict into the open. But they then withdrew and allowed outsiders to act as the strangers and put the formal motions which actually split the committee and temporarily the village. After the first two meetings an outsider was blamed, and after the third Charley – a member of the church and a miner. The Chair throughout was taken by those a little removed in social position from the general run of committee members.

Thus villagers were able to preserve their unity in a difficult situation. They were able to fall back on a verdict which none was in a position to deny. They could have managed all right but outsiders *would* interfere and cause trouble.

I believe that many of the features I have described for Glynceiriog exist in similar systems elsewhere. When I first talked about Glyn in Manchester, an eminent Indian sociologist, Dr Srinivas, first playfully accused me of a satire on university life and then said: 'It is just like my village.' This is a refrain I have heard many times since.

The social relationships and mechanisms built up in the nucleated village based on an economy which includes more than agriculture, but which is still, compared with towns, relatively undifferentiated, are the high peak of those based on multiplicity of social ties and social redundancy. In the following chapter on a larger mining village – a town without a town economy – we begin the downward slide (or the upward climb) to the culture and social organization of the city.

CHAPTER 5

The Town that is a Village: Ashton

THE West Riding of Yorkshire is an area where 'from the inception of the industrial revolution to the present time industry has been the keynote of life for the majority of its inhabitants' (Dennis, Henriques and Slaughter, 1956).

At about the same time as Williams was in Gosforth and I was in Glynceiriog, two anthropologists and a sociologist were looking at a mining town in the West Riding which they called Ashton.

Ashton is set among other towns famous for the production of wool textiles and machine tools. It grew as they grew, because it provided them with a basic raw material – coal. Its population in 1951 was 13,925. In 1851 it had been between 600 and 700.

In 1868 the first colliery, Manton, opened; by 1871 the population was 2,265. The first shaft at Ashton colliery was sunk in 1877, and deepened to reach a second seam in 1885; by 1891 the population reached 7,528. And it grew until it reached its peak of 14,955 in the 1931 census.

The population of Ashton has thus grown as the coal beneath it has been increasingly exploited. Its size as a town and the character of its housing reflects this too. In 1951 it had about 4,000 houses ranging from mine-owner's mansion through suburban semi-detached council houses and artisan terraces to early nineteenth century back-to-backs.

There are in fact only about a hundred back-to-backs in Ashton but their significance is greater than their numbers suggest. There is a general feeling sometimes admitted to in Ashton itself, and widespread in the West Riding as a whole, that Ashton is 'a dirty hole'. These houses are cited in support of the view. Their accommodation consists of a living-room-kitchen, bedroom, box-room, and cellar. There are blocks of shared lavatories in the middle or at the end of the row.

The next oldest are artisan terraces built in the 1870s. They are an improvement on the back-to-backs. They have two bedrooms, and a separate living-room and kitchen but they still lack bathrooms and private lavatories.

The overall impression given by Ashton comes from the thousand or so houses built between 1891 and 1911. They have three bedrooms and their own lavatories. They are conspicuous in comparison with the council and Coal Board houses built since because they were erected along the sides of the roads. The fact that the 1,300 houses built between 1911 and 1953 are less noticeable arises from their siting off the main roads. They owe to this also the fact that there was room to give them reasonably-sized gardens. For most of the population of Ashton these are the best houses available.

Ashton people are people who live in Ashton; it does not follow from this that they work, play, or shop there, for Ashton is by no means isolated. The town of Castletown with a population of 23,000 is five minutes away by bus. The bus journey to Calderford, which has a population of 43,000, takes only fifteen minutes. It is important that Ashton people do not think in terms of miles away but of bus times. The authors compared Ashton with another similar town ten miles away from Barnsley. To this town, Fullwood, Barnsley was the nearest bigger town than itself. Fullwood had twice the number of registered clubs and nineteen clothing shops as against Ashton's seven. Thus both men's leisure and women's shopping (for other than day-to-day food) seemed to be more internal in Fullwood than Ashton. The authors think that, on balance, this is to be explained by the ease in getting away from Ashton.

Women especially are forced out from Ashton to work and to shop. Areas whose economy is based on coal are notoriously short of opportunities for women to find employment. In 1911, 38 out of every 100 people in Ashton were working for a living. In 1931, 42 out of every 100. Seven of these 42, or 16 per cent, were women. While this is a 6 per cent increase on 1911 it is small compared with the national figures (for 1936) of 25 women for every 100 men employed, and with the figures for the twelve leading towns of West Yorkshire which have 55 for every 100 insured men. In both 1911 and 1931, 30 per cent of the women of Ashton who worked were in domestic service outside the town. In 1944 Ashton was scheduled as an area in need of facilities for women to work. By 1952 there were two small clothing factories and a very small macaroni factory. The last employed only 10. The clothing factories employed 167 and 29 women respectively of whom a total of 163 were from Ashton itself. In 1951 the number of women between the ages of fifteen and sixty-five in Ashton was 4,826.

If most women do not do paid work, and those who do have to look outside Ashton for it, the situation for men is very different.

Most men between fifteen and sixty-five are working in industry for wages and the dominant occupation is coal-mining. In 1911, 76 per cent of the men employed were miners, and in 1931 68 per cent; and while the authors give no figures for 1951 they leave us in no doubt that miners are still in a clear majority. There is no other major industry and those workers not in mining are, except for those in the clothing industry, in trades and services ancillary to it.

But not all Ashton's miners work in Ashton, nor are Ashton's mines worked exclusively by Ashtonians. The authors estimate that there were about 3,700 miners living in Ashton in 1952 of whom 2,300 work at the two remaining collieries. There they are joined by 600 miners who live elsewhere. Nearly 1,500 Ashton miners must travel each day to work outside the town where they live. This journey to work is characteristic of mining areas. During a study in South Wales I collected figures from all the collieries in one Coal Board Area, and these showed a similar pattern. There is, however, a qualitative difference between this journey to work and that of Glynceiriog men. Ashton miners travel by bus in a culture where this is commonplace. They work side by side with others who, while not from Ashton, are from towns where housing conditions, life chances, and styles of life are essentially similar.

Is Ashton then anything like a community in the sense in which we have been using the term?

Certainly Ashton people and especially miners and their families think that it is, and behave as if it were. When in August 1933 Manton colliery closed down, the manager was optimistic to the point of complacency about the absorption of the 650 redundant men elsewhere. By May 1936, 76 per cent had been absorbed, but the transferred miners had great difficulty in adapting themselves to the strange customs and practices of their new work places. For while coal-mining unites all its workers in an experience of dark and dirty conditions and of industrial battles unknown in other industries, it also divides them through highly developed local customs. The colliers' skill, seniority, and even knowledge of technical terms are often not transferable from pit to pit, let alone village to village, district to district, or coalfield to coalfield. This may be a factor binding miners to their home towns and their home collieries.

Again, while all miners share a largely common history of strike, lock-out, and unemployment, each pit or village has its own special variant of the general pattern. It matters a great deal with whom one shares an experience. Sentiment arising out of shared misfortune may be both exclusive and lasting. The Ashton riots of 1893 when two men were killed and many injured are still part of the community's consciousness of being a community.

Ashton is no economic paradise or beauty spot. It is dominated by 'spoil' and slag heaps and its air is heavily polluted. Unemployment there in the twenties and thirties was less widespread than in Durham or South Wales which were dependent on export markets. But the very existence of near-by manufacturing towns which provided a market for Ashton coal emphasized the contrast between Ashton's own poverty and the relative lack of poverty of its neighbours and enhanced its sense of community.

Ashton people are sensitive about their background of poverty and drabness and quick to defend their town against potential detractors. Social relations in the pit, like the

abhorrence of those who 'blackleg' in strikes, spread outwards into social relations in the homes and streets.

So it does remain true of Ashton that 'a man's workmates
are known to him in a manifold series of activities and contracts [sic], and often have shared the same upbringing'
(Dennis et al., p. 19).

The women too have had experiences in common. The
struggle of each and every family to maintain themselves
during the lock-out and the depression was, as it were,
carried on in full view. People who have 'got on' and are
thought to be giving themselves airs still in the 1950s earned
the comment, 'I don't know why he should think so much
about himself – his father was only a collier same as anybody else. . . .' (Dennis et al., p. 80).

Nevertheless, there is not the homogeneity about the
Ashtonians' participation in the community that there was
in the other societies we have discussed.

There is a continuum of degrees of involvement. At one
end is the old miner who followed his father into the local
pit and has worked there all his life interrupted only by
periods of general unemployment. His whole life of work and
play is bounded by Ashton. At the other extreme is the
woman who left school and Ashton at fourteen to go into
domestic service in Huddersfield. She may since have worked
in Leeds or Bradford, and if still single or with grown
children may now travel daily by bus to work in near-by
towns. For shopping or the cinema, too, she may go off by
bus. To her Ashton may almost have become a dormitory.

In general in Ashton, as not in Glynceiriog, it seems to be
the men rather than the women who preserve the pattern
of the community and give it its character. The character
that they give it arises in turn from the social position which
they derive from the interrelated facts that they are wage-
earners, miners, and inhabitants of a specific area.

The special nature of the area we have already discussed.
The fact that they are wage-earners they share with the
majority of the population of working age in the whole
of England. Ashton is not merely not physically isolated.

Discussion of its way of life is inseparable from discussion of economic class in Britain as a whole.

The miner of Ashton is required to present himself, summer and winter, spring and autumn, on at least five days a week at the pit and to put his ability to work at the disposal of an agent of the employer. This agent will tell him what to do and if the miner wishes to have money on which to live, within limits, he will have to do as he is told. Today the employer is a public corporation, the National Coal Board, but the Ashton miner is as unlikely to meet members of its Board of Directors as he was to meet the directors of the colliery company or an individual coal owner. Neither coal owners nor Board members would live in Ashton, nor would they spend much, if any, time there. The miner, like other wage-earners, works at the ultimate direction of people he never sees.

In return for his agreement to place his time at the disposal of these mysterious and distant powers, the miner, like other wage-earners again, receives a wage in money with which to buy the food, clothing, shelter, and entertainment he requires. The exact amount he will receive in any week depends on many factors. It depends especially on a complicated process of negotiation between the buyers of his ability to work, his employers, and his representatives – trade union leaders. It is, as we shall see, one of the peculiarities of mining, that one section of miners, the colliery face-workers, takes a direct part in the negotiations which determine their own wages.

The product of the miner's labours is coal. Once he has produced it, the miner has no further control over its ultimate disposal. In sharp contrast, then, to the small farmers of Wales, Ireland, and northern England, wage-earners like the miners of Ashton are linked to the consumers of their product only through their employers. Even this relationship to their own employers is reduced to an economic one. It does not have any overtones of social redundancy. If they knew their actual employer they would be hostile towards him, as they are to other employers. To some extent at least, work, which is integrally woven into the life of the small farmer, has become a thing apart. If the miner wishes to spend time when he should be at work on some other activity he cannot normally do so. If he finishes his allotted task more quickly he cannot leave. To do so would be to endanger his security and that of his family. Work still involves cooperation between director and those who carry it out. But the cooperating parties no longer meet as equals. Times of labour shortage and high wages do arise when some measure of freedom to work or not to work is there. Even in such periods, other groups may make accusations of 'absenteeism'. If the worker's life is seen as a whole such times are rare.

'The worker experiences his tie to the enterprise as a continual and binding necessity. When a man receives his wages every seven days, and these are on the whole not a great deal more than enough for comfortable survival he is *bound* to his work. By Sunday night the collier who starts work at 6 a.m. on Monday is not enjoying himself with the same abandon as he did the night before' (Dennis *et al.*, p. 29).

As Alan Sillitoe has pointed out, what is worthwhile in life may seem, in these circumstances, to reduce itself to what can be fitted into 'Saturday night and Sunday morning'. A job becomes an absence of freedom endured during the days, which makes freedom possible in the evenings and at weekends.

In Ashton, the working men's clubs hold weekly draws with prizes up to thirty pounds. A side bet may bring the possible prize money up to sixty pounds. The winner of such a draw who turned up to work on Monday morning would be considered somewhat odd by his mates.

There are other features of life in Ashton which arise out of this fundamental situation.

The pit officials whose job it is to see the work is done are seen as enemies at least during working hours. The very fact that in Ashton, but not in other Yorkshire towns, officials belong to the same clubs as the ordinary workers may in itself be indicative of this hostility. Thus one of the three under-managers in Ashton who belonged to and frequently visited two of the Ashton clubs said to the authors:

'When I'm out for a drink, a chap is liable to get a bit drunk and come over to me and start being nasty. If I'm in a pub there isn't much I can do about it. In the club all I have to do is to call a committee man, tell him what is going on, and I can be sure of redress' (Dennis *et al.*, p. 142).

Any possible way of outwitting these officials without suffering financial loss will be used. This is something which arises out of the social situation and is independent of personalities involved. A miner in South Wales told me how on his first day in the pit his uncle told him the first thing to remember was that all deputies (the supervisory grade) were rotters. A few days later the deputy had just gone off and his uncle remarked what a decent fellow he was. The youth said, 'I thought you said they were all rotters', to which the older man replied, 'So they are, but there are decent rotters and lousy rotters. He's a decent one!' In *Coal is our Life*, the story is told of a collier of left-wing views who became a bookmaker, and had employees of his own.

I remembered how the bosses used to treat the men, [he said], and I thought I'd try and rule by kindness. But I soon found I was being swindled; they thought I was soft and took advantage of me. You see they'd got so used to ordinary employers that they thought this was just a good chance to get the better of me. So I had to change my methods and now I have to rule them with an iron hand. I don't like doing it but I find I can't make it pay any other way (Dennis *et al.*, p. 33).

These rather negative reactions are not the only way in which wage-earners respond to their situation in society at large. There is also, and especially among miners who exercise a high degree of both skill and strength, a pride in being workers who add to society's riches and an expressed feeling that others are parasites living upon them.

Wage-earners also are subject to a fundamental insecurity. Wages are calculated by the shift and paid weekly.

No one knows when an accident or sickness is going to end his ability to earn. Although there was full employment in Ashton in 1952/3 most miners could remember prolonged unemployment either in their own lives or in those of their fathers. Cyclical unemployment arising out of 'a general decline in demand for goods on an international scale' (Dennis *et al.*, p. 19) was experienced in Ashton from 1929 to 1933.

Forty-eight per cent of all the insured workers in the Ashton Labour Exchange area were unemployed in 1937. In the years between 1928 and 1936 unemployment among mine-workers in West Yorkshire never fell below 21 per cent and in 1933 reached 57 per cent. In some years unemployment arising from a specific lack of demand for coal complicated the more general situation.

In 1952/3, Ashton miners were not confident that this could not happen again. Events since then in the coal industry have shown that they were not being entirely unrealistic.

The chance of real social mobility for the Ashton miner is very small, as it is for most wage-earners in Britain. It is true that, as we have seen, one became a bookmaker, but he was exceptional. The growth of large corporations, both nationalized and private, makes it unlikely that most workers will ever become their own bosses. Only the treble chance on the pools holds out a remote hope. Most wage-earners will remain such until they become old age pensioners. Lack of training, leisure, and income cut them off, now and forever, from 'the ideals of behaviour, the good things of life, in short the cultural ends of the society in which they live' (Dennis *et al.*, p. 31).

The authors conclude:

In terms of national economy and society, the inhabitants of Ashton are part of a class-divided society. It is interesting to note here that Ashton itself, far from being a microcosm of that national framework, is representative of only one part of it. To all intents and purposes the inhabitants of Ashton are all of the working class. In relation to the stratification of our society, they are all in the same category. In this, Ashton is typical of mining villages (p. 37).

We have now seen that what characterizes Ashton in general derives from its inhabitants being all of one class – wage-earners. What characteristics does it derive from being dominated by one industrial category – coal-mining?

Firstly, it must be said that class relationships seem to be intensified in mining areas. There are a number of reasons for this, which arise out of the nature of the actual work of miners.

There is, of course, the obvious point that mining is dark, dirty, and dangerous, which sets miners apart from other manual workers, let alone non-manual workers and employers.

Secondly, since pits can only be sited where there is coal to be found, miners tend to live in *relatively* isolated villages inhabited mainly by other miners, and not in towns with mixed industries.

To stay alive and to earn money as a piece-worker at the face usually involves close cooperation among a team of workers. This solidarity at work is carried over to the trade union organization which is usually dominated by face-workers and ex-face-workers, and from there to the social institutions of society at large. The trade union organization derives its strength partly from the daily bargaining for piece-work allowances between colliers and the deputy. In contrast to many industries such bargaining is carried on at the very place of work – in the coal face. Colliery face-workers are thus directly involved in the negotiation of their own wages and, hence, determination of their own status in a way which is rare in general industry. The militancy which this engenders carries over into other situations.

Finally, and for the same reasons, past hostilities between employer and employed are kept continually alive 'by the basic physical fact of coal getting'.

'The old system of industrial relations characterized by a fundamental conflict between management and men, is kept healthily functioning' (Dennis *et al.*, p. 79).

The dangers in mining are not confined merely to risks of being killed or maimed. The greatest impact, perhaps, on the miner and his family is made by those relatively minor mishaps which reduce earning power temporarily or permanently. The boy recruit to mining is at first poorly paid, but his wages (if he is lucky in getting a place on the coal) rise by the age of twenty-six to a comparatively high sum. Here they may remain until in his forties he is no longer strong enough to do the work. For the rest of his life as an underground repairer or on the surface he will be reduced once more to the low day-wage man's rate. He may not, however, be lucky enough to stay uninjured until he is forty. At any time his earning capacity may be permanently or temporarily cut in half.

This pattern of earnings during the miner's life cycle contrasts with that of the ordinary manual worker who reaches a lower peak in his early twenties but who can expect to remain at about the same real level until he retires at sixty-five. It contrasts also with the professional pattern of a very low initial income which may continue to rise into late middle age.

Many of the features of family and personal life and some of the features of recreational activity in Ashton are explicable in terms of this pattern of earnings. Parents, for example, assured the investigators that their sons would not go down the mine. Young men themselves said the mine was not for them. In the event most of them ended up there. This was partly, of course, because there was little else they could do. It was, in part, because initial wages, while low compared with colliery face-workers, compare favourably with those of the kinds of alternative work available – builders' labourers, busmen, and railwaymen.

Finally, to be a miner in Ashton is to be in the swim and share the life-experience not only of the majority but also of the group which almost completely dominates social life.

The general uncertainty whether the high level of earnings, or indeed life itself, will continue leads to two extreme attitudes to life being prevalent among Ashton miners – the very frivolous and the very sober. These two views of course are not confined to villages based on the mining industry.

Jenkins in *Welsh Rural Communities* divides a Welsh village into similar halves (Davies and Rees, 1960). But in the mining villages, these views, like many other features, are seen in sharp relief, because of the rarity of the middle way. The authors illustrate the point neatly by reference to two ballads commemorating mining disasters. The first, written in 1882 after the Trimdon disaster, draws the conclusion:

Oh let's not think of tomorrow, lest we disappointed be.
Our joys may turn to sorrow as we may daily see.
Today life may be strong and healthy, but soon there comes a change,
As we may see from the explosion that has been at Trimdon Grange.

The attitude of 'eat, drink and be merry for tomorrow we die' seems to be dominant in the leisure activities of all, and the family life of some, of the Ashton miners.

The second ballad quoted concerns the Seaham disaster in 1890 and concludes:

Death to me short notice gave,
And quickly took me to the grave.
Then haste to Christ, make no delay,
For no one knows his dying day.*

There is a substantial minority of Ashton miners who behave as if they took this more serious view. They do not seem to be as numerous as those one found in South Wales, at least until recently, where the 'protestant ethic' was stronger (see Brennan, 1954).

The second view, giving thought for the morrow, is not given much encouragement by the general social conditions which surround life in Ashton. Thriftiness is a case in point. There is little point in a miner saving for a rainy day since no amount of saving would be adequate to meet prolonged incapacity. If he saves for a sunny day, to take a holiday or to buy something special, he is quite likely to have to spend the savings unwillingly on making up the difference between

* See A. L. Lloyd, *Come All Ye Bold Miners*, quoted in Dennis *et al.*, p. 132.

his receipts from National Insurance and his requirements for living. In 1952 there was no sick pay scheme in the mining industry. By and large, miners fix their living standards on a basis derived from their early earnings as day-wage men. They then fix a sum as their wife's wages and continue to pay it, come rain, come shine, for as long as they can. They insulate this sum from large rises or falls in their income by spending the surplus on leisure. A good husband will work harder for a few weeks to help pay for a holiday or an expensive item of domestic furniture.

If there is a third attitude between the 'abandon' of the frivolous and the 'thoughtfulness' of the serious it is nearer the latter. It is held by a small group which wants to change or at least improve the situation in which Ashton miners find themselves. In work they are to be found on the committee of the trade union branch, and at leisure in the 'best room' of club or pub.

The sphere of life where these contrasting attitudes make the most impact is in the family and, within the family, especially in the relationships between miners and their wives. For while the miners derive their views from experience in the pit and at leisure, the family derives its pattern of life as well as its income from the father.

Nearly all Ashton families live on wages derived from mining, but very few women have seen the inside of a pit or have any accurate idea of work underground. This division of sex roles is found in every aspect of Ashton life almost from the cradle and almost to the grave. In the authors' words:

The Ashton family is a system of relationships torn by a major contradiction at its heart; husband and wife live separate, and in a sense secret lives. Not only this, but the nature of the allotted spheres places women in a position, which although they accept it, is more demanding and smacks of inferiority (Dennis *et al.*, p. 228).

As soon as children can walk and even before, the different roles of the sexes are impressed upon them. Girls are given presents of dolls, aprons, and the like; boys get cowboy sets, guns, and toy soldiers. While a father may take little interest

in his children of either sex, if he can be persuaded to take
one of the children to the gardens or to the cinema when he
is on the afternoon or night shift, it will always be the boy.
It is a common sight in Ashton, we are told, to see a father
romping with his small sons while a little girl looks on
excluded even at this stage from the wider social life. This
is to be her fate throughout. Adolescents and even younger
girls are expected to help their mothers in the day-to-day
tasks of the household. Adolescent boys, like their fathers,
are excused. This would be a sissy occupation and they are
encouraged to go off with a gang of their friends to play football or knock around the streets. These groups of male age-
mates or peers are a most significant feature of life in
Ashton. Men may continue to take part in them throughout
their lives. Boys of first school age form groups of six or seven
who play together. In adolescence, such gangs go to dances
together, and make forays into neighbouring towns and
villages, where, as the 'Ashton lads', they may get involved
in scraps.

It is this group and not the family of origin which is
threatened with break-up by marriage (see Allcorn, 1954).
When, in their twenties, young miners start serious courtship, it is from this group that opposition comes and from
which they have to fight to escape. After marriage the links
to the group are bound to be weakened, but it is a point of
honour among the men to keep some time for drinking and
attending sporting events with their mates. In middle age,
when children are grown and expenses less, when the
novelty of the early days of marriage has long worn off, men
return once more to the company of their peers in club, pub,
trade union, or betting office.

These groups may be seen as isolating the men from their
families and as deliberately excluding women. Women certainly see themselves as involved in an economic and social
battle between the demands upon their men folk of the
family and the demands of the group of male work-mates
and friends.

The men even speak differently when they are on their

own and this serves still more rigidly to segregate the sexes. In all mining areas one hears references to 'pit language'. The authors describe how the incidence of 'obscene' swear-words in conversation intensifies as men go down the pit and to their working places. Any remark below ground is punctuated with obscene words. Below ground also, men discuss sex and their experiences freely but always imper-sonally and without reference to specific wives and daugh-ters. In the pubs and clubs also, on week nights, obscene language is used and stories told. But in the presence of women or their families miners' language is more restrained. Milder blasphemous expletives are commonplace but sexual swear words are out. A miner who hears another use these words in front of his wife would probably knock him down. I myself have seen many such fights after closing-time (stop-tap) on Saturday nights in South Wales. If, however, a woman trespasses on to male preserves, she will not be treated with this respect. Thus a miner who rebuked a friend for swearing in front of his girl friend in a pub on a week-night at first received an apology. When the offence was re-peated he was told that if he wanted to protect her he should not bring her to the pub. An older woman who went to the betting office to place her disabled husband's bets was sub-jected to ribald comments and suggestions. Although these were offered with good humour, they had bite, and she would not have had to suffer them elsewhere.

This change in habits of speech marks a change in social role from men among men to men as members of families. But, of course, as fathers, husbands, and boy friends, miners may find themselves playing two roles at once. These situa-tions lead to an embarrassment which reveals the import-ance of the more usual segregation of roles. Thus fathers and sons who work together in the pit are inhibited in their swearing. One collier aged fifty-seven described an experi-ence thus:

'I'm like any other miner. I can swear as well as anybody, and, of course, my son can as well – after all he's 27 and he's working at the face. But we've never sworn in front of each other. In fact I don't think he's ever heard me swear. But one day I was sitting waiting to go out of the pit and a group of colliers came and sat ready and he was one of them. They started talking and they swore just like any other lot. My lad didn't know I was there and so he swore as merrily as anybody else. Well I've never felt so awkward in my life before. I could feel myself blushing and managed to creep away without him seeing me. I'm glad I did because we'd both have felt very awkward' (Dennis *et al.*, p. 218).

Again, the authors tell how, in a bus queue after a film showing Marilyn Monroe, two girls deliberately teased their boy friends by hinting at the sort of discussion on sex which they knew the lads had when they were alone with their work-mates.

On the other side of the obscenity barrier, girls too, of course, grow into a social life with those of the same age and status in the life cycle. They tend to go in pairs when single and to remain more closely attached to their mothers and sisters even when they are married. The social life of women outside the home, especially after marriage, consists mainly of such informal but frequent contact with neighbours, their mothers, and married women kin. The forbears of most Ashton families came to the town during the period 1895–1908 and so neighbours are often also kin. Ashton, unlike neighbouring Calderford, is small enough for women to maintain contact with kin even after moves to new areas and council housing estates. Women call frequently for cups of tea and gossip in each other's houses. They call this 'callin' or 'having five minutes off'. Just as the men discuss their work in their leisure, so the women discuss theirs, their houses and their children. While the men's discussion not only of work but also sex is impersonal, the women discuss their personal lives and their husbands' habits in some detail.

Despite the isolation of their work interests, common to wage-earners everywhere, but intensified by the special conditions of a *mining* village, men, women, and children are united – at least for part of each day – in a household.

This must (and the women's gossip groups just described ensure that it usually does) 'provide a sound and comfortable place to eat and sleep for parents and children, a place where they can enjoy privacy, if they ever feel the need of it, and very important, a haven for the tired man when he returns from work' (Dennis *et al.*, p. 179).

Home is seen as the very antithesis of the pit. The one with food, cleanliness, tidiness, comfort, and warmth is cosy; the other dirty, dark, impersonal, and a place of toil is not. To provide her husband with one, the wife must ensure he spends time in the other.

For the man's part in maintaining this, however, is seen in essence as a purely economic one. A 'good worker' in the Ashton wife's view is one who does not miss shifts and pays her each Friday her wage. After that it is up to her. Thus the administration of the household, and the care of the children, falls upon the women. At the time of the study a collier expected to give his wife £7 to £8 a week and a surface man £6 to £7. The collier may have earned £9 or even £14 but his wife's wage would remain the same. Most of it she would spend on food in local shops. Large items and clothing might be bought on tick or hire purchase and paid off week by week. Really large items she would ask her husband to help with. Similarly if he ran out of chewing tobacco money on Wednesday or Thursday he would ask her for a 'sub'.

Even serious-minded husbands who spend their time at home making things for the house do so on their own or with the help of men friends or their sons and not in cooperation with their wives.

It is true that the roles of husbands and wives in maintaining the household and raising the children are still complementary as in the other societies we have described. But it is a cooperation mediated only by cash. There are (in the opinion of the authors) in most Ashton families few activities which 'demand cooperation or encourage the growth of companionship between husband and wife' (p. 183).

In fact, in Ashton marriage 'there is a business-like division of duties and of work to which the development of affection and companionship is accidental'.

The same customs which make the wage the subject of a battle between the husband's contradictory desires to keep in with his mates and to do right by his family tend to develop companionship and affection between mothers and their children and especially their daughters. The mother-son tie, however, is also strong. Children see their mothers as their protection against a capricious father and they offer her protection in their turn. The authors tell two stories illustrating this. In one a father introduced a mistress into his wife's house. The mistress was turned out and the father set upon and thrashed by his four daughters of ages ranging from sixteen to twenty-nine. In the other case daughters who went out to work took days off when he did, so that he was forced to work himself or have no money coming into the household.

Miners who were children in the depression were particularly attached to their mothers. They saw them especially as being the bulwark of the family, because to some miners the depression was a challenge to maintain their leisure-time way of life. Such men continued to drink and gamble as a gesture of defiance, hiding a real concern for their families, which they considered it unmanly to show.

As in many societies, old men and old women, especially after widowhood, may lose their distinctive sex-roles. The old women go to pubs and ignore or enjoy the ribaldry, the old men visit their daughters and daughters-in-law and dandle grandchildren on their knees.

But during the greater part of the life-cycle woman's place is in the home and with her kin. She sees her man at table and in bed. The rest of the time he is at work or in the club. She is excluded from the world of ideas because she is excluded from the actions of Ashton men.

'. . . the club, the pub, the bookie's office, the trade union, all the places where men do talk together are closed to women . . .' with one significant exception – the Labour

Party. It is to these, the voluntary formal organizations of Ashton, that I now turn.

The activities of miners and their families outside working hours can once again be divided into frivolous and serious. Overlapping this division is another distinguishing those activities connected with the pit and those independent of it.

The major voluntary association connected with the pit is, of course, the trade union branch. Not all workers in the pit are equally attached to it although all must belong. The branch leadership and the rank and file members who attend general meetings are in fact drawn mainly from among the contract workers. This is not surprising since it is only they whose wages are directly affected by activities at this level. Surface workers and other day-wage men have their wages and conditions determined by negotiation by N.U.M. leaders, at the nearest, in Barnsley and more usually in London.

Only two branch officials in Ashton were not in fact contract workers at the time of election. Most of them were, in fact, fillers, that is face-workers. For it is this group that is most likely to secure election. They work in the largest teams and because of their working conditions are involved in most disputes.

The authors consider that the trade union does not have importance in leisure situations outside the colliery. This is a conclusion which even on their own evidence is hard to accept. They argue it by pointing out the lack of emphasis placed on the Friendly Society aspect of trade unionism in the area.

In fact, however, the characteristics required of the Branch Committee must, in my opinion, ensure that they have a more widely relevant prestige. They are contract workers and fillers – the elite in skill and pay of the industry.

They attend work regularly, being therefore 'good workers' in the women's definition as well as the men's. They are good talkers, and are expected to hold to the slogan 'the miners – right or wrong'. Whereas the miner expects his ordinary mates to be heavy drinkers, he requires his union leaders to drink only in moderation (cf. Doherty, 1955 and Sigal, 1962).

The main leisure centres of Ashton for men are, as we shall see, the pubs and working men's clubs. In each of these, there is a 'best room' where the conversation ranges more widely than in the general rooms. In these rooms meet 'an important part of what can be regarded as Ashton's "intelligentsia"' (Dennis *et al.*, p. 145). Here groups of ten to twenty men, most of them colliery contract workers, discuss the topics of the day. On one such evening described, talk ranged from a local rugby league match, through international boxing to government road and housing policy. The opinions of 'best room' men are respected by their fellow Ashtonians. The urban district councillors are 'best room' men. The trade union branch committeemen meet informally but regularly in the 'best room' of one of Ashton's hotels.

Another way in which the importance of the union and its leaders extends outside the pit is the way in which union decisions may be enforced by community pressure. Before the closed-shop such pressure could make the life of the non-unionist and his family isolated and uncomfortable. Ashton people tell the story of one of the few who blacklegged in the 1926 lock-out. When he died in 1946 even his sons refused to attend his funeral. Blacklegs in Ashton were very few. I know one mining village elsewhere where, even in 1960, there were two separate groups to be seen waiting to go down the pit. One was of miners who had gone back to work early in 1926 and those of their sons who stood by them. The rest who stood separately did not speak to the pariah group.

Apart from the union the other activities associated with the colliery do not involve many people, directly or indirectly. The most important is the Ashton Workmen's Band. This is supported by a levy on the miners, but is not a colliery band in the sense of getting special privileges. Some men's shifts are occasionally re-arranged to help the bandmaster but even this is rare.

The band is said to enter fully into the life of the town and people feel it is 'their band'. It even plays at celebrations affecting only two or three streets. It has also an external function like the rugby team of maintaining Ashton's prestige 'in the numerous competitions in which brass bands customarily engage' (Dennis *et al.*, p. 120).

It does not seem, however, to have the importance in social life ascribed to similar institutions in Glynceiriog. The authors conclude:

'For most people the satisfaction of hearing of the success of the band is the limit of their interest. Ashton people know nothing of the competitions in which "their" band does badly. But if it does well there is widespread comment' (p. 121).

The rugby league club rouses stronger passions. 'Each game is an occasion on which a high proportion of Ashton's males come together and participate in the efforts of Ashton to assert its superiority (through its representatives) over some other town (through their representatives) (p. 156). . . . Attendances at home matches vary from 2,800 to 10,000. Even on one occasion when a rugby league international was televised in full, 3,400 turned up to watch the home team. Only nine watched the International in the T.V. room of one of the clubs. It is a standing joke in Ashton that the number of "teas thrown at t'back o't'fire" on Saturday night depends on the relative success or failure of the Ashton team.' There were thirteen supporters' clubs in Ashton and like Glynceiriog's small equivalent already described 'they organized dances, social events and selected a "Rugby League Queen". In this case she competes with "Rugby League Queens" from other towns in an attempt to show that Ashton possesses beautiful women as well as strong and skilful men' (p. 158).

Other institutions connected with the colliery which earn prestige in external competitions are the cricket team and the St John Ambulance Brigade.

Intermediate between voluntary associations based on the colliery and those run independently within the community are the activities of the statutory Miners' Welfare. This was set up in two stages after Royal Commissions on mining in 1919 and 1926 and is today run jointly through an organization in which both the National Coal Board and National Union of Mineworkers participate.

Among its many activities is the provision of institutes and halls in mining villages. The largest building in Ashton is, in fact, the Welfare Hall. Although this looms large in the town according to the authors, it plays but a small part in the lives of miners over twenty years old. The amateur musical and drama society put on a few performances there each year and it is used for charity and publicity concerts. There was one in aid of a Road Safety Campaign, for example. The union branch committee meets there once a fortnight and the local Labour Party also uses it as a meeting place. Though the authors regard the hall as largely a white elephant, the union branch in 1953 raised *its* contribution towards it by 1¼d to 3d per member, and £4,500 was spent on renovating it.

To the youth of Ashton, those between fifteen and twenty-two and especially between seventeen and twenty years old, it is an institution of vital importance.

Here each Saturday night throughout the year there is a dance attended by 400–500 young people out of the 700 in this age group. At holiday times, more than one dance is held. The programme of dances at Easter 1953 was Saturday 7.30 to 11.30 p.m., Easter Monday 12.15 a.m. to 4 a.m., and 8.15 p.m. to 1 a.m. on Tuesday morning. It is at these dances that the male and female social worlds of Ashton intersect for long enough to make courtship and marriage possible. Any young man can ask any young woman to dance, even if they have not seen one another before. Such a request is rarely refused. Dancing makes conversation in the early stages of acquaintanceship inessential. Indeed, the crowd even makes much knowledge of dancing superfluous. If after one dance the couple do not feel inclined to pursue the friendship it is open to the boy not to invite the girl again or for the girl to refuse.

For young women this may be looked back on as the only period of full social participation in other than the society of other housewives in their lives. For the young man, even at twenty, dances at the Welfare are a small part of his social life outside home and pit. His main amusement is beginning to be centred with the rest of the men in the major social institutions of Ashton, the clubs and the pubs. His main interests outside the affairs of his work at the pit are likely to be in betting and rugby league football.

There are six working men's clubs in Ashton with a combined membership of about 6,850. There are also seven pubs which fulfil broadly similar functions. Club members are nearly all men since only one of the clubs admits women members. The others explicitly exclude women from membership, and even from the premises except for Saturday evening and Sunday afternoon and evening concerts. Many men are members of more than one club and so membership is half as much again as the number of men over eighteen.

The object of all the clubs is said to be that they are 'established for the purpose of providing for working men the means of social intercourse, mutual helpfulness, mental and moral improvement and "rational recreation"' (Dennis *et al.*, p. 143).

At all the clubs the bar is very important. It provides the financial basis. In one Ashton club an annual income of £12,500 included £12,200 bar-takings and £40 membership subscriptions. The rest was cash in hand from the previous year.

The main activity is simply talking over beer. Conversation is free and easy and the men concerned have known each other in school, pit, club, and pub all their lives. Except in the 'best rooms' already described, conversation is concrete and down to earth. The two main topics are work, the incidents of the day, and sport, the incidents of the weekend. At weekends there are concerts to which women are admitted. Local performers sing mainly musical comedy songs. The pattern is reminiscent of Old Time

Music Hall. These concerts form one of the ways in which individual Ashton families are integrated into a wider community.

'When the performance first began [about 8 p.m.] there were groups of four or six sitting at each table. Many of the groups sat for considerable periods in complete silence. What conversation there was, was between couples. As soon as it was announced that the artist was about to sing there was quietness. By 9 o'clock there were very few silent groups, and all the people at each table leaned forward appreciatively listening to whoever was speaking. The Master of Ceremonies found it increasingly difficult to secure the required degree of silence. It is as if the performance was quite subsidiary to social intercourse, and was indeed used merely to facilitate it by filling in the gaps in the conversation. Later on there is constant liaison between the members of different groups. The whole audience, which was originally composed of individuals and pairs rather loosely associated in groups of four or six, has become a series of groups – now somewhat larger – about six or eight – associated with other groups – in an audience now much more like a unity' (Dennis *et al.*, p. 147).

The concerts are sometimes replaced by 'housey-housey' or 'bingo' which adds the thrill of gambling to a social process of being drawn together. The authors do not describe an actual bingo session, but in my own experience there is much joking and chaffing between tables as the evening goes on. It is one of the few ways in which women can participate in the gambling interest of the men.

Bingo or housey is not the only form of gambling carried on in the clubs. I have already mentioned the weekly club draw. Side-bets are placed on games of dominoes and cards, and a bookie's runner is usually in attendance.

The main centre of gambling in Ashton was not the club but the bookmaker's shop. One of these has a turnover of £700 a week in the flat-racing season. There were four main bookmakers in Ashton and each had about forty regulars who (at least until the Betting Act) used his shop as a club.

Other men and a few women walked in and out to place bets as they would go to any other shop. The fate of women who lingered in the betting shop has already been mentioned.

The working men's clubs (and some of the pubs which are very similar to them) do provide other facilities besides drink, talk, bingo, and concerts, but they are little used. Billiard tables, radio, television, books (rarely), and newspapers are examples. An important element of the clubs which the authors perhaps underestimate are the subsidiary interest groups, the angling clubs, tourist clubs, etc., which form part of all the major clubs. It is true these cater for only a few – the angling club described had only thirty-six members. One suspects that, given overlapping membership and overlapping interests, they may form a framework to leisure in Ashton which is concealed by the obvious surface pattern of drinking and betting.

Seen in the mass, the leisure time lives of Ashton miners may seem purposeless and wasteful. If the activities and interests of each individual at different times of his life were to be studied the mass might seem less homogeneous.

Nevertheless, we can accept as largely substantiated the authors' view that the uncertainty of miners' lives, and their hazardous conditions of work, help to impose upon the majority of them a leisure in which their major organizations are thriftless cooperative societies for the purchase and sale of beer. In my experience in South Wales, clubs can provide companionship, a pleasant physical background, and a sense of belonging which inspires in many of their members remarkable loyalty and enthusiasm. The fact that members run them themselves through an elected committee, and the profits are 'ploughed back', enhances their ability to engender this *esprit de corps* and differentiates them from the pub.

A part of this feeling of solidarity is directed against the women, who are identified with the necessity to attend at the other pole of the miner's life – the colliery. It is perhaps significant in this respect that women are admitted only at weekends, when the memory of the informal pressure of the family driving the man to work can be put aside until Monday morning.*

There are some leisure activities in Ashton, however, in which women are allowed a part. The least overtly social of these is reading. There is no bookshop in Ashton, but there is a library with over 2,000 registered members and a monthly issue of books fluctuating between 5,000 and 6,500. 'Reading must therefore be ranked with the clubs, the public houses, sport and gambling in respect of the number of people concerned' (p. 167). A quarter of the books issued were non-fiction but 'westerns' for men and 'romances' for women were the most popular.

Radio and television provide a constant background to domestic life in Ashton. The cinema for both teenagers and married women, usually going without their husbands, is another more or less social recreation.

The only voluntary association in which women partici-pate fully in Ashton is the Women's Section of the Labour Party, which has a hundred members. This meets fort-nightly and draws twenty to forty middle-aged and elderly women to each meeting. Although its activities are mainly social, its core members are also the leading lights of the Ashton Ladies Labour Choir; its activities have resulted in the election of two women district councillors. The Labour Party Women's Section is preoccupied with social activities which are tolerated by the men because men regard them as the sort of frivolities appropriate to women. Nevertheless, behind this façade, it seems to me possible that even in Ashton women are moving into a position where they will

* The authors devote a little over a page to the churches of Ashton which have, they say, declined in importance since the 1920s. In 1953 there were two Anglican churches, one Anglican mission, eight Non-conformist and one Roman Catholic church. The largest Methodist church had eighty members, mainly women. Average Sunday morning attendance is said to be eight women, four men and twelve children. Sunday evening has a somewhat larger adult attendance with twenty-two women and ten men. One of the Anglican churches and its Mission recorded one hundred communicants each Sunday(!) but the authors say that tradespeople were over-represented for their numbers in the town.

acquire the sort of importance in decision-making in the community which they have elsewhere. A comparative study of the linked question of the role of women and of clubs and welfare institutes in the various coalfields of Britain would be of great interest.

In this chapter I have described life in Ashton. It remains a village, but combines multiplicity of ties and sense of community with urban values and environment. It has not been as easy to say 'this is so' for Ashton as it seemed to be for the communities in our earlier chapters. I have tried to follow Dennis, Henriques, and Slaughter in showing the intimate interrelation between the miner's work, his family, and his leisure. I have tried to show also that there is an additional dimension to what appear at first sight to be the sociologically meaningless activities of drinking, betting, swearing, and Saturday night hops. Whom the miners drink with, and above all, the people whom they do *not* meet, and the things they do *not* do, give us a means to understand the differentiation of social groups and categories which interact in the daily life of a segment of industrial Britain.

CHAPTER 6

Small Towns: Glossop and Banbury

In this and the next chapters we are going to town. Like all those who leave the countryside we shall be presented with problems.

In their study of Glossop, A. H. Birch and his collaborators did not concern themselves to see social life as a whole. They were interested in the specific problems of grass-roots politics in Glossop. Birch says they were interested in public and not in private life. This means that they give no information on kinship and the family in their book. On the other hand, Willmott and Young in their two books were interested in family life and not in politics, so they give us no information on voting, or political party and trade union membership. Margaret Stacey in her book on Banbury gives both sorts of information because the problem she sets herself, the relationship of traditional patterns to change, makes both of them relevant.

The fact that it is possible to write about politics and leadership in Glossop without details about kinship, and about kinship and class in Bethnal Green, Greenleigh, and Woodford without details about politics, shows that the multiplicity of ties and social redundancy characteristic of the rural community are here less important.

Before turning to a more detailed discussion of Glossop, it is useful to put some of our towns and town segments into perspective by a simple comparison.

Sixty-five per cent of the inhabitants of Glossop were born there, but only 41·4 per cent of Banbury's were born in Banbury. Bethnal Green has the highest proportion of native-born of any London Borough. Fifty-three per cent of Young and Willmott's general sample were born in Bethnal Green. In Woodford only 12 per cent were native born.

In Glossop, of those classified as wage-earners, over 36 per cent voted Conservative. In Banbury the figure is 30 per

cent. While no figures are given for Bethnal Green or Woodford, it is suggested that the figures would be low in Bethnal
Green and high in Woodford.

Forty-one of Glossop's workers, against 31 per cent of
Banbury's, are employed in traditional relatively small-
scale industry. Again there is no information from Bethnal
Green or Woodford. One would guess that Bethnal Green's
figures would be lower and Woodford's lower still. Social
class in Glossop is to a great extent cut across by the unity of
old Glossopian families against incomers. This is not true of
Woodford of which Willmott and Young write, 'There were
still two Woodfords in 1959 and few meeting points between
them' (Willmott and Young, 1960).

GLOSSOP

Glossop is a small industrial town only thirteen miles away
from the centre of Manchester.

Nevertheless 'it is sufficiently isolated to have a distinct
community life of its own'. It owes this to the nature of the
moorland countryside which surrounds it. This is bleak,
pastoral country, too wet and cold for wheat, rising to
between one and two thousand feet above sea level. Eighty
per cent of its employed residents work within the borough
and nearly two thirds of its present inhabitants were born
there.

Like Ashton, it is a creation of the industrial revolution
but here cotton rather than coal was king. At its peak, in the
years between 1900 and the end of the First World War,
there were nine large firms in the town; eight were engaged
in cotton goods manufacture and one was a paper mill. The
owners were all relatively speaking very rich and all lived
in the town. The population rose ninefold during the nineteenth century, mostly in its first half. By 1851 Glossop could
be described as one of the great seats of cotton manufacture.
At that time, its population was about 17,500; 38 per cent
of the adult men and 27 per cent of the women were employed in cotton.

Perkin, who wrote the historical chapter in Birch's book,

distinguishes four stages in the town's history. Between 1821 and 1866 it took shape as a town. When Wesley preached near by in 1761 the area was virtually uninhabited. In 1819 'Howard Town', the only settlement, was a thin straggle of cottages parallel to the Glossop brook. In 1821 the Snake Pass route from Manchester to Sheffield was opened as a major road to give Glossop its first importance. By 1846, 'it had all the appurtenances of a town; shops, railway-station, gas-works, high street, and central square fronted by a "handsome town hall and market house with a prison and an office for the agent of the Duke of Norfolk – a noble range of buildings in the Italian style" ' (Birch, 1959). There was no initial conflict between lords of the manor and industrial developers, for they coincided in the Howard family, Dukes of Norfolk.

It was ideally suited for cotton textiles being near to Liverpool and Manchester, 'the chief port for the raw material and market for the product. Glossopdale had an established connexion with the trade, the humidity necessary for the spinning of the yarn under tension and above all an abundant flow of remarkably soft water, for power and the finishing processes of bleaching, dyeing and printing' (Birch, p. 10).

The Howards were joined by other families of mill owners nearly all of local stock. In Glossop people still say that each of these families founded a church, a school, and a mill. They competed with each other in their championship of the various religious groups and associated political parties, a point to which I will refer again in the description of present-day Glossop. It is to the way that the mill-owners took a paternal and competitive interest in the town's social life that Perkin attributes his belief that bitter class struggle hardly developed in Glossop. This is the more surprising in the light of the trials of the Lancashire Cotton Famine, 1861–4, and turbulent events in neighbouring Hyde and Stalybridge. Another view might be that lack of alternative work drove rebels and would-be rebels out of the district.

Perkin writes:

Glossop's comparative industrial peace cannot be ascribed to higher wages. For most of the period wages in the Glossop mills, though higher than in many other occupations were no better and sometimes worse than in the towns nearer Manchester. The cause is to be found in the superior industrial relations of the Glossop masters, in their success in maintaining contact with their workers not only in the mills but outside in the churches and chapels, the reading-rooms and clubs, at public lectures and on the sports field. The masters demanded a loyalty that went far beyond obedience in the mill, and they seem to have received it. Antagonisms in Glossop were not between classes but between rival religious groups, representing complete vertical sections through the class structure (Birch, p. 21).

The second phase in Glossop's history, its heyday, dates from its receipt of a Borough Charter in 1866 to the long decline which began in 1920. During this period in Glossop as elsewhere the number of looms and output generally increased while the number of enterprises declined. Twenty-six enterprises of 1831 had become nineteen by 1884 and thirteen by 1900. In 1920 there were eleven enterprises owned by five or six firms. In this period also, the paper industry was started, and by 1920 it employed nearly a thousand workers or one twelfth of the insured population.

Relatively free from economic worries and the competition of ducal landowners, the leading industrial families, like Italian Renaissance princes, competed between themselves for political power and social influence.

They saw eye to eye on all important matters, attended the same functions, and shared control of such paternal institutions as the cricket club and the Volunteers (Birch, p. 26).

The Catholic Howards stood aside and the major struggle was between a Tory, mill-owning Anglican family – the Woods and Sidebottoms, and a Liberal, paper-manufacturing Nonconformist family – the Partingtons. It is interesting to note the part played by sport in this rivalry. A Partington built the cricket pavilion and his son patronized rugby. A Wood sponsored the football club so effectively that for one season it even reached the first division of the English league. This last Wood, Sir Samuel Hill-Wood, raised the prestige of Glossop through sport in still wider fields by being Chairman of Arsenal F.C. and Captain of Derbyshire's cricket team.

Glossop's third phase was the depression of the twenties and thirties, and this phase lasted roughly from 1920 until the outbreak of war in 1939. The biggest firm, the Woods, went bankrupt in 1924. Unemployment reached 14 per cent in 1929, and 55 per cent in 1931. After attempts to bring in new industries in 1931 (the first since 1884) unemployment in 1938 was still 36 per cent and in 1939 23 per cent. The combination of cyclical crisis and the specific problems of cotton textiles gave Glossop a record of unemployment as bad as many of the mining areas of South Wales.

Since the war, Glossop has regained some of the population loss of the thirties, and while it is still heavily dependent on cotton, 59 per cent of its nearly six thousand workers in manufacturing are in other industries which include rayon, wool and silk, clothing including gloves, paper-making, food-canning and rubber.

Seen in retrospect at least, the status divisions in Glossop just before the First World War seem straightforward enough. At the inaccessible top of the tree were the Howards, secure in riches, ownership of land, and pedigree. Next to them and of increasing importance in local life, as the Howards increased in importance nationally, were the industrialist millionaires. Below them in status there were then ranked the shopkeepers, professional people, office workers, and finally factory hands.

The authors say it was possible to move upwards in prestige and power by making money in business. None except the Howards had secondary education and humble origins were no bar to social acceptance. I suspect this is an over-simple view. The rich Catholic families in fact sent their children to private Catholic schools and the rich Protestants sent theirs to public schools. A cursory glance at *Who's Who* reveals that present-day descendants of Sir Samuel Hill-

Wood were educated at Eton. It may be true that the old elite of Glossop was recruited locally by making money, and the new elite is recruited outside through the grammar school. Both maintain their social prestige by sending their own children to private or public schools. It seems to me possible that the authors underestimate the importance of this point.

The old pattern of leadership by rich local industrialists who were borough councillors, presidents of Glossop's many voluntary associations, and leaders of its churches, disappeared as the industries became larger and external to Glossop. To some extent the old pattern may be just another case of strangers being manipulated by a self-governing majority. I am sure that shrewd devotees of cricket, rugby, and soccer among the working class and burgesses in some situations, manipulated Partingtons and Woods in this way. Nevertheless, unlike the Outsiders of Glynceiriog, these local industrialists wielded real power over the working lives of Glossop's people. There was an accepted hierarchy, unlike egalitarian Glynceiriog, and Sir Samuel Hill-Wood was a genuine national leader in sport.

Local leadership and the relationships between classes and status groups have changed in Glossop as the growth of large-scale industry brought with it centralized government and centrally oriented political parties.

Glossop now has many citizens who, while running industry and government, do not own the former nor control the latter. These are the group for which we have already introduced Watson's term of *spiralists*. It was in fact the findings of the Glossop study which originally suggested the concept.

In Glossop, these men 'unlike the self-made men of an earlier generation, have rarely worked their way up in the town in which they were born. Most of them secure advancement either by moving from one post to another, which may well be in quite a different area, or by promotion within an organization which has branches in several places' (Birch, p. 37).

Thus nearly a third of each group of 114 children in

Glossop enter the grammar school, which is the first hurdle that non-public school spiralists have to cross. This compares with a national average of under a fifth.

Less than a third of the boys who leave grammar school stay in Glossop and only just over half of the girls. In the case of secondary modern school pupils, around 70 per cent of the boys and just under 90 per cent of the girls leaving school find employment in the town.

The other side of the coin is the fact that nearly two-thirds of the professional and managerial workers of Glossop are immigrants, compared with just over a third of the adult population as a whole.

The authors estimate that about four-fifths of the most influential people in the town, 'the chief industrialists, the senior public officials, the clergymen, the headmasters', are immigrants.

The picture emerges of a group of immigrant leaders of industry and government who have no roots in the town and do not play a prominent part in its social and political life – the spiralists. These face 65 per cent of the population born and bred in Glossop and wage-earning. In between are the 'burgesses', like the local shopkeepers, who combine the *relative* wealth of the former with the local background of the latter.

I have said that spiralists *face* the rest of the population, in point of fact they rarely do. The voluntary association membership of Glossop does not cut across status-group lines. The authors counted about a hundred such associations. Some set out to limit membership. Examples are working men's clubs and industrial welfare schemes on the one hand, and the Rotary Club, Inner Wheel, Chamber of Trade, and Employers' Association on the other. While others do not specifically aim to have members of one status group, in effect they do. 'Thus nearly all the members of the Golf Club are business or professional people, Tennis Club members are mainly professional or white-collar workers, and the supporters of the Amateur Bowling League are largely industrial workers' (Birch, p. 40).

Similarly, the Brass Band attracts industrial workers and the music and repertory clubs, professional and white collar workers.

The churches, which are thought in the past to have been institutions which cut across social and economic if not political divisions, can no longer do so effectively since only about a third of those interviewed claimed to attend even once a month.

Significantly, perhaps, since most women in Glossop have their occupation in common, only the two women's organizations – the Townswomen's Guild and the Women's Institute – appear to be exceptions to the general rule.

Social classes, and immigrants and natives do however mix in two contexts – the Magistrates' Bench and the borough council. The magistrates' activities only touch marginally the lives of Glossopians. Seven of the eleven are former or present borough councillors (four Labour, two Liberal, and one Conservative). Although the Bench includes four house-wives, two industrialists, a retired locomotive driver, an executive civil servant, and a retired postman, it lacks industrial workers. Of its members, two are in their forties, five in their sixties, and four in their seventies. One wonders how justified is the author's statement 'that the Bench as a whole is in touch with all the sections and activities of the community' (Birch, p. 143).

When Glossopians were asked whom they regarded as the six most influential people in Glossop they showed little consensus. A quarter of them gave no answer and few named more than three. Thirteen per cent gave answers referring back to the Glossop of its heyday. But of the thirteen people most frequently named eleven were borough councillors, and one had been in the past. Seventy-two per cent of persons named were in fact politicians and only one per cent were magistrates other than politicians.

The borough council then is where the Glossopian tends to see the representatives of his community. It is in the borough council also that one can see most clearly the division between immigrant and native.

The council of Glossop 'has 24 members consisting of 6 councillors and 2 aldermen from each of the 3 wards' (Birch, p. 113). Each ward elects two councillors each year. They hold office for three years. The elections for councillor are, and always have been, contested on political party lines. Aldermanic and mayoral elections are conducted by the council and the ex-mayors respectively on the basis of seniority.

Although each candidate carries a party label, few electors vote a straight party ticket. Personality, general friendliness, and reputation are therefore important. 'Of twenty-six candidates over the years whose votes showed them to be more popular than their running-mates, eighteen were in a group of occupations in the public eye. Only five of the less popular were in this group of occupations' (Birch, p. 117).

The Conservatives on the council, as in Glossop as a whole, are a party of tradesmen. For the past thirty years at least half of their councillors have been shopkeepers. The Liberal candidates immediately after the First World War were all business proprietors or managers; in the last few years half of them have been office or factory workers. The Labour Party has moved in another direction. From putting up all industrial workers in the twenties, they have progressed to having professional or white-collar workers as half their council members.

The age of councillors varies from early thirties to the early seventies. There are two distinct groups of members divided according to length of service on the council. Eight members (three Conservative, three Labour and two Liberal) have served for over twenty years. They form a group whose long interaction has led to a sentiment which often over-rules their party differences.

Party membership, and who has the majority, determine the chairmanship of committees. In the past Conservatives decided this; now it is an alliance of Liberal and Labour. The majority do not take all, but merely the key positions like Finance, Housing and Town Planning, and Health. But 'the influence of party affiliations in the subsequent work of the council is not easy to trace. The Liberals do not believe that their council member should be tied to any particular policy and they do not hold caucus meetings; the Conservatives generally regard party agreement as desirable, but they have abandoned the practice of holding caucus meetings and frequently disagree during debate; the Labour members still hold caucus meetings but no binding decisions are taken there and it is quite common for Labour councillors to be on opposite sides during Council debates' (Birch, p. 119).

The main issues which divide the council are firstly, economy, and secondly (and relatedly), being businesslike. On economy there are old Tory diehards who cry 'keep down the rates at all costs' and young Labour hotheads who say 'choose the right policy and damn the cost'. The majority of the councillors take up an intermediate position not clearly related to party affiliation.

The issue of being businesslike is the one which causes the division between professional immigrant and traditional Glossopian to come into the open. The rate-making proceedings in 1953/4 illustrate the point well. The debate was conducted in an extremely forthright and blunt manner:

In the former year there was a large increase of 2s 5½d in the county precept, and the majority of the council decided to soften the blow to the ratepayers by reducing the Council's capital reserves by an amount equal to the proceeds of a 1s 5d rate. When some councillors objected that this would only postpone the evil day they were told that in the following year the position might, in some unspecified way, be easier. To a limited extent this optimism proved justified, as during the next twelve months the completion of new houses increased the product of a 1d rate and an extra exchequer grant equivalent to a 5d rate was made available to the borough. During this year, in addition to drawing out balances, the Council overspent by an amount equivalent to a 2½d rate, and in 1954 the county precept was increased by a further 2d in the pound. As a result of the new housing and the grant, however, and by cutting expenditure by an amount equivalent to a 2d rate, it was possible to meet the estimates for 1954–5 by an increase of only 8d on the existing rate, and this was proposed. As this would have been a very complicated story to explain to the electors, the Chairman of the Finance Committee, introducing the motion, said that the increase of 8*d* should be regarded as equivalent to an increase of 2*d* for housing, 2*d* for improved services, 2*d* for salary increases, and 2*d* for the increase in the precept. In the pre-war Council such an explanation would not have been questioned, but in 1954 one of the immigrant councillors – belonging to the same party as the chairman – went through the statistics and made the chairman explain to the Council why it was necessary to increase the rate by only 8d instead of by 1*s* 9½*d*. Some of the Glossop-born Council members patently regarded this as a waste of time.

Two amendments were proposed during the following debate. One, moved by an immigrant Labour councillor and seconded by a Liberal, was that the amount allocated for the purchase of library books should not be reduced; this was opposed by a Liberal and a Conservative (both natives) and withdrawn on the advice of a Labour alderman (a resident of forty-eight years' standing). The other motion, moved by a Conservative and seconded by the one Independent in the Council (both natives), proposed that the rate should not be increased; this was put to the vote and heavily defeated by an alliance of members of all three parties. The new rate was then adopted by the same majority (Birch, pp. 120–1).

Some Glossop-born councillors showed their hostility to immigrants by commenting sarcastically about the councillor who did not want to cut book-buying: 'Of course, X is an educated man and he feels happy when he sees a lot of books around'. Similarly, another immigrant councillor who asked whether, to save corrosion, the swimming-bath roof ought not to be painted, was taunted with not having paid rates. It is possible, although we have no way of knowing, that traditional Glossop councillors were protecting themselves from the informal pressures of their own social network by blaming inevitable rate increases and capital investment on councillors whose own networks related them with professional colleagues often outside Glossop and relatively indifferent to rises of rates within the town.

At all events debates in Glossop Council bridged across party divisions and emphasized other divisions. I want to turn briefly to the characteristics of these parties and their relationships to divisions of social class and status. Here, too, we shall find that blurring of sharp edges which a multiplicity of ties and social redundancy still creates in micro-urban Glossop.

Although in a sample survey the authors found that seventy-five per cent of those they interviewed had at some time met a borough councillor, the voting in borough council elections is as low as elsewhere in Britain. In national elections nearly 85 per cent of the population vote – a proportion that must be very near to the maximum possible. Nevertheless, the political parties of Glossop are organized more for social and recreational activity than for political objectives. At the centre of each party is a social club. The parties in fact resemble one another much more than do their equivalents in the cities. The Labour Party lacks the elaborate organization and attention to procedure which characterize it elsewhere. The Conservative Party lacks its usual flourishing women's section and Young Conservative group. Within all the parties only a minority of the membership is active at all, and there is wide disagreement on policy within each party. What there is much more agreement about is what sort of people ought to be associated with each party. Parties in Glossop were seen as the places for particular social groups. In fact, however, reality was more complex.

Thus the Conservative Party claimed a thousand members, three hundred of whom were members of the club. An attendance of fifty was exceptionally good. The party was dominated by businessmen and professionals from whom its councillors and committee were selected. Many Conservatives would have liked their party to be governed by aristocrats or at least tycoons. The rank and file looked on near-by Buxton's colonels and gentry with envy. The Glossop leadership were irritated by Buxton's lack of understanding of local business problems. Although only a sixth of Conservative members were women, the party had a fair cross-section of the town by occupation. Its most remarkable characteristic was the over-representation of Anglicans. While

45 per cent of the community were Anglicans, two-thirds of the Conservative members were Anglicans. In the general election 41 per cent of Birch's total sample voted Conservative.

The Liberals claimed six hundred members in six associations and three clubs. The Liberals seem to form the social activists of Glossop. Few of their members were industrial workers and three-quarters were Nonconformists (compared with just over a quarter in the population as a whole).

The Labour Party is the smallest in membership but in many ways the most interesting because it is the most political. It is seen by all as the party of wage-earners and especially industrial workers, yet most wage-earners do not belong to it and many vote against it. It claims only 160 to 180 members of whom 60 per cent are in fact industrial workers. Most of the rest are also wage-earners, yet four out of its nine councillors were professionals or managers. The only people in these categories who joined at all seemed to be those with political ambitions. A half of Labour Party members were Nonconformists and a quarter Roman Catholics. Although some of the remainder said they were Anglicans, it was the familiar use of C. of E. as a residual category, for none were really active churchgoers.

There were in fact within the leadership of the Labour Party three distinct groups. The first and the most influential were the four older Labour councillors. All four were over sixty, three had been born in the town, and one had lived there for forty-eight years. None of them had industrial experience. Like the other traditionalists on the council they were concerned to keep down the rates. In pursuit of their policies they formed alliances with the Liberal councillors even against the younger Labour councillors. These, backed up by the wife of one of them and an officer of the Labour Party, made up the second group. These six were all in their thirties or early forties and all except one were immigrants with some formal education. They believed in organization and efficiency rather than tradition and local pride. The third group is the largest and probably includes all

the trades unionists in the town. It had only one representative on the borough council but made up all the trades
council. All its members were industrial workers and leaders
in the trade unions who had left school at fourteen. They
described themselves as thinking men and the authors say
'they are all class conscious working men of the type that
have been the backbone of the Labour movement' (Birch,
p. 59).

Although they dominated the Executive of the local
Labour Party, they had little political influence in the town
outside the Trades Council.

In a sense the understanding of this group's position is
the key to Glossop. For as the authors point out, in Gorton
or Greenwich – where studies of politics have been carried
out – they would be the dominant force in the Labour
Party (Benney and Geiss, 1950 and Donnison and Plowman,
1954).

If all wage-earners in Glossop (or in the country) voted
Labour, the Labour Party would have a permanent
majority. In fact, were the industrial workers in Glossop
Labour Party to support this last group of leaders, they
would dominate the party. The table below reproduced from
Small Town Politics, however, shows that we must share the
author's conclusion that in parliamentary elections 'the
business and professional groups are fairly solidly Conservative, but there are numerous exceptions to the rule that
industrial workers vote Labour' (Birch, p. 106).

In fact the votes of wage-earners in a town like Glossop
may be associated with their own view of their social status
(44 per cent of industrial workers who said they were middle-
class voted Conservative as against 31 per cent of the others.
Sixty-seven per cent of the white-collar workers who said
they were middle-class voted Conservative as against 33 per
cent of the others) (Birch, p. 109).

Secondly, Conservative voting is associated with membership of the Anglican Church (46 per cent of Anglican
industrial workers voted Conservative as against 33 per cent
of industrial workers as a whole).

One must agree with the authors that the assumption 'that industrial workers who vote Conservative are people who have in some way been led astray from their natural tendency to support Labour' (Birch, p. 110) is totally unhistorical.

TYPE OF OCCUPATION AND VOTING IN THE GENERAL
ELECTION OF 1951

Type of occupation	No. of electors	% voted Conservative	% voted Liberal	% voted Labour	% did not vote
Business proprietors	38	73	8	8	11
Professional and managerial workers	73	65	15	12	8
White-collar workers	129	47	3	31	19
Industrial workers	417	33	8	42	18
Total	657	41	8	35	16

In a town like Glossop, especially, relationships between economic classes are not simply mediated by the cash nexus. They are less multiplex than they were fifty years ago but they are still multiplex. The older the worker and the nearer he was born to Glossop, or the longer he has lived there, the more this is likely to affect his behaviour. This is a point to which we return in more detail below in reference to Banbury.

BANBURY

While it is possible to speak of Glossop as a community in the sense in which we have been using the term, this is more difficult for Banbury. Margaret Stacey in her conclusions in fact states explicitly that Banbury is not a community. She believes it is not because of '. . . the complexity and overlapping of ties within the town, the ties with groups outside the town, and the lack of strong shown tensions among the disparate groups' (Stacey, 1960).

I think her first reason as she has stated it is a bad one,

but her overall judgement commands acceptance. She distinguishes between non-traditional and traditional Banbury. I shall accept this distinction in fact but change the terminology in a significant way. The lives of people in Banbury may, on the one hand, be Banbury-centred. On the other hand, they may take place in Banbury but look for reference groups and foci of interest elsewhere. The social life of anyone in the town may approximate to one or other of these two extremes or lie between them. In this it reflects the kind of continuum I am suggesting for Britain as a whole. Banbury does, unlike our other communities, approximate to a microcosm. Like most towns in Britain, Banbury is the meeting-point of at least two cultures – local and national. This distinction cuts across that between immigrant and Banburian, and to some extent across divisions of class and status. In so far as Banbury has in the past generated and continues today to generate its own style of life, it is a community like the others we have studied. In so far as it provides merely a residence for those whose interests and values are derived from other systems, it is not. The task of description and analysis is at once made easier and more complicated by the existence of those whose ambition or education leads them away from their starting-point in a Banbury-centred culture. In addition, in Banbury as in Glossop, there is a category whom Watson describes as 'blocked spiralists', who have reached the limit of the social and geographical mobility they are likely to attain and who hence find themselves 'deposited' in Banbury. It is from this category that many formal leaders are selected. For convenience of reference I adapt Merton's terms *local* for Banbury-centred individuals, institutions, and groups, and *cosmopolitan* for the others.

Some working-class individuals in a small town will behave in accordance with *local* status group norms. Others will identify themselves not with wage-earning and other groups of the locality but with the national category of the working class. The former are locals; the latter cosmopolitans. The same division can be made in other sections of the population. I believe that as one moves from rural to urban, one sees the results of a process of proletarianization in which *local* gives way to *cosmopolitan*, and multiplex to undisguised class relationships.

Banbury is a town of about 19,000 inhabitants in central England. There is no other town of comparable size within twenty miles. It lies about forty miles from Birmingham and seventy-five from London in the centre of a band of hills about twenty miles wide. This band, rising to four or five hundred feet above sea level, crosses England from northeast to south-west, dividing the Midlands from the South. Banbury is neither one nor the other.

The town is the centre of an agricultural district with roads radiating from it. The borough council estimated for the benefit of a Royal Commission that it is the marketing centre for a population of 40,000. There has been a settlement at Banbury for 2,000 years and a town for 800 years. 'Every market-day for the last 400 years, the people of the district have gone into Banbury to buy and sell and, not less important, to gossip' (Stacey, p. 4).

It has not, however, been just a market town. As early as 1830 when its population was already 6,400, seven hundred of its families were engaged in 'trade, manufactures and handicrafts' as against 130 in agriculture. The manufactures and handicrafts were, however, ancillary to the activities of the countryside around. It was the centre of plush-weaving and horse-girth manufacture, although these trades were cottage industries in which much of the actual production took place outside the town. There still exist a printing-works, a timber yard and a brewery which were already established in 1830.

The first major industrial development in the town came in 1848. An immigrant bought the business of a local ironmonger who had invented a turnip-cutter and set up a foundry. He built a factory 'in alien brick and in vivid contrast to the local stone', as well as workmen's cottages to go with it. By 1871 when the population reached 11,700, the factory employed 2,000 men, many of them immigrants.

The railway came at the same time, but although the factory found international markets, since it produced agricultural equipment, it maintained its local character. After 1871 there was a period of stagnation and, with the lessening importance of handicrafts connected with harness for horses, almost a decline. In 1933 the foundry closed down, and in the same year an aluminium factory employing 2,000 people started production. Now it employs a quarter of the town's working population. When a shopkeeper or publican in Banbury speaks of 'good' or 'bad' times he refers to the state of the aluminium·market.

The 'Alley', as it is sometimes called locally, stands outside the town and outside its traditions. It represents the coming of cosmopolitanism. It is part of an international company whose executives are sometimes in Banbury and sometimes in Geneva or Montreal. It works three shifts, 6 a.m. to 2 p.m., 2 p.m. to 10 p.m., 10 p.m. to 6 a.m. 'Working life is out of time with home life, with wives' cooking and shopping and sleeping, and with the children's school life, out of time too with the social life of other people' (Stacey, p. 9). With the cosmopolitan factory came cosmopolitan shops – Woolworths, Boots, and other chain stores – and cosmopolitan people. The population rose between 1931 and 1951 from 13,000 to 19,000.

Many of these newcomers are immigrant, and it is significant that born Banburians not only call them foreigners but think that they are mostly 'Scots, Irish, and Welsh' with a few of 'those Northerners' thrown in. In fact, Welsh, Irish, and Scots make up only 15 per cent of the immigrants, and those from the Midlands and the South outnumber the rest by two to one. Nearly 15 per cent come from within twenty-five miles of Banbury. Their real foreignness lies in their socially *cosmopolitan* outlook. 'Many of the men were used to working in large-scale industry for absentee owners; they had been brought up to take it for granted that a worker belonged to a trade union' (Stacey, p. 14).

These workers, like the foundry workers before them, had to be housed. More than a thousand new council and

private houses were built on the town outskirts to house
them.

In 1830 Banbury was 460 yards across; today it is over a
mile, 'and every twenty minutes buses bring people from
the new estates – the acres of new brick houses, of new
concrete roads, and of gardens cut from turf – into the
town centre, still the main focus for shopping, commerce,
and entertainment' (Stacey, p. 10).

Like Ashton, Banbury has many different sorts of houses
ranging from slums to mansions. Stacey arranges them in
order of status, taking a sample of about nine hundred. Of
these nearly a third are old nineteenth-century houses
lacking bathrooms, inside lavatories, and often back doors.
They are found in the town centre in terraces hidden between the shops and the canal and at the east end of the
town across the canal and the railway. Most of the category
which Stacey calls 'rough' working class live in these
houses, although they also house many of the older skilled
workers. 'These are the older, independent, "respectable"
craftsmen whose homes are "clean and decent" and who
"keep themselves to themselves" ' (p. 95).

In contrast with Ashton, the first impression that the
visitor gets of Banbury may be of comparatively new
houses. Nearly a quarter of the houses in the sample are
council houses mainly post-1914. They lie on the outskirts
near the main roads entering the town. They are three-
bedroom, semi-detached or short terraces. They have bathrooms, fixed baths, and usually indoor lavatories. These
house the unskilled and semi-skilled workers of Banbury.
Another group of old houses proved difficult to classify.
These are large houses in and about the town centre, with
five or six bedrooms, attics, and cellars, nearly three
quarters of them lacking bathrooms and lavatories, but
privately owned. They make up nearly 15 per cent of the
total. They seem popular with clerical workers and some
traditional craftsmen.

Next, in ribbon development along the entry roads and
making up a fifth of the sample, are what elsewhere would

be called suburban semis, the homes either of manual
workers who rent them from the companies they work for,
or of clerks, schoolteachers, and lower civil servants buying
them on mortgage.

Finally in the sample are the houses of the prosperous
tradesmen and the senior officials on the outskirts, and the
'good old houses' of the town occupied by the best people.
These last, like their equivalents in other towns, often become offices or boarding-houses as their inhabitants die or
move to the rural outskirts.

Many of Banbury's really well-off choose to live in the
villages around rather than in the town itself. It is here, too,
that the local gentry and county have always lived, some in
what are literally mansions.

Types of houses are not, of course, mixed at random in
Banbury. They tend to cluster in distinct ecological areas in
which social status and social patterns are to some extent
closely related. Types of house are not necessarily homogeneous in social status. The prestige of a house depends not
only on what it is, but on where it is and who lives in it.
Thus one street is considered lower in status since council
houses were built at the end of it. On council estates those
known to have been occupied by people from slum clearance
areas enjoy low prestige.

Patterns of relationships between neighbours vary from
district to district.

Banbury, as we have seen, is a town where people live
next door to one another. 'All households in the interests of
a quiet life if nothing else have to come to some working
arrangement with the people next door' (Stacey, p. 101).
These people in Banbury are not necessarily kin; they may
have a different cultural outlook in terms of *local* and *cosmopolitan*; they may be regarded as of higher or lower class
status. There is clearly no uniform pattern of neighbouring
relationships.

Households of wage-earners need each other's help apart
from general sociability. They expect to give and receive it
in the small emergencies of daily life. If, in a working-class

Banbury street, a neighbour runs out of sugar or salt, she will borrow. If a minor accident means a visit to hospital, a neighbour will look after the other children. This sort of exchange is reciprocal but not formally so. There is an informal norm that people help one another. In a situation of weekly wages this is almost inevitable. The degree of necessity varies with the stage of the life cycle that people have reached – the very old and the young married with children will have the greatest need. This, however, is aid in the acute crisis. To deal with chronic crisis requires the bringing in of kin (or in their absence social agencies). For the chronic crisis is likely to infringe on the possibility of reciprocity. Thus the so-called 'rough' working class are in perpetual chronic crisis and are in fact forced back upon their kin by the partial ostracism of 'ordinary' and 'respectable'. The 'respectable' or 'aspirant', as I called them in Chapter 3, are not willing to be under obligation to their neighbours. For they hope their neighbours will soon be, if they are not already, their social inferiors. The 'ordinary' are secure in their ability to borrow and repay. Even the ordinary in chronic crisis needing sustained help summon relatives from afar. This is especially the case in childbirth, when mothers come to the aid of their daughters from a considerable distance.

The inhabitants of the suburban semis borrow and lend such things as garden implements; the best people living in their own grounds may regard as their nearest neighbour someone who lives several hundred yards or even several miles away.

To the majority of Banbury's inhabitants neighbours form a greater number of nodes in their social networks than do their relatives even if the relatives live in the same street. 'It is only where relations with neighbours are poor for other reasons, differences in social status for example, that kinship plays a dominant role' (Stacey, p. 111).

There is, however, a wide range of variation in knowledge of, and relationships with, kin outside the elementary family. Lineage is not important to most Banburians. There is an important exception in the case of the burgesses who derive prestige from their old established businesses. This group used to dominate town politics and justify the belief that it is 'the old families who still run Banbury'.

The family of aunts and uncles, cousins, married sisters, and above all mother remains important to the young married woman. This is a vestige of the social and economic importance of kin in the countryside which I have described in earlier chapters.

Few married women work for wages outside the home in Banbury. When they do it is often as secretaries or teachers – jobs in which they remain in the traditional female roles of helpmate to man or career of children. Most Banbury women are housewives only, and of them it is true that 'a wife cannot resign from her work without breaking from her husband and children, nor can she leave her husband without losing her job. Her occupation is rightly returned as "married woman". *This is a unique status in a society otherwise based on individual contract, specialization, and separation of function*' (Stacey, p. 136; *my italics*).

It seems, therefore, that the change in technology which changes the social patterns of men's lives reacts differently upon those of the women. The norms of the married women's social life lag behind.

This, however, is modified in Banbury by the short-lived nature of what Stacey calls the immediate family of husband and wife and their children. As has been reported of town life elsewhere, early marriage leads to an early end to the tie between mother and home. Forty-six per cent of the sample households were lacking in the sense that they had no children, children who were already leaving home, or had a widowed head (Stacey, p. 135).

While this figure is not available for the other communities we have discussed, one suspects that this is a relatively high proportion.

While initially social status, and political and religious affiliation are determined in the elementary family, they are consolidated and symbolized elsewhere. This process, however, can only be described in terms of the division in Banbury, already mentioned – that between *locals* and *cosmopolitans*. Stacey expounds this by contrasting examples within different status categories, and with some modifica-cation I will follow her plan.

The locally oriented 'upper-class' county or gentry are few. They are exemplified by Sir William who is from an old local family and feels he should give local service. He went to a public school, is Anglican and Conservative. He sits on the county council and the Bench and is President of the British Legion. Sir William's recreation is hunting. His equivalent among the cosmopolitans is a Lord. Lord A was not at public school himself, but his son goes to one. His religion is unknown, his interest in Banbury is slight. He is chairman of a group of engineering companies which takes him to America or London more often than it keeps him in Banbury. Both Sir William and Lord A read *The Times*, the former starting on the court page, the latter on the stock exchange reports.

Mr Shaw is *local* – a burgess in Watson's sense. He is the third generation of Shaws to have a business in Banbury and has been mayor of the town. Also an Anglican and a Tory, he drinks in the White Lion. I cannot guess his newspaper reading habits. Perhaps Mr Grey, another burgess but a Methodist and a Liberal used to read the *News Chronicle*. He plays bowls at the Chestnut Bowling Club. Being a tee-totaller he sees relatively little of Mr Shaw and his friends. The *cosmopolitan* equivalent of Mr Shaw and Mr Grey is Mr Brown. He has a degree from a provincial university and is a leading technologist at the 'Alley'. His social aspirations are within his firm, and he is prepared to travel where they send him. He is, in fact, a spiralist. While he is in Banbury he meets his like at the Banbury Players, an amateur drama-tic club. If he becomes a blocked spiralist, he may join the Rotary and there meet the burgesses, or take a more active interest in politics than merely voting Tory. He very likely reads the *Daily Telegraph*, and may even have friends who read the *Guardian*.

Burgesses and spiralists used to meet at the Tennis Club, but it split on a very characteristic issue. The burgesses wanted it 75 per cent social, 25 per cent tennis; the spiralists were interested in technique and played to win.

The working class in Banbury can also be classified according to a differentiation between *locals* and *cosmopolitans*. The *locals* are Anglican George and (additional to Stacey's list) Baptist John. George goes to the pub on the corner of his street and belongs to the British Legion. For twenty-five years, interrupted only by war service, he has worked for the same firm. He votes Tory and thinks Sir William and Mr Shaw are natural leaders who know what is best for the workers. John has also worked for many years in a locally based, traditionally run industry. He is Baptist, Liberal, and T.T., and plays bowls at the borough club.

Ted, their *cosmopolitan* equivalent, is a union man and votes Labour; he has been a Labour councillor and does not recognize the complicated system of status and prestige 'assented to' – to use Mogey's term (Mogey, 1956) – by George and John. To him there are just bosses and us – the workers. He is inactive in religion.

These pen-pictures are obviously to some extent caricatures but they do give some idea of the distinction between *local* and *cosmopolitan*. To adapt Stacey (p. 173), the town is bisected two ways. It is cut down the middle by the line which divides *locals* from *cosmopolitans* and it is cut across the middle by the line which divides middle class (burgesses and spiralists) from workers. Outside the town but sometimes active in its affairs are the *local* and *cosmopolitan* rich. The *locals* are a group, or rather an interconnected network of face-to-face groups, based on family, neighbours, occupations, associations, and social standing. Banbury is their principal frame of reference, and their key question is one about ascription – who *is* he? What is his family? *Locals* have a *total* status in all activities.

Cosmopolitans are a category; although united by the fact that all live in Banbury, they have their frame of reference in a wider society. Their key question is one about achievement – What does he do? What has he done? As the answer to this may be different in different fields of activity, *cosmopolitan* status is not total but fragmented.

The way status and prestige, localism and cosmopolitanism interact in social life may best be seen in the organization and leadership of voluntary associations and political parties in Banbury. As the author points out, these are ideal fields for the investigation of social status in a town since they are both voluntary and small in membership. Since voluntary associations connected with religious and political beliefs attract only the more active adherents, they provide sources of information on the larger bodies which would otherwise be difficult to reach.

Banbury is an ancient borough with a Charter four hundred years old. But like other local authorities it has steadily lost power and prestige to the centralized county council and national government. The *local* middle class, the burgesses, regret this as bitterly as they regret the invasion of their own preserves by *Labour* cosmopolitans. To many in this group, as to the local gentry, 1945 and the simultaneous victory of the Labour Party nationally and in the borough still seems to be the end of the era of reason. The borough returned Liberals to parliament throughout the nineteenth century. Its first Tory was elected in November 1922, during the same election at which Labour stood for the first time.

Whatever the social and religious differences remaining between burgess and spiralist, *local* and *cosmopolitan*, Liberal and Tory, they are united by a common fear of socialism and the domination of working-class outsiders (in every sense). The fact that *local* wage-earners and the inhabitants of the rural hinterland of the constituency share their views results in the continued return of a Conservative M.P. In the town itself, Stacey's survey revealed that Labour voters out-numbered Conservatives and Liberals together.

The Liberal Party in Banbury does not share the social

advantages of its equivalent in Glossop. Its main non-political connexion is with the Free Churches. The Liberals have no councillors but their leaders 'are much the same sort of people as the Conservative leaders' (Stacey, p. 45). Fifteen out of the 24 members of its committee are employers or self-employed, 6 are office workers and only 1 is a manual worker. The Conservative committee of 12 has no manual workers: 8 are self-employed and 4 are office workers. The Labour Party committee of 11 are all employed workers, 4 in offices and 7 manual. Eight out of 12 on the Conservative committee are born Banburians; 2 out of 11 of the Labour Party committee were born in the town.

The characteristics of the 24 borough councillors point the differences still more. Eight in 16 Conservative councillors are born Banburians; 2 in 8 Labour councillors. Fifteen Conservative councillors are non-manual workers. The other is a wage earner. Five Labour councillors are wage-earning manual workers, one is a full-time trade union official and two are shopkeepers receiving their income from profits (Stacey, p. 45).

Eleven of the 16 Conservative councillors are members of Churches (8 Anglicans, 2 Roman Catholics and 1 Baptist). One of the Labour councillors is an active Methodist.

Both among the leadership and in the rank and file it is clear that politics in Banbury reflect occupation, social class, and status divisions. But there is a complication: while all locally-oriented of whatever class tend to Conservatism, it is not true that all cosmopolitans tend to Labour. Among the cosmopolitans, 'class vincit omnia'; wage-earning cosmopolitans vote Labour, salaried and self-employed, with few exceptions, vote Conservative.

There is, as we shall see in more detail shortly, a clear association between Conservatism and Anglicans, and Liberalism and the Free Churches. The recreational social life of Banbury is built round these divisions and hostile political and religious views are rarely confronted in informal situations. When political and religious views may clash, as when two councillors of opposing parties are present at the same ceremony, open conflict is avoided by silence or by joking. Banbury is at an ideological frontier between *localism* and *cosmopolitanism* and between class and class, hence the hidden conflicts are bitter. Stacey feels that in these circumstances 'parliamentary election campaigns appear to perform a most vital function of the "safety-valve" variety. They provide a licence to say in public

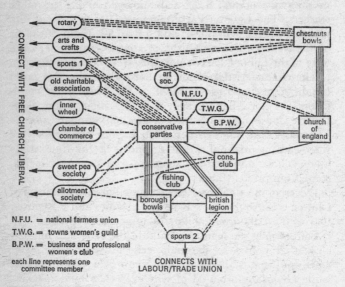

FIG. 3. The Conservative/Anglican/Bowling connexion in Banbury.

about a political opponent or his politics what it is otherwise taboo to say' (p. 55). She adds that councillors get to know one another and their hostile sentiments towards one another are modified by their constant interaction. One might add further that none of the divisions are absolute. There *is* a Baptist Conservative councillor, and there *are* Labour trades people. The lines of cleavage are clear but there are still bridges. One feels that only a little in the nature of an economic or social explosion is needed to blow the bridges up. This impression is confirmed by the organization of voluntary recreational associations in Banbury.

Stacey counted 110 such associations, of which thirty-nine had direct religious or political content and seventy-one did

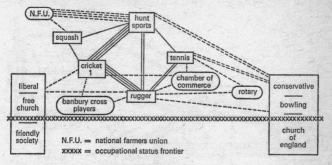

Fig. 4a. Sports I in Banbury.

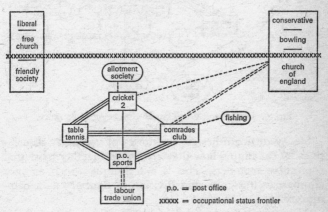

Fig. 4b. Sports II in Banbury.

not. The seventy-one she groups into eight categories which she calls sport, hobbies, cultural, social, social service, charity, mutual aid and occupational associations. They all have in common the fact that their membership, and especially their leadership, are male, middle-aged, and

higher than average occupational class status. Thirty-nine
of the seventy-one are run by men only, and six by women
only. The religious, social and social service associations are
the only ones with a high proportion of women members.

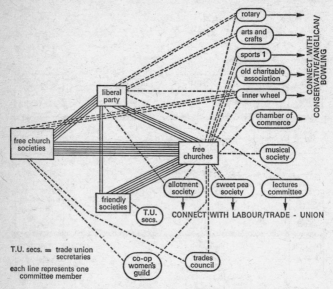

FIG. 5. The Liberal/Free Church connexion in Banbury.

Stacey distinguishes six territories of voluntary associations by examining how they are linked together by shared
committee members. This is a technique which at once
emphasizes the unity and division of Banbury as a community.

These territories are (i) the Conservative/Anglican/Bowl-
ing associated with (ii) Sports I and (iii) Sports II (see
Figs. 3 and 4), (iv) the Liberal/Free Church/Friendly
Society (see Fig. 5), (v) the Labour Party/Trade Union
(see Fig. 6), and (vi) Cultural (see Fig. 7). Significantly she
treats the women's clubs quite separately from these six.

The four main women's organizations are the Inner

Wheel, the Townswomen's Guild, the Business and Professional Women, and the Co-operative Women's Guild. None of them shares a committee member with any asso-

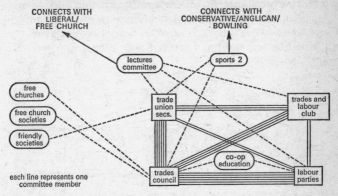

Fig. 6. The Labour Party/Trade Union connexion in Banbury.

ciation in the Labour–Trade Union connexion. Only the Co-op Women's Guild comes below what is called the occupational status frontier (see Fig. 8). Only one man sits

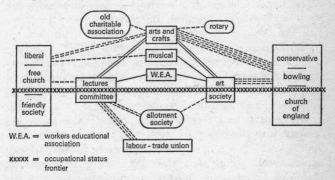

Fig. 7. The Cultural connexion in Banbury.

on committees which lie on both sides of this frontier. He is on the Chamber of Commerce and the Sweet Pea Society. All three of the higher status associations have links with the

Conservative connexion, and the Inner Wheel and Co-op Guild have links with the Liberals (see Fig. 8).

Perhaps the most interesting sector is the linked three territories of Conservative/Anglican/Bowls, and Sports I and II since this is the core of *local* Banbury. Its voluntary association component is divided into two parts by the status frontier, the links across the frontier being political and religious.

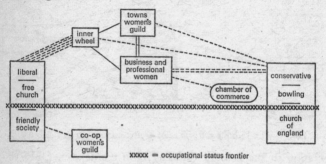

xxxxx = occupational status frontier

Fig. 8. Women's Clubs in Banbury.

The upper Conservative territory is associated with the Chestnut Bowling Club and the parish church; the lower with the Borough Bowls, the Conservative Club and the British Legion. Members of the Chestnut Bowls are 90 per cent Conservatives, which includes three Conservative ex-mayors and two Conservative Borough councillors. It is closely associated with Rotary (a link with the Liberal connexion) and with the Freemasons.

The gentry and farmers from outside the town are brought into this charmed circle by their association with Sports I which is made up of the rugger, squash, cricket, tennis, and hunting group. Here again there are many links with the Freemasons. This group is made up of large farmers and landowners outside the town and the more prosperous professionals within it. They are *cosmopolitan* but Conservative and, with the exception of one Free Church-man, describe themselves as Church of England.

The lower Conservatives have links with the hobbies associations and with Sports II. They include a few wage-earners and no self-employed professional men or bank managers. The dominant occupations are assistant managers of shops, some clerical workers, and owner-managers of small shops and businesses. Sports II includes another cricket club, but squash is replaced by table-tennis. Odd-

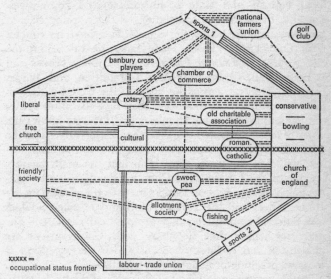

FIG. 9. Non-political connexions in Banbury.

fellows, Foresters, and Buffaloes replace the Freemasons of Sports I. Committee members in Sports II are of lower social status than those in Sports I. 'Thus we find that cricket club A in the Sports I group has a committee of occupational-status classes 1, 2, and 3, while cricket club B in Sports II has classes 3, 4, and 5. The same is true of the Chestnut and the Borough Bowls' (Stacey, p. 88).

The Labour/Trade Union connexion is, at least as far as the leadership is concerned, socially isolated. Only one Labour/Trade Union leader is involved in Sports II, and he is a born Banburian. This does not mean, of course, that no Labour voters follow sport. Similarly, only one man links Labour leaders to the cultural territory and he rarely attends the university extension lectures committee to which he belongs. Labour leaders do not in general meet Liberals at all, except on government advisory committees. They meet Conservatives only in the formal environment of local council and state organizations and committees. Socially, the voluntary associations of the working class in Banbury, and especially the *cosmopolitans*, have no contact with those of other classes. Their leaders operate within the closed circle of Labour Party, Trade Union, Trades and Labour Club, Co-op Education Committee, and Trades Council. They sit across the table to the Conservatives in local government, as those they lead face the other classes only as employers and as shopkeepers. If it were not for the votes of locally-oriented workers, the Conservatives like the Liberals would be excluded from the formal political leadership of the town. This is in fact the main characteristic of the Liberal/Free Church/Friendly Society connexion. Whereas Liberal leaders meet Conservatives on the Inner Wheel and the Rotary Club and in some hobbies and cultural committees, they are politically isolated. The activities which they do share with Conservatives are charitable and social service and, with the exception of Rotary, preclude prolonged social contact.

But however socially divided and politically isolated, Liberals share with Conservatives a hostility to Labour. 'When the middle class do come across a member who is a Labour supporter, they are surprised and shocked. They avoid social relations with the recalcitrant' (Stacey, p. 53). Paradoxically, the non-political Rotary Club provides the recreational symbolism of the town's 'middle-class' unity.

'In sum, two main factors decide what associations a man joins, his political-religious adherence and his social status. Of these social status is dominant, since two men of common adherence will join different associations if their occupational status falls on different sides of the frontier; on

the other hand, given a common occupational status two
men may well join the same association despite differences
of religion and politics, provided there are adequate taboos
on religious and political discussion. In practice in Banbury
this means that while Liberals and Conservatives of similar
status will join common associations, Labour is isolated
because there is neither parity of status nor of outlook'
(Stacey, pp. 89–90).

In this chapter the complicated social relations of class
and status have been explored against a background of the
local new-microcosm of a small town. As far as the inhabitants of Banbury are concerned, they feel themselves to be
part of a society divided by class, and they do not distinguish,
as we have tried to do, between this and status. (See above,
p. 70 *et seq.* and below, Chapter 10.)

To all Banburians, stratification is a fact of life, they only
differ in their views of whether or not it is acceptable and
inevitable.

CHAPTER 7

Communities in Conurbations: Bethnal Green

THE village community is associated in people's minds with rural organization. A community-like social group sometimes survives or grows, however, in the midst of a conurbation. Bethnal Green is such a place. It is not surprising therefore that it should have attracted many students to its study.* It has a rarity value. At least we think it does. We have not enough studies of other urban neighbourhoods to say how typical it is. Nor can we say precisely why it has maintained or rather created this sort of character – but there are some indications to which we can point as we describe it.

The importance of the Bethnal Green studies we have, and especially of the 'Bethnal Green Trilogy' of the Institute of Community Studies (Townsend, 1957; Young and Willmott, 1957; Willmott and Young, 1960), is the way that they show the 'extended' family acting to overcome the potential disorganization which I suggest may go with increase in scale. This is a point to which I return below.

Bethnal Green is a metropolitan borough in the East End of London totally embedded in the conurbation. It has the important characteristic, like Glynceiriog, of being densely populated and not having any main highway passing through it.

[In 1946] a three-halfpenny bus ride from Liverpool Street Station brings you into the very centre of Bethnal Green, the crossing of Bethnal Green Road and Cambridge Heath Road. But you immediately get the impression, unusual in London, of having come in to a backwater. There are few reasons for going through Bethnal Green in order to get to some place of general importance.

* Compare Firth, 1956; Jephcott, 1962; and see on Bethnal Green Glass and Frenkel, 1946; Marris, 1958; Robb, 1954; Townsend, 1957; Willmott and Young, 1960; Young and Willmott, 1957.

The Borough is always by-passed, whether travelling from the City to the east, the north-east or the north.

Further, the Borough is so compact: it is almost a rectangle, two miles east to west by one mile north to south. To walk out of Shoreditch into Poplar along the Bethnal Green Road and Roman Road takes thirty-five minutes, and from Hackney to Stepney along the Cambridge Heath Road only twenty minutes (Glass and Frenkel, p. 39).

Its population in 1955 was about 54,000. This was greater than the 1946 estimate of 48,000, but then the ravages of bombing, evacuation and men still away in the forces distorted the picture. In 1901 it housed 129,686 people. Between the wars the population dropped steadily from the 1911 census of 128,183 to 117,234 in 1921, and 108,194 in 1931. At the time of the National Registration in 1939 there were 68,476 residents (Glass and Frenkel, p. 43).

It is mainly, but not entirely, a one-class borough in economic terms.

SOCIAL CLASS OF OCCUPIED MEN

	Bethnal Green general sample 1955 %	Great Britain census 1951 %
Higher professional	1	3
Lower professional	5	15
Clerical	12	8
Skilled manual	49	45
Semi-skilled manual	11	16
Unskilled manual	22	13
Total	100	100

Here, as elsewhere in this book, we use the Registrar-General's classification of social classes. Occupations are assigned to one or other class in *Classifications of Occupations*, 1950. 'Higher professional' coincides with the Registrar-General's Class I; 'Lower professional' with his Class II; 'Clerical' and 'Skilled manual' with Class III; 'Semi-skilled manual' with Class IV; and 'Unskilled manual' with Class V. The source for the data for Great Britain is the *1 per cent Sample Tables, Census*, 1951 (from Young and Willmott, p. 93).

In the terms of Young and Willmott:

> The overwhelming majority of Bethnal Green men are manual workers, with a particularly high proportion of unskilled people. It is worth noting, too, that the professional classes are not like those elsewhere. The local government officers, teachers, doctors, welfare workers and managers of the borough do not, on the whole, live within its borders. They travel into their work every morning from outside. More than half of the 'white-collar' people in our general sample actually living in Bethnal Green were shop-keepers and publicans, in many ways more akin to the working class people they serve than to the professional men and administrators with whom they are classified. The tone of the district is set by the working class (Young and Willmott, pp. 93–4).*

Robb in fact classified the traders as working-class on the grounds that their level of education (leaving school at fourteen) and standard of living were not very different. Both books would have had added clarity on this point if they had distinguished between class and status-group. What both authors are saying is that within Bethnal Green, despite a class division between traders and workers, there is little status division. Conversely, salaried administrators have consumption standards, particularly in housing, which set them apart as a status group from ordinary Bethnal Greeners. They are also likely to be spiralists excluded from local culture and kinship. One wonders whether the traders vote with the wage-earners or if they make up the few opposition votes to the overwhelming parliamentary and Borough Council Labour majority.

Bethnal Green is not entirely homogeneous, however. There are distinct ecological areas with differing styles of housing and prestige.† In fact it is this differentiation coupled with its 'isolation' which, in my view, helps to keep Bethnal Green a community. Bethnal Greeners have a segmentary set of loyalties to their street, their locality, their district of Bethnal Green, Bethnal Green itself, the East

---

* Page references are to the Penguin edition.

† The discussion of the districts of Bethnal Green is mainly derived from Glass and Frenkel.

End, and to London. Their active kin relationships cut across all these and reinforce them.

It is possible to distinguish six districts within the borough, five of which have housing conditions which are broadly similar.

Save in the area immediately west of Victoria Park, you meet at every step the same monotonous rows of two or three-storey grey-yellow brick cottages. Here and there are some fresher colours, red and grey nineteenth- and twentieth-century tenements, four to six storeys high (Glass and Frenkel, p. 40).

Young and Willmott describe one, built in the 1870s:

... on the first floor two bedrooms, and on the ground floor a living-room, a kitchen and a small scullery opening on to a yard which has a lavatory at the end of it and a patch of earth down one side. Many of the yards are packed with clothes hanging on the line, pram-sheds, boxes of geraniums and pansies, hutches for rabbits and guinea-pigs, lofts for pigeons and pens for fowls. The only difference between the houses is the colour of the curtains and doorsteps which the wives redden or whiten when they wash down the pavement in front of their doors in the mornings (pp. 37–8).

To Townsend, however, the monotony was broken by the parks and squares and 'by the width of some of the streets of terraced cottages, by their neatness and dignity and by the number of small backyards and gardens'.

Before the war 32 per cent of all Bethnal Green dwellings were in blocks of flats – 'the buildings' – the first of which was erected in 1862, supposedly under the direct influence of Dickens. Townsend describes them as 'huge forbidding buildings set in narrow paved yards, rather like outcrops of granite, overlooking unpretentious escarpments'. They are far from modern or convenient, with water taps and lavatories on the landings and half a flight of stone steps up or down.

Of all households in Bethnal Green 89 per cent had no bathroom in 1946, and 78 per cent no hot water systems. There is still much overcrowding despite the fact that the population halved between 1931 and 1951 while the number of rooms remained the same. In 1931 there were three households for every two dwellings; in 1951 five households for every four. In 1931, one in four people lived two or more persons per room; in 1951 only three in a hundred (Young and Willmott, pp. 23–4). The gloom of 1946 had, according to Townsend, been a little relieved by 1956: 'Since the war the landscape has been made even more varied by large scale building of new council flats of varying design and colour.'

All the Borough which lies east of the Regent Canal is referred to as 'Bow', the name of the Borough which with Poplar it adjoins. 'It is a highly-respectable neighbourhood: the small houses are remarkably well kept, with gleaming windows, shining door knobs and whitened doorsteps' (Glass and Frenkel, p. 40).

In this part of the Borough most dwellings house one family only, with the chief wage-earner in stable, but often poorly paid, occupations. The council employees, whose status has declined so much since the war, are likely to live here (Young and Willmott, pp. 96–7).

Separated from 'Bow' by the Canal and across 'Twig Folly Bridge' is what Glass and Frenkel call the black spot of the Borough. The houses here, between a hundred and two hundred years old, are dilapidated and poverty-stricken. This was the area where unemployment and casual labour were the rule and where fascism operated in pre-war Bethnal Green. Adjacent to the Roman Road near Victoria Park is the third area: 'the only one with middle class pretensions'.

'The fourth area is delimited merely by the fact that it is quite clearly not a part of any of the other neighbourhoods in the Borough. This, the Bethnal Green Road area, is large and amorphous; stretching from behind Victoria Park Square, over the Cambridge Heath Road, as far to the west as Gibraltar Walk and Fuller Street; bounded on the north by the Hackney Road; on the south by the main L.N.E.R. line.

'Within it there is considerable diversity street by street.

Here are the weavers' cottages. Here are many of the mixed houses and workshops of the cabinet makers, bootmakers and tailors who succeeded the weavers. Before the war there were also in this area a few distinctly Jewish streets, Blythe Street and Teesdale Street, which since then have become more mixed in character' (Glass and Frenkel, p. 40).

The fifth area in contrast to the last is very 'markedly differentiated', for it is the foreign quarter around Brick Lane and the L.C.C. Boundary Street Estate. Living quarters, shops, and small workshops are inextricably mixed, a policy adopted both by local people and the L.C.C. as early as 1890 (cf. Jacobs, 1962).

This quarter, foreign though it is, is still essentially regarded as part of the Borough. The sixth area, however, which was peopled by the L.C.C. with rehoused 'strangers' who make up 40 per cent of the tenants, looks more outwards, towards Hackney, than inwards to Bethnal Green.

Bethnal Greeners regard these areas as sufficiently different to refuse to move from one of them into another. 'Many stories are told of families who would rather camp in the kitchen of their uninhabitable blitzed houses or sleep in public shelters than accept accommodation in another area of the Borough' (Glass and Frenkel, p. 43).

But within the areas mobility was (before the blitz) considerable and made possible by a diversity of house and flat sizes and types. Young and Willmott show that this is mediated through kinship, street loyalty, and a network of acquaintances and connexions built up through long residence. For example, the family who lived in the house described on page 177 above were a husband and wife and two children. The family had married in the last year of the war and at first lived with the wife's parents in a house the latter had been given after being bombed out. For four years after the war and demobilization the family lived in two small rooms at the top of the house, sharing sink and lavatory. Then the wife's widowed grandfather went into a Home, moving out of a house he occupied in the next street. This arose because 'he had been looked after by an aunt who lived near by, but when the council pulled her house down, after declaring it a slum, and moved her to "one of those estates outside London", she could not care for him any more' (Young and Willmott, p. 39). The wife's mother then spoke to grandfather's rent collector and secured the tenancy for her daughter who lives there still.

The rent collector is one of the key figures in the distribution of non-council housing. He operates through the system of relatives 'speaking for' their own, lubricated occasionally by a 'bit of dropsy'. In the case of houses this operates informally to favour kin; in the case of 'the buildings' it is often official policy. In the case of the council it is 'nepotism' and not allowed (Young and Willmott, pp. 37–43).

Townsend, however, tells the story of the 'extraordinary lengths' that mothers and their daughters went to in order to live near each other. They repeatedly visited the local housing offices and arranged complicated exchanges with third parties.

In one of his interview reports he records:

They explained to me that originally they had been offered a place in Hackney but they made very strenuous efforts to get near their youngest daughter, and finally found that they could obtain a flat from two single women who wanted to move out of Bethnal Green. Because they were entitled to a place in Hackney, they have arranged for these two women to go into that place. Mrs Tilbury said she had to go up to the housing office several times, 'to tell them' (p.34).

The other key person is (as in much else in Bethnal Green) mother.

A neighbour dies, a family moves upon change of job, Mum bumps into a friend in the pub, the collector remembers you as a child, your home is pronounced a slum, a son has tuberculosis – chance often seems to be the distributor of houses. But, despite the galaxy of accident, there is, as we have seen, a tendency for residence to be matrilocal (Young and Willmott, p. 42).

Intense loyalty to particular streets is part of Bethnal Green life. This is one of the areas of the famous East End street parties at times of national rejoicing – Coronation, jubilee, and victory. In the twenties there were also frequent street fights especially between 'Jewish' and 'Gentile' streets. The children play games in teams organized by streets or blocks of 'buildings'. During the war the 'streets' reproduced themselves in informally demarcated areas of deep underground shelters. These street loyalties even have their external material symbolism. 'In one street is a row of six houses with an aspidistra in each front window, rarely found elsewhere; in another a line of four alsatian dogs and, in a third, a succession of curtains of a particular hue, dark blue, rose pink, yellow ochre' (Townsend, 1957, pp. 12–13).

Kinship links people across these street divisions and also encompasses them.

Young and Willmott counted thirty-eight households which had relatives in other households in a street of fifty-nine. Two blocks with fifty-two and 176 households respectively had twenty-eight and sixty-four with relatives in other households.

Part of Bethnal Green's cohesion arises out of the shared poverty and lack of social and geographical mobility of its inhabitants. This is explicable both in terms of history and of its present economy.

Bethnal Green was first referred to as an area in Tudor times when, as part of Stepney, it was 'a pleasant hamlet where wealthy city merchants, bishops, judges and Lord Mayors built their country houses. But in the seventeenth century, the urban invasion began' (Glass and Frenkel, p. 38).

So close to the city and yet outside its boundaries, laws against housing the poor could be and were defied there. Slums and tenements grew up to be joined, after the revocation of the Edict of Nantes in 1685, by the cottages and tiny workshops of Huguenot refugee silk weavers. A few French names still survive, as do the allegedly Huguenot habits of growing flowers and breeding cage birds.

The Society for Protestant Refugees from High and Low Normandy still flourishes and serves many local people who could not claim French blood. But in the Huguenot families – and especially those with the French names which still stand out on the electoral rolls – the connexion is a source of special pride.

They rarely have documentary evidence of their ancestry. One local informant not in the sample was exceptional: he brought out an old paper written in somewhat strange French in the year of the Revolution, which as far as could be made out was a petition from a man who was his ancestor beseeching the Governors of the French Hospital in Hackney to employ, and at the same time treat, his granddaughter. Others did not know the details of their genealogies, nor were even sure of their relationship to other local people of the same name. Mr Michaud thought that some other people were the offspring of his paternal great-uncle, but they were 'not quite up to Mum's and Dad's standard'. Mr Berthot told us that he had once by accident met a girl who was probably a relative. 'Once a girl came up to me at work and said "You look just like my Dad, what's your name?" It turned out that her name too was Berthot.' But though the details were hazy, they did claim to come of Huguenot stock – as one man put it, 'My people came over from Lyons with the weavers.' For them, and to a lesser extent for other local residents, the fact that their 'people' as well as themselves were born in Bethnal Green helps to keep alive a very personal sense of history, and this sense of history reinforces the feeling of attachment (just as it does in a regiment, a university, a trade union or a political party) to the community and to its inhabitants (Young and Willmott, p. 114).

The Huguenots have been followed by successive waves of immigrants from European persecutions.

Bethnal Green became a separate parish in 1743 and a Metropolitan Borough in 1899. Meanwhile slums were cleared and schools and tenements were built.

But the most marked changes took place in the social activities and relationships of the Bethnal Green people. In the middle of the nineteenth century, observers were still struck by the singular absence of public buildings. Churches, chapels, taverns and beer-houses were the only meeting places. Some fifty years later, Bethnal Green was noted for the very opposite; there was then, and there is now, an abundance of institutions; settlements, clubs, missions, besides the old Churches, the Town Hall, health and education services and an unusual number of pubs. There are various crowded shopping-centres and the traditional street markets. In terms of its institutional equipment Bethnal Green is far richer than the more well-to-do parts of London and the newer suburbs and housing estates.

The very poverty of its people was largely responsible for this wealth of institutions. Charitable and benevolent organizations, missions and individuals came into the area to look after, or to convert, the poor (Glass and Frenkel, p. 39).

We have no data on the part played by voluntary associations in present-day Bethnal Green.

Whatever its degree of social self-containment, Bethnal Green is not economically isolated. 'The Borough has by itself a more diversified economy than some countries. But the Borough has no frontiers: it belongs to the economy which stretches down both banks of the Thames' (Young and Willmott, p. 89).

Its first industry was Huguenot silk-weaving. The last handloom weaver disappeared in 1939 and the last mill in 1955. A trade ancillary to this at first but then of increasing importance was furniture making, still very much in evidence. In 1946, 42 per cent of all industrial and wholesale establishments were concerned with it. Boot- and shoe-making and tailoring followed on. There are breweries and railway depots. The type of industry peculiar to Bethnal Green is small-scale. These types of industry 'struggle on in sawmills, caster-making, locks, hinges, dowels, glass, organ-building'.

'One of the most characteristic sights of the streets is a pile of legs, shelves and chairs being trundled on a hand-cart from one sub-contractor to another' (Young and Willmott, p. 91).

Glass and Frenkel suggest that this accentuates the self-contained village characteristics. Buildings used for industrial, commercial, and residential purposes are intermingled. This means that 'Bethnal Green husbands may find employment in any one of these local industries, their wives can do all their shopping right on their doorstep'.

Local industry, however, is continuously declining. In 1921 already 58 per cent of the working population were employed outside the Borough. By 1951 this had increased to 68 per cent, although two-thirds of them worked in adjoining boroughs or in the City of London (Young and Willmott, p. 91). There is plenty of work for women near at hand and nineteen of the forty-five wives in Young and Willmott's marriage sample were in paid employment in spite of having young children. There is still available work which can be done at home on the modern version of the putting-out system.

This diversity of jobs may in some sense diminish the unity of experience between father and son, although it must be remembered that nearly all jobs are manual work of some kind. On the other hand diversity serves to aid the stability and fails to promote the mobility of the family.

When dependent on one or a few industries, the family is as vulnerable as the district. Their economic foundation is treacherous. When the coal, steel and other heavy industries of areas like South Wales were hit by the pre-war depression, men had to desert their native hearth in search of work, and when they left home they had to leave many of their relatives behind. East London is less vulnerable because it has many industries to lean on, and while it cannot avoid being harmed by a general contraction in trade, particularly in overseas trade, at least there is a good chance that even then some of its industries will be able to save themselves from the general decline. When people lose their jobs in one employment, they can usually get jobs elsewhere within daily travelling distance and, if that happens, they do not have to leave their homes (Young and Willmott, pp. 91–2).

This does not mean that the depression of the thirties had no effect in Bethnal Green. Many were unemployed, and local authority jobs were sought after and, if achieved, brought status and security. Such jobs were handed on from father to son. The jobs of attendants in women's lavatories, baths, and wash-houses were reserved for the

widows of council employees. Among dockers and market
porters and a small number of other jobs, sons still follow
their fathers. For the most part, however, it is now employers who seek workers, rather than kin begging jobs for
their sons, daughters, brothers, and sisters.

There is still advantage in economic variety even in good
times.

In the one-industry town or village the son must follow his
father's occupation because there is no other: unless he is to leave
home, the son of a miner or farm-worker must become a miner or
a farm-worker too, which is one reason that those with no love
for coal or land do go off to the city, even when mining or agriculture are themselves prosperous and short of labour. By contrast,
East London offers such a bountiful choice that sons and daughters
can usually take the job of their liking without leaving home. The
city which does so much to create change, by holding up a thousand
different models of behaviour, compensates in this way for the
vicissitudes which it fosters. Some of those evacuated in the war
remarked on its merit. Mrs Glass was delighted with the friendliness of the small Lancashire town where she stayed with her husband, yet wanted to come back all the same.

'It wouldn't do to stay there. In London if he has words with the
boss or doesn't like anything, he can walk out and get into another
firm. In Lancashire there was only one firm in his trade' (Young
and Willmott, p. 92).

This stability which accommodates to economic change
is the background against which can be seen the operating
of kinship and community in Bethnal Green. In Robb's
words:

One consequence of this immobility is that everyone is surrounded by people very like himself, most of whom he has always
known. Bethnal Green has many points of similarity with a village,
or rather with a whole series of overlapping and interlocking
villages. The opportunities for close, long-term relationships are
greater than is usually the case in a large metropolitan residential
area.   The likelihood of an inhabitant having neighbours who are
strangers, or whose way of life is very different from his own has
until recently been very slight. This immobility also makes it

essential for him to be on good terms with his neighbours, as they are likely to be there, for better or worse, for most of his life (Robb, 1954, p. 57).

The comparative stability of Bethnal Green means that the individual lives in an environment of people whom he knows and to whom he is connected in many ways.

> . . . People have a number of links or ways of orienting them-selves to the same person: he was at school, he is a relative by marriage, he lives in a well-known neighbourhood (Young and Willmott, p. 116).

It means above all that he, or especially she, lives sur-rounded by cognatic kin (see p. 49). There is of course wide variation in the numbers available and the nature of social interaction with them. In Peter Townsend's survey of old people he met an unmarried woman who was an only child of an only child. He also met a woman who had had seventeen children, whose mother had had eighteen, and husband's mother twenty-two (Townsend, 1957, p. 28).

Nevertheless, despite individual variations, Willmott and Young found that their 'marriage sample' of 45 couples had between them 1,691 relatives (siblings and their spouses, uncles and aunts, nephews and nieces, and grand-parents, but not parents or cousins) of whom 902 or 53 per cent lived in Bethnal Green or a neighbouring borough. On average, each couple had thirteen relatives within the Borough and forty-one of the forty-five couples had some (Young and Willmott, p. 87).

They had expected to find what Townsend calls 'the immediate family' important. They were surprised to find that the term family as used by Bethnal Greeners meant much more in Bethnal Green. Thus the child of one of the researchers, asked at school to draw his family, drew his mother and father and brother, and commented: '. . . Isn't it funny, the others were putting in their nannas and aunties and uncles and all sorts of people like that' (Young and Willmott, p. 14).

Young, Willmott, and Townsend found it useful to distinguish between the *immediate family*, the *extended family*, and an environment of kin.

Townsend defined the immediate family as consisting 'of one or both parents and their unmarried children living in one household. Any two of its members stand in one of three relationships to each other: wife/husband, parent/unmarried child, unmarried sibling/unmarried sibling' (Townsend, 1957, p. 108).

Departing from the strict anthropological meaning of the term, Townsend goes on to define as an important institution the *extended family* which consists of '. . . more than an immediate family who live in one, two or more households, usually in a single locality, and who see each other every day, or nearly every day. At least two of its members stand in a relationship other than the three possible relationships of the immediate family described above' (Townsend, 1957).

Townsend explores the significance of this second group from the point of view of the aged, Young and Willmott from the point of view of the young married couple. Both find it important especially in the case of the women. The strongest link between kin in Bethnal Green is between mothers and their married daughters. Looking at this tie in terms of the whole cycle of life makes its *reciprocal* nature apparent and emphasizes the *continuity* in the extended family. Townsend makes the point most sharply:

Childhood ties with grandparents, parents and brothers and sisters are only gradually replaced and supplemented by others with husbands, wives, children and grandchildren (Townsend, 1957, p. 122).

and again:

The grandmother may be of as much value to her daughter in looking after the grandchildren as the daughter is of value in looking after her mother in illness and old age (Townsend, 1957).

Surprisingly perhaps, at first sight, marriage may bind a daughter more closely to her mother than she had been bound while single. While she was single, the working girl lived to some extent in a man's world. She 'behaved in many ways like a man, clocking on at a factory like her brother and earning her own money to spend as she chose. But when she marries and even more when she leaves work to have children, she returns to the woman's world and to her mother. Marriage divides the sexes into their distinctive roles and so strengthens the relationship between the daughter and the mother who has been through it all before . . . They share so much and give such help to each other because in their women's world they have the same function of caring for home and bringing up children' (Young and Willmott, p. 61).

There is thus a special unity between a grandmother, her daughter and her daughter's child which may limit the range of the extended family by separating off this core from other kin including in-laws, who may be regarded as 'outlaws'. Mother and daughter are more likely to co-operate than mother-in-law and daughter-in-law. One of the reasons that young couples are more likely to share houses with the wife's mother than the husband's is that mother-in-law and daughter-in-law 'are strangers, and, what is worse [in the early days of marriage], rivals for a stove and a sink – and may be for a man' (Young and Willmott, p. 32). But even between mother-in-law and son-in-law there may be tension, and tactful *avoidance* may be practised or even over-jocular behaviour. Thus Townsend knew of married sons who visited their parents on the way home from work unaccompanied by their wives. Daughters, too, see their mothers and sisters when their husbands are at work, and sister may hastily leave if her brother-in-law arrives home while she is still chatting. Where conflict ripens into open dispute it may well be between a husband and his wife's kin since he is likely to meet his affines more often than his wife is to meet hers.

This avoidance of each other by groups of affines and the

tendency that goes with it for pre-marriage associations and cooperation to continue for both husband and wife leads to a measure of *segregation* between man and wife in their financial, domestic, and family roles. This is consistent with Bott's hypothesis, to be discussed in Part Two below, that 'the degree of segregation in the role-relationship of husband and wife varies directly with the connectedness of the family's social network'.

Townsend stresses this role segregation much more than Willmott and Young, who write:

The man's earnings may still be his affair, but when it comes to the spending of the money, his part of the wages as well as hers, husband and wife share the responsibility. 'To be truthful,' said Mrs Sanderson, 'I don't know how much he earns, I only know what he gives me.' But she later went on to describe the discussion she and her husband had recently had about whether to buy a television set, which he would pay for, and to mention that 'my husband does a lot of cooking; he's a good cook'. In the home there are still 'men's jobs' like cleaning windows, mending fuses and decorating, and 'women's jobs' like cleaning, cooking, baby care, washing dishes and clothes and ironing. There are still plenty of men who will not do 'women's work' and women who think 'it's not a man's place to do it'. But for most people it seems, the division is no longer rigid. Of the 45 husbands, 32 gave some regular help to their wives with the housework; 29 had, to take an index trivial enough in itself but perhaps significant, done the washing up one or more times during the previous week (Young and Willmott, p. 27).

Young and Willmott's marriage sample was made up in fact of people much younger than those that Townsend interviewed, so the difference in emphasis may merely result from accurate observation of either changes implicit in the age-cycle or from a real change in social mores. In any case, there is a danger of taking what is in one sense an analogy with pre-literate society too far and seeing the use made of kinship ties in Bethnal Green as a formal kinship system – a charter which must be obeyed. Kin behaviour in the *extended family* is much more fluid and adaptive than a formal description would suggest. Willmott and Young admit that they inquired much less closely into other than kinship ties. Townsend states the adaptive nature of the extended family very clearly:

The family is continually regenerating itself through the cycle of birth, marriage and death, enrolling new members as old members die. As time passes, an individual marries and so gains a new set of kindred. As he gets older, children and grandchildren begin to take the place of parents and siblings as intimate companions. Wife takes the place of mother, and (in some respects) daughter of wife. Even when there are no children, there are usually nephews or nieces or cousins, if not siblings, who partly compensate. An orphan brought up by his mother's sister calls her 'Mum'. One thing brought out time and again in the course of the previous analysis is the way an individual's relationships adjust to variations in family composition. Childless and single people see more of siblings than people with children. Those with sons but not daughters see more of daughters-in-law than other people. Those with fewest relatives seem often to intensify their contacts with them. Even the unmarrieds or the childless are often drawn into a three-generation family. One of the chief functions of kinship associations is to provide replacements for intimate kin lost by death, or migration. A second function is to compensate for the absence of children, grandchildren or siblings, by providing substitutes or preserving into old age some of the ties of childhood and adolescence. There may be substitutes for siblings and children as well as parents. In one meaningful sense the extended family of three generations is a self-balancing or self-correcting institution to which the principles of *replacement* and *compensation* are fundamental (Townsend, 1957, p. 113).

In this way the mother–daughter tie is seen as less absolute. It is modified and adapted by links between other relatives which may serve similar functions.

The extended family, as Townsend has defined and described it, is a group. Such families and the individuals who make them up also form nodes in networks of interaction composed of kin, friends, and neighbours. This is the aspect of kinship that I now discuss.

It is once again mother who links the extended family and

the individual into the wider network, and when she dies, the texture of the network may become thinner. Thus '35 per cent of the 162 married, widowed and divorced women in the general sample with their mothers alive had seen a sister in the previous day against 16 per cent of the 242 whose mothers were dead' (Young and Willmott, p. 78).

Sometimes the memory of mother serves to maintain a network of siblings and their affines. One family met each year on the anniversary of their dead mother's birthday. Other family groups organize family credit clubs and one member may act as treasurer for Christmas savings. If accidents of geography separate siblings they keep in touch through Christmas and birthday cards. Wider kin maintain ties to a different extent at different stages in the cycle of family development. When grandparents die, ties with uncles and aunts are weakened; when parents die these are weakened still more. When the uncles and aunts themselves die the links with cousins are broken. The way in which ties are attenuated and new kinship ties created is demonstrated in the behaviour surrounding funerals, weddings, and christenings.

The funeral brings in the widest span, since kin are actively sought out and invited to attend even if previously contact had been completely lost. It is here that the line is drawn which inhibits family expansion beyond a person's grandparents and their descendants, since young children are, by convention, excluded. Similarly christenings are attended only by the parents of the couple and their siblings. Nearly two thirds of the godparents of the children of the marriage sample were siblings of either husband and wife, usually one from each side. This particular ceremony re-emphasizes and yet makes more limited the uniting of kindreds which a wedding brings about. While the average attendance of adult relatives at a wedding was twenty-one, that at a christening was only seven (Young and Willmott, p. 85).

Young and Willmott's description of a wedding celebration highlights the social processes involved.

In Bethnal Green, it is evidently the party that follows the ceremony, rather than the ceremony itself, which provides the sociologically significant ceremonial.

Matrimony is a relationship of social groups as well as individuals, the two principal partners representing the two 'sides' from which they come. The two-fold division which gives rise to the need for such far-reaching adjustments can well be observed at any wedding in Bethnal Green; and since observation can here supplement interviews, we start by describing one of them, between Sylvia Hanbury and Harry Buxton, she from the Bow end of Bethnal Green and he a docker from Shadwell.

The reception was held at the bride's home. After the wedding in the late afternoon, the bride and groom moved off from the church in their hired Rolls-Royce and the wedding guests followed in smaller cars. Once arrived in Mr. Hanbury's front room, most of the guests stood about rather stiffly, holding glasses of beer and sniffing the pickled onions. The Buxtons, that is the bridegroom's family, were grouped by the window looking disdainfully at the chipped china dogs on the mantelpiece, the worn linoleum on the floor, and the pictures of country scenes which did not quite conceal the damp patches on the wall-paper. Mrs Alice Buxton, the mother, said, 'I don't know whether I'm the bride or not. I'm shaking like a leaf.' Mr Hanbury, with a slightly forced joviality, called out the first toast, and they all turned with raised glasses of beer to the smiling bride and bridegroom, who were standing behind the small table by the fireplace on which towered the tiered wedding cake. 'They must have got Mowlems to put that up,' said one of the Buxtons when the toast was over.

The thirty-two guests squeezed down at the cramped tables for the wedding breakfast of ham and tongue, salad and pickles, trifle and jelly, washed down with ale and Guinness. The heat became greater, the faces more flushed and the talk louder. After an hour, the meal and toasts over, the telegrams read, the trestle tables were cleared and stacked away. Sylvia and Harry concentrated on trying to bring the two families together. They were not to go off to their honeymoon – a three-day stay at Clacton – until the next morning. In Bethnal Green, where they were born and bred, couples do not fly off to a honeymoon when the first reception is over. 'I'm going to stay to the very end, that's if we ever get away. We haven't actually booked,' said Sylvia, 'I wouldn't miss a minute of it.'

Harry took off his new jacket and carried a tray of drinks around the by now smoky room. Before long he anxiously asked his wife's grandmother, who was sitting close to the fire, 'It's going very well, isn't it, Gran? Everybody's mucking in, I mean, you can't tell which side is which, can you?'

At nine o'clock the men decided to go over to the pub, where they all contributed a £1 a head 'whip' for the purchase of drinks. Soon the wedding party filled the saloon bar of the City of Paris, where it had been joined by some of Sylvia's and Harry's workmates; not being relatives, they were not invited to the reception, but they dropped in to the pub 'to wish you luck'. Sylvia's brother, Jack, on his way to the 'Gents' stopped for a word with some friends in the other bar. 'Didn't Sylvia look lovely?' said a bent old woman, a neighbour from along the street who said she had been present when Sylvia was born; she had stood at her doorway that afternoon, waiting excitedly for the bride and groom to come back from the church in the Rolls. 'How's it going, Jack?' asked a red-faced man who pressed Jack into having a drink with him. 'All right,' Jack said, 'very well really. But they're a funny lot. Greedy too. You should have seen the drink they put away this afternoon.' He gave the bar-counter an authoritative rap. 'It won't last if you ask me. Sylvie'll be back home within a week.'

When the pub closed some of the relatives living in Stepney, Dagenham, or East Ham went home, the others returned to the Hanbury's, and many newcomers arrived. Two men could be heard talking about the bride's mother. 'She's a funny woman,' one of them emphatically declared. 'I told her off this afternoon when she said she was tired. "Of course you're tired," I told her straight, "we're all bleeding tired." She didn't take no notice though. Like water off a duck's back.'

'She *is* a funny woman,' the younger man answered seriously. As the husband of one of the bride's sisters, he was talking about his mother-in-law. 'I've tried, Bert, I've tried ever since we got married, to be friends with her, but we just don't seem to get on.'

'To tell you the truth, Frank,' the other leaned forward conspiratorially, 'I don't think I could ever get on with that woman. Anyway,' he added with an air of finality, 'you married Ethel, didn't you? You didn't marry her bleeding family.' Despite these sentiments, the two of them rejoined the party and soon all of them, including the two mothers, were dancing and laughing around the room together, in the early hours of the morning, one family indistinguishable from the other (Young and Willmott, pp. 62–4).

This account does not tell us who attended the church nor who were the newcomers who arrived after the pubs were closed. What is evident is that the two families were not the only witnesses to their union. Work-mates were a party to the proceedings and at least one neighbour, even if neither category was invited to the house.

Membership of an immediate family turns attention outwards to the extended family: the extended family in turn links its members into a kindred. Members of the kindred live in different streets, have different affines, different school friends, different neighbours. The kindred forms 'a bridge between the individual and the community' (Young and Willmott, p. 104).

Phyllis Willmott, wife of one of the researchers, accompanied a Bethnal Green resident, Mrs Landon, shopping. In half an hour Mrs Landon met fourteen people with whom she was acquainted. To some she spoke and some she acknowledged with a nod. For a week she kept a record 'of all the people she saw in the street and whom she considered herself to "know"'. There were sixty-three such people of whom thirty-eight were related to at least one other person of the sixty-three. Some she saw many times (Young and Willmott, p. 107).

Like people at the rural end of our continuum, the Bethnal Greener is 'surrounded not only by his own relatives and their acquaintances, but also by his own acquaintances and their relatives' (Young and Willmott, p. 105).

In what then do the differences lie? Firstly, the Bethnal Greener lives and takes some of his recreation side by side with kin and local acquaintances; he does not necessarily work with them. Secondly, in economic terms, the immediate and extended family may consume as a unit but they do not necessarily or even usually produce as one. It is for this reason that some anthropologists have objected to the use of the term *extended family* in this sense. Thirdly, it is possible without distortion for Young and Willmott to study one aspect of social life and to say nothing, for example, about politics and voluntary associations. Another aspect of this is the existence of nearly 54,000 people in one residential bloc who appear to be broadly free from prestige, status, and class differences. Perhaps the most striking difference, however, is revealed by the methods imposed on the researchers. Although they wished to use personal observation as much as possible, they were forced to rely mainly on interviews of a sample of the population. Young and Willmott in fact used two samples: a general sample of every thirty-sixth person on the electoral register (987 people) and a marriage sample of forty-five married couples chosen at random from the general sample. This means that as they themselves write they 'can only report what people say they do, which is not necessarily the same as what they actually do'. Despite the importance of the family as a face-to-face group in Bethnal Green, it is still a part of a society which requires mainly door-to-door study.

CHAPTER 8

Urban Housing Estates

IN the last empirical chapter I want to say something about the social life of the three and a half million British house-holders and their families who live on council housing estates. There is a large and growing literature on this which I cannot hope to describe exhaustively. I wish merely to continue into this area some of the lines of pro-gression that have developed in the discussion on 'tradi-tional' societies. Such estates vary in size from Dagenham – Becontree (100,000 inhabitants) and Wythenshawe (90,000 inhabitants), to the small housing estate in Glynceiriog which was an integral part of the village.

These estates differ one from another in many ways. Thus in Watling the minority of slum clearance immi-grants were moved at a time when London County Council policy was to break up the residential patterns of the in-habitants of slum streets and distribute them widely about a new estate.

The Liverpool estate was, in origin, not a council estate at all but built for the Ministry of Aircraft Production to house workers in a specific factory; its inhabitants were drawn from widely scattered parts of the country (Lupton and Mitchell, 1954). In Watling, people of high status with small families use the community centre; in Liverpool, people of low status with, I suspect, large families.

The Sheffield estate (Hodges and Smith, 1954) was a slum clearance estate which was moved in, street by street, preserving the patterns of physical proximity of neighbours to each other.

The estates also vary in the stage in their own develop-ment when they were studied. Durant, for instance, studied Watling ten years after it was started.

Despite these differences, there are some common features in all these estates which can be related to the ideas of community discussed in other chapters. In the first half of this chapter, I shall describe the public social life of such estates – voluntary associations and community centres. In the last half I shall describe private social lives on estates – kin, friends, and neighbours.

Town planners and housing authorities in general see the houses and estates they build as more than just aggregations of dwellings. There is a view, sometimes explicit, but often implicit, that estates should be communities and that the way to achieve this is to set up *neighbourhood units* the inhabitants of which should not only live side by side but come to be 'good neighbours and friends' as a result of their constant interaction at home, at the shops, and at work. Such planning and ideology seeks to impose an idealized version of village life on the town dweller in council estates. This chapter does not attempt fully to describe housing estate life, but to examine some of the ways in which estates, despite or because of the authorities which set them up, become like or unlike the communities in the earlier chapters.

In the Irish, English, and Welsh countryside, we found people who lived together and prayed, played, and worked together. In the housing estates to be discussed, people live together or at least side-by-side. To what extent do they work together, play together, or pray together?

Before I consider any estate in detail, I will consider what each has in common with the others. Estate inhabitants are virtually all manual workers with their wives and families. Otherwise the local authority would not have selected them for a house. With some exaggeration the would-be council tenant has been characterized:

'The man who set about it efficiently would get an essential job, marry young, father a child a year, find himself a slum flat, share it with another family, and develop chronic ill-health' (Alderson, 1962, p. 94).

On new estates there is likely to be a demographic peculiarity in that young married couples and children under sixteen years old will be over-represented compared with their incidence in the general population. In 1962, three out of five council tenants had children under sixteen. This pattern, of course, changes with time but does not change into a 'normal pattern' unless council policy is adjusted to make it do so.

Although council rents are subsidized, they are often high compared with the rents of the property from which tenants come. This may result either in preventing the very poor from accepting tenancies or in making life very hard for them if they do so. For added to the increase in rent are the expenses of removal and new furniture and fittings. Thus when the Sheffield estate was built in 1927, 40 per cent of the householders were unemployed and newspapers had to serve for curtains. A study of Stockton on Tees council house tenants in 1927 showed a rise in mortality associated with malnutrition arising from the necessity to spend earnings on goods other than food. While this is unlikely to be happening in the 1950s and 1960s, the extra expenses may have other social effects on the relationships between people and their neighbours and in the formation of voluntary associations (see M'Gonigle and Kirby, 1936, Jefferys, 1964, Mogey, 1956).

New estates are not, so to speak, built *in vacuo*; their siting has two probable features. Firstly, they are likely to be at a distance from the people's original homes. Thus Greenleigh is twenty miles from Bethnal Green; South Oxhey is seventeen miles, and Watling is some way out of London. The Sheffield estate is exceptional in being only a mile from the centre of the city. This suburbanization has social effects in terms of a journey to work which costs money and time. It may complete the segregation of living from working and working from playing. In the case of Greenleigh, as we shall see, it may effect also reversal of sex roles in the kinship organization similar to the one already noted as marking a difference between Llanfihangel and County Clare on the one hand and Glynceiriog on the other (see Chapters 1, 2, and 4).

The second feature in relation to siting is that often there were privately tenanted or owned houses and a long established community near the estate site. In all the studies there is a history of conflict between the new and the old which goes far to determine the social patterns of the new. The old inhabitants did not choose to have a council estate and indeed often fought bitterly against its being built (see Benney, 1947, Collison, 1963, Jefferys, 1964).

If it is true that the old inhabitants suffer from compulsion, so do the new tenants.

By and large, council tenants did not choose where they would live. By slum clearance or through the shortage of housing, they were forced to live wherever there was a council house available for which they were eligible. Circumstances compel them to live in a certain place and with particular neighbours. The kind of house they live in is thrust upon them without consultation; they may be forbidden to keep pets or compelled to have a dustbin, or a garden, or no garden. It is true that the village dweller did not choose his village nor the parishioner of Llanfihangel his parish, but compulsion by birth is different from compulsion by letter from the council when your pattern of living is already set. It is also true, however, that once you have one council house, it is sometimes possible to change it for another and thus exercise an element of choice of neighbours and of site. Nevertheless, most council tenants have to make some social adjustment to neighbour and neighbourhood as the price for house, kitchen, and bath.

Since rents are relatively high and most council house tenants are manual workers on daily or weekly engagements, there is a sense in which, despite their council house, they are fundamentally and patently insecure. This was very evident in the twenties and thirties and emerges clearly from the Watling study. An indication at the present day is the difficulty which manual workers experience if they should try and get Building Society Mortgages to buy their own house. The very reason that a relatively highly paid skilled worker lives on a council estate may be the recognition by financial institutions of his uncertainty of future (Jefferys, 1964).

Perhaps the most telling of the social factors affecting life on the council housing estate is not the uncertainty of the future but the uncertainty at present.

In the last chapter I quoted Robb who said about the Bethnal Greeners that their immobility ensured that they were surrounded by people like themselves. People not only know how their neighbours expect them to behave, they also know the likely effects of their behaviour on others. They know what will happen if they flout the norms governing behaviour in Bethnal Green and they know what will happen if they keep them. The housewife who moves to a new estate does not know how her neighbours will react to friendliness or to coolness. She may be nervous to try and quick to withdraw if the response is unfavourable or even unexpected.

Behaviour in the communities I have described in previous chapters is sanctioned by the fear of gossip – 'what will people say?'. The sanction is reinforced by hearing what people actually do say in actual situations. In the housing estate, gossip chains may be less extensive – the sanction may then be 'what will people think?'. Since these thoughts are often unexpressed – the sanctions may become those of advertisers in mass media – if *Woman's Own* thinks it is all right, Mrs Jones two doors away cannot think it wrong (cf. Mogey, 1956).

This state of uncertain or merely passively sanctioned norms seems to me to make possible the emergence on housing estates of a society alienated from norms – the classically anomic society (see page 277 below). Empirical studies from Watling in 1939 to the Bristol Social Project, still in process, suggest that housing estates are for this reason difficult places for youth to grow up in. Educational and recreational facilities for adolescents are almost non-existent on many estates (Wilson, 1963). The Bristol estate had only street corners, Watling, the warmth and dryness of Burnt Oak Tube station.

Separated from work and from play, from beer and from
books, paved with good intentions, the social life of housing
estates seems as far as it is possible to get from the utopian
dreams of a village fellowship made urbane by town
civilization.

WATLING 1939

Although nearly twenty years older than most of the studies
I have used in this book, Ruth Glass's (then Durant) study
of Watling* still remains perhaps the most relevant and
apposite to my theme.

This is partly because she sets out to answer not some
minor administrative problem, but the key question, 'Has
the new housing estate grown into a community?'. By
community, she means 'a territorial group of people with a
common mode of living striving for common objectives'
(Durant, p. ix). A second feature of the study is its emphasis on 'how people lived and what they did rather than
on what they said'. In the last chapter I quoted Young and
Willmott's self-imposed dependence on what people said
rather than on what they did.

The site of Watling in Hendon, north-west of London, was
virtually undisturbed farmland until 1924. There were a
few middle-class houses built in the early 1900s and in 1920.
In 1924 the Tube reached Edgware. In 1927 the first
families moved into the London County Council estate. By
1936/7, when Glass studied it, there were 4,032 dwellings
on the estate with a total population of just over 19,000, of
whom it was estimated that nearly 10,800 were over
eighteen, and 5,000 between five and fourteen. They came
mainly from St Pancras and Islington. About 30 per cent
came through rehousing schemes but only 15 per cent as a
result of slum clearance (Durant, p. 2).

Rents were higher than in most L.C.C. 'cottage estates',
as they were then known, but this does not mean that

* Ruth Durant, *Watling: a Survey of Social Life on a New Housing Estate*
(P. S. King), London, 1939.

Watling was inhabited by an elite stratum of London wage-earners. They were however at an elite phase in their family cycle. The estate was characterized by three types of family which had distinctive economic characteristics. 44 per cent were small families with one wage-earner enjoying a relatively high wage. These were economically secure and geographically immobile; if not the elite of the London working class, the elite of Watling. Twenty-six per cent were large families with one wage-earner enjoying relatively high earnings. Finally, as an unstable and mobile minority, 21·5 per cent were large families with several wage-earners but relatively low earnings.

Although the small one wage-earner family with a comfortable income gave Watling a well-off look, like other council estates its tenants were nearly all wage-earners. Semi-skilled workers and labourers made up a quarter of all residents. Just over a half of the householders were slightly better off as skilled, transport, and black coated workers, police, and members of the armed forces.

Thus about half of the residents were in an economically precarious position.

'Economic crisis or a rise of prices, unemployment or sickness, death or sometimes even marriage of earning children causes disruption of the household economy and often compels removal from the estate' (Durant, p. 7).

Shopping was more expensive in less familiar markets; rents were at least three times greater than in the tenants' area of origin. Husbands had to pay fares to work and for meals out.

'The new home needs new linoleum, new curtains and even new furniture and all is bought on hire purchase. In the old "mean street", people were not tempted by the example of their neighbours to acquire fresh impedimenta. At Watling, where more households with better incomes have settled, the wireless next door becomes an obligation to bring home a wireless' (pp. 7–8).

This factor of economic uncertainty was only one of the features which led to an uncertainty about staying or going.

In the first ten years of its existence 3,900 families came and went. This is nearly as many as lived there at any one time (4,032 families). Watling seemed, however, to be peopled by two distinct groups: those who came, stayed a short time and then moved, and those who came and stayed. If a tenant stayed more than five years he had come for good. People moved back to London because, on the one hand, they 'had underestimated the demands, financial as well as psychological, which new environment would make, and on the other, because frequently domestic or external events upset people's precariously balanced budget' (p. 17).

There were 1,431 families transferred to other L.C.C. estates. Some families lured on by the prospect of a house of their own, re-emigrated from Watling to Burnt Oak. There was 'a considerable exodus from the municipally owned estate to cheap, privately built houses near by, which try to compensate for the inferiority of their plans, looks, and solidity by a sense of superior social status which they inculcate in their inhabitants' (p. 18).

The final social composition of the estate then arises by selection and re-selection, by council selection, and self-selection. Those who remain are alike; manual workers with a tendency to small but young families supported by one wage-earner per household.

Men were not attracted to settle in Watling by the promises of local jobs – for the most part in 1937 they continued to travel in the Tube to London – 'that vapour bath of hurried and discontented humanity' (Morris, William, 1963, p. 183). The same underground railway line encouraged the growth of local industry which did provide, directly or indirectly, employment for the women and dead-end jobs for the youths. There were plenty of unskilled jobs for those in their teens. Once, however, they reached the age to receive the adult rate, local jobs were unobtainable. While it is true that Watling boys married Watling girls, they had to go to London to find lodgings and unskilled work. Watling houses were too large and the fares and rents too high for the young married. To those fortunate enough to qualify for a skilled trade there was neither local training nor work facilities. Watling was for them merely a dormitory.

So the L.C.C. having chosen moderately sized, moderately prosperous family groups, economic and social conditions preserved this pattern. The young and the old, the rich and the poor, moved away. The people left shared the same problems, the same life styles, the same life chances. A shifting population concentrated the interests of the survivors but denied them the stability to pursue them.

In the early days, Watling was a frontier and its inhabitants pioneers. Like many pioneers, they had to contend with a hostile environment and hostile natives. Both were conducive to the fostering of community spirit and community organizations – 'antagonism from without breeds association within' (Durant, p. 21).

This antagonism made Watling people class conscious in opposition to the hostile middle classes who surrounded them. It also led them to seek an active social life of their own. 'So far as amenities did exist they were barred for the council tenants.' The first stage was the formation of a Residents' Association in January 1928, the second the production of a local paper, the *Watling Resident*, which appeared in May the same year.

The residents came from different parts of London and if a large number of people did come from the same area they were separated. The only integral social group which survived the move was the family. However, the situation was different from that described by Kuper (1953) for Coventry. One might not know the neighbours as individuals but they did come from a common background in north London.

The first associations at the small scale level were between the women. As housewives they had, by changing their place of residence, also changed their place of work. Their work had also become more difficult, shops were farther away, schools non-existent, neighbours strange. They got to know each other in the backyard and through the children's play groups. The men met on the way to the station and in the Tube to town. For many families, getting to know their neighbours ended there. At most they joined those local associations which made it easier to make a family, home, and garden-centred adaptation.

The men (for it was with one exception men who pioneered the wider communal associations) came to the estate already having experience of public organizations. This is an observation which has also been made elsewhere – the conclusions of *Neighbourhood and Community* for example, emphasize the existence of such people on the Liverpool estate as a major difference from the Sheffield estate. Durant illustrates what manner of men they were by listing the characteristics of the seven candidates from the estate who stood for the four seats on Hendon U.D.C. in the election in April 1930. They were in fact all leading lights in the Residents' Association who had campaigned for municipal representation. The three anti-socialists were all ex-service and two were civil servants. The four Labour candidates were all active trade unionists and workers in the Co-operative Society. The jobs of the Labour party candidates are not directly revealed, but the trade union affiliations of two of them indicate craftsmen, and the other two were a railway clerk and a transport worker. The discussion of leadership roles and strangers in earlier chapters should discourage us from making the facile judgement that unskilled workers are incapable of organizing public activities (cf. Birch, 1959).

The Webbs in their *History of Trade Unionism* stress in their definition of a trade union the fact that it is a *continuous association*, not merely an *ad hoc* body. The history of individual unions shows how such continuous associations came into being in response to attacks from outside. Residents' Associations seem to develop in a similar way.

In December 1927 an insulting letter about the Watling people appeared in the *Hendon and Finchley Times*. This led first to a meeting of six men and then in January 1928 to a public meeting of 250 people in a church hall. A still

bigger meeting followed and formed the Watling Residents'
Association with as its objects:

(a) promotion of the interests of the residents on the
Estate, and

(b) for their well-being in such social and other activities
as may be found necessary (Durant, p. 31).

It was the Residents' Association which started the
monthly *Watling Resident* which had spectacular success. At
its peak in March 1929 it sold 2,636 copies. (In 1947 it was
given free to members and was read by others as a local
newspaper. It had in 1947 a circulation of 1,000.) (*Planning*,
1947.)

'It was the practice of the circulation manager during
that period to visit every month the people in the road
which was just occupied. "Where I could not effect a sale I
gave them a back copy," he said in an interview. "If they
did buy the book next month I offered them a whole set of
back issues at a very reduced price." In that way the *Resident*
reached nearly every house on the estate during the summer
and early autumn months of 1928. Systematic visiting of
newcomers to the estate was thus assured, and they were
informed of all previous events of common interest'
(Durant, p. 37).

The Residents' Association thus succeeded in establishing
a link between all the inhabitants. At the same time it
agitated for municipal representation and was treated as
being semi-official by the L.C.C. and other authorities. It
represented the people of the estate to each other and to the
outside world. It kept estate dwellers aware of the outside
world both in Hendon, and, through links with other community associations, with other estates. Finally it attempted
to secure the affiliation of special interest and hobby groups.
A Distress Committee, District Nursing Committee,
Children's League, drama circle, and a fête and gala were
all organized as offshoots of the original Association.

At first all this activity was conducted from meetings held
off the estate since there was nowhere on the estate to meet.

Later the Association used churches, church halls, and schools. Finally, it set out to form a Watling Centre and Hall under the slogan 'all Watling for a Watling Hall'.

This was partly in response to a decline in the support that the Association received. As early as August 1928 the *Resident* said: '. . . The committee alone cannot put life into an Association . . . the first business of the associates of an Association is to associate. This is difficult until there is a house in which to associate for indoor pleasures, and ground on which to associate for outdoor pleasures' (Durant, p. 41).

Subsections began to disaffiliate and membership fell from 400 in May 1928 to 94 in May 1929. Competition replaced cooperation and the committee began to quarrel among themselves. This, of course, did not make Watling less like a village community but more like one. In Watling, however, there was not that unity of purpose and history of shared experience which enables village conflict to provide a focus around which to cohere.

Watling people did not work in Watling. The factors which divided people in Watling came from outside and not from within the estate itself. For this reason they were not compensated for by ties which cut across them. Given the high turnover of tenancies, there were evidently many tenants who had not shared in the battle for amenities and recognition which had originally given the Watling Residents' Association birth and life. There were now three types of local voluntary association: firstly, the Horticultural Society, the District Nursing Association, and the Loan Club. In these, people associated at one level in order to function more effectively as family isolates at another level. This group had 4,820 members in 1936.

Secondly, there were Watling or Burnt Oak branches of national organizations – Old Comrades, Townswomen's Guild, Co-operative Guild, Labour Party, and Conservative Association. These had a total of 800 members in 1936. The churches drew in about a thousand adults each Sunday.

Thirdly, the old Residents' Association, renamed the

Watling Association, which had, during 1936, 809 members.

Durant points out that there were special features in Watling which led to the breakdown of the Community Association:

(a) the depression, which made poverty more worrying than loneliness and sharpened class division between secure and insecure;

(b) the filling of the estate, which made immigration an individual rather than a social event;

(c) the high turnover of population.

She considered that had the Centre been built earlier these factors might have been overcome. Subsequent research in other estates suggests that she was over-optimistic. As it happened, 'the Centre was almost the last building of public importance to be built. Watling's corporate life had shown symptoms of anaemia prior to that event . . .' (Durant, p. 49).

The Centre and Voluntary Associations in 1936

By 1936, when Durant studied it, Watling was no longer an isolated 'island colony' in a middle-class neighbourhood. Other estates had been built round it. There was a cinema, a pub, and a lending library near by, and shops on the estate itself. With the help of outside organizations, one of which paid the salary of a full time organizing secretary, the new Community Centre was finally built and opened in January 1933 by no less a person than the Prince of Wales. Of its 1936 officers only two were associated with the old Association before 1931. It still helped those in distress and difficulty and it now provided premises for a 'poor man's lawyer'. It still took the lead in organizing such public affairs as the Peace Ballot. Most of the other organizations on the estate would have nothing to do with the Watling Association. Churches and political parties had little association with it. It was not even the main centre for meetings since it was small and inconveniently situated in a new part of the estate. The Association had become separated from the older part of the estate; most of its members lived within three hundred yards radius of the Centre in a specific part of the estate.

'Membership is concentrated in certain parts of streets and in rows of houses which are close to each other. As in Watling's early days, streets or parts of streets still seem to function as the units of association. But the genesis of such relationships is no longer quite so plain. People bring their neighbours to the Centre, but perhaps only there do they become really friendly with each other. The Centre certainly cements friendships started in back gardens and Tube compartments' (Durant, p. 98).

The numbers deeply involved with the Centre are small. The total membership during 1936 was only 6 per cent of the adult population, 809 people. Two per cent or 276 people paid their subscription for more than twelve months during 1935 and 1936. Only 73 paid over the full two years.

At the Centre itself, it was possible to distinguish five distinct and conspicuous groups of people – the officers, ordinary adult members, adolescents, children, and the old age pensioners.

The organizing secretary held a full-time paid post, but he was not paid by the members but by outside bodies. The other officers were voluntary and unpaid, but each was in charge of only one aspect of the Centre's work. It appears that the organizing secretary's connexion with external authority and his bird's eye view of the Centre gave him considerable power.

By 1947 there had been three full-time paid secretaries, each one an outsider.

Leading members of its council maintain that an outsider is, by and large, more likely to be satisfactory than an ex-member secretary. Moreover, the Middlesex County Council rule that their grants to the *Association* depend on the quality of the educational work undertaken makes it desirable to have someone with more experience in educational activities than most Watling members possess. The decision to continue to appoint an outsider rests on deeper issues. They argued (when appointing a new secretary in 1946) that they must have someone with new ideas. This suggests that they felt the need for a man who was capable by character, education and experiences of having a vision which, because it was wider than their own, would stimulate them. The women's societies feel a similar need for one outside personality who can see ahead of themselves, 'a good brisk jokey chairwoman'. Possibly any group with a homogeneous composition and no very concrete objectives feels this need for one person who can raise its own standards (*Planning*, 1947).

The officers were easily met since they spent a great deal of time at the Centre. 'Some almost live at the Centre, and so do their wives and their children.' All certainly live with the Centre (Durant, p. 104).

They spent time at the Centre and sat on more than one committee. They were active as members as well as officers.

'Of 138 office-holders, 130 fulfil or attend other functions at the Centre; of 202 members of social and education activities, only 107 do so; of 77 members of sport and hobby groups, only 25 are interested in other aspects of the Centre' (Durant, p. 105).

Durant carried out a special study of twenty-one of the principal officers of the Association and their families. The families included another sixteen officers, of whom nine were wives, two were husbands, and five adolescents. They all either had jobs near at hand, or jobs which gave them free time. Four were housewives with small or grown families. Two were pensioners. Six had jobs which in any case brought them into contact with other people. Eighty-one per cent of all the officers worked locally in contrast to 32 per cent of the total Watling population. Not one of them was of the large family, one wage-earner type. Nearly all of them came from the small family, one wage-earner type, which has the most money and time. This, of course, is also the least geographically mobile group.

Apart from the officers the members were also a highly selected group – they were not drawn from the poor, the ill, or the overworked.

Women predominated, especially those who had neither large families nor full-time jobs.

A special group of attenders, but not necessarily members, were the devotees of whist who spent almost as much time at the Centre as the officers. 75 per cent of them came regularly. Average attendance at Monday drives during 1937 was 120, with seventy at the Wednesday and Thursday sessions. This compared with eleven at the Men's Adult School and thirty-two at the Women's. There were four regular whist drives a week during the winter and three in summer, with additional drives for charity and on special occasions. Durant well describes the social functions they fulfil for those who attend them.

Whist drives promise money and they promise prizes. They provide attractions which are peculiar to them. They plunge the players amongst a crowd of people without forcing them to be stiff and formal or to make conversation. It is much less difficult being 'social' if everybody has something definite to do. There is no helpless standing around and searching for the right approach. Each is assigned a place, is bound to cooperate as well as to compete, and thus immediately to make contacts. Moreover, during the whist drive the player constantly changes partners and he experiences what never happens to him in his everyday life, effortless moving from one group of people to another (Durant, p. 109).

Early each evening, the Centre, like the Tube station, had a crowd of adolescents just hanging around, waiting for something to happen. Apparently nothing to interest them ever did, but they had to go somewhere. There was conflict between these youngsters and the Centre members, who were for the most part not their parents. By and large, although they attended dances and played billiards, they were not welcome inside.

There were several children's groups attached to the Centre. There were eight different activity groups for children, but these and especially one called the 'Moggies' were as selected a group from all Watling children as all the members were from all Watling adults. There were

seventy-two of them and their school records were more
distinguished than their age mates.

In 1937 there were only seventy-seven old age pensioners,
fifty-eight of whom belonged to an Over Sixty-fives club at
the Centre and their meetings had an average attendance
of fifty.

Possible rivals to the Centre, for the allegiance of Watling
people in 1936, were the churches and other social and
political groups.

The churches were organized as parishes or congrega-
tions on a different basis to the estate. Watling lies within
two Anglican parishes. St Alphege's vicarage was, however,
the first house to be occupied and the church itself was
opened in 1927, the church hall in 1930. Fifteen thousand
inhabitants of the estate were its technical parishioners, but
a quarter of these belonged to other denominations. Three
thousand parishioners live off the estate, but only fifty of
these attended the church compared with four hundred
estate dwellers. But St Alphege's, like the other Anglican
church, John Keble, is geographically marginal to the
estate. John Keble is in fact across the bridge which marks
the class boundary between Watling and Mill Hill. People
from both sides of this boundary shared church offices,
mixed at socials and gatherings, but separated at the bridge;
'so much so, that if women from the Estate happen to leave
a church function together with inhabitants from the other
side, they try to avoid confessing in which direction they
have to go' (Durant, p. 53).

Nonconformity in Watling was more popular and tried
to express fellowship rather than churchmanship. Plymouth
Brethren and Wesleyans both had halls in the busiest parts
of the estate and regarded their members as 'workers' and
(every second one) officers respectively. The Wesleyans had
four times the number of their adherents using their hall and
belonging to various societies and clubs. The Brethren
attracted 1,100 to their Sunday Schools. Some children
spread their favours, attending the services of one church
and belonging to social groups of another.

The Roman Catholic congregation on the estate is, naturally, more self-contained. The spiritual and social needs of its members are met from the cradle to the grave, and since most of them belong to large families, which have to struggle for their existence and cannot afford a number of leisure activities, their attachment to their religious organization tends to be exclusive. About ten per cent of the Watling population are Roman Catholic, 2,000 people, and the clergy say that almost every other one is in contact with the Church of the Annunciation, situated in a favourable position, next to the park and the station. A hall, in which weekly whist drives and occasional dances are held, and a Roman Catholic Elementary School are adjacent to the church. There is, in addition, a Roman Catholic Central School on another part of the Estate (Durant, p. 55).

Thus, all the churches stress sociability and gregariousness almost to the point of conflict with the religious aspect of their work. This led from time to time to a restressing by the clergy of the religious differences. Hence the churches united the inhabitants by dividing them. They offered a choice of venues for the same activities like whist and dancing (concerts and communal games for the Wesleyans). They also divided the whole by closely uniting small sub-groups in loyalty to common, differentiated, religious beliefs and practices.

Only the Anglican churches are affiliated to the Community Centre. John Keble church is in the same area, but apart from a few very active families there is little overlap. Wesley Hall in fact provides a rival to the Centre although it did not set out deliberately to do so. 'It stands in the heart of the Estate. It is three times as large as the present headquarters of the Association; it houses a number of local societies; the Estate is the sole area of its activities' (Durant, p. 57). Durant does not give an analysis by family size, occupation, or social status of its members. I suspect in fact that it, too, like the Centre is 'class' selective, but in another direction.

In addition to churches, there were political party branches, loan clubs, and Nursing and Horticultural

Associations, but these were all at the service of their members rather than making demands upon them.

'People's contacts are not much more enlarged by joining them than they are by buying water from the Metropolitan Water Board. Of course the utility of these societies is considerable, but they do not help to cultivate a social circle' (Durant, p. 60).

Durant concludes that if membership of local organizations is taken as a guide, 'it appears that the men and women on the Estate are more concerned with their family problems than with either communal recreation or traditional and modern creeds'.

Watling was settled in the 1920s and studied in the 1930s. The background to the study was depression not 'affluence', and yet the report has a familiar ring. If television is substituted for wireless, and bingo for whist it seems to have a consistent pattern with more recently established and studied estates. There is a familiar pattern of initial loneliness followed by unity against the outside world, giving rise to an agitational Residents' Association. This achieves its task and most of the inhabitants settle down to a home-centred but small group oriented, social life.

A minority continues the public social life of the Community Centre. This minority is drawn from one status-group, in Watling – the respectables (see Dennis, 1961).

The next estate I shall describe, built in wartime Liverpool, shows a similar pattern, but here it is the 'rough' status group that carry on with public social life and the small family respectables who wholly, instead of in part, keep themselves to themselves.

LIVERPOOL 1951

The Liverpool estate studied by Lupton and Mitchell in 1951 is not strictly a council housing estate. It was built for the Ministry of Aircraft Production in the wartime conditions of 1942 to provide housing for workers in a local armaments factory. The land on which it lies was originally scheduled as part of the Green Belt and is exposed, flat land, some eight miles out of Liverpool. The houses are of the type usually known as prefabs and were not built to last. There are 496 of these semi-detached bungalows with unplastered walls, concrete floors, and two-inch, breeze-block party walls which are far from soundproof. About 2,000 people lived on the estate, 60 per cent of whom came from Liverpool, 20 per cent from neighbouring districts and 20 per cent from farther afield.

Although the houses themselves are not of high standard the general layout of the estate is good. There are gardens, back and front, to the houses. A shopping area of Co-operative stores, grocer, tobacconist and confectioner, milliner, and a telephone kiosk are centrally situated.

The first families moved in in June 1942, and by the end of 1943 not only were most of the houses on the estate finished but a Community Centre had also been provided. This and the administration office are the most solidly built structures on the estate. The Community Centre has a hall seating 150 people comfortably, a small club room and a committee room. Its committee is also the committee of the Residents' Association.

The inhabitants of this estate were not coming from squalor to comparative comfort. Quite the contrary, many had left better built and more comfortable homes. They accepted the move because it was wartime and because in many cases it meant an end of separation from their families. Like other new estate dwellers, however, they faced the hostility of the near-by village and a lackadaisical attitude on the part of the authorities to finishing the estate to the satisfaction of the inhabitants.

When the first inhabitants moved in there were only bare concrete floors and glass-substitute windows. Footpaths were unpaved muddy tracks.

The near-by village contained an Anglican Church and a school. The village pub was not welcoming to the new-comers. The village regarded the whole estate as an intrusion on their privacy and referred to its inhabitants contemptuously as 'the people on the property'.

Even in 1951 '. . . apart from casual contacts, such as those made in the village post office which serves both communities, and activities organized in connexion with the parish church, opportunities for social intercourse between villagers and estate residents include evening classes and meetings of the Parent–Teacher Association at the school in the village, the British Legion Club which now meets in the village, and the Village Club with its cricket pitch and bowling green, but none of these activities attracts many people from the estate. On the other hand, only about ten of the villagers have been attracted to the community centre and most of these only by the whist drives. The two communities differ in tradition and outlook, and contact between them is slight. Relations are more amicable than they were ten years ago, but they remain two separate entities' (Lupton and Mitchell, 1954).

In fact, despite the peculiar origin of the estate there was a situation which is commonly reported from such estates. These two kinds of external opposition are precisely the factors which lead to the formation of Residents' Associations and one was duly formed in September 1942. While its primary purpose was to represent the inhabitants in their corporate relations with the outside world, its leaders also set themselves the task of giving the estate an internal social and recreational unity.

In its first capacity it had to deal initially with the Ministry of Aircraft Production for matters concerned with the buildings and equipment, and the City Council on such matters as rents and re-letting.

A complication was that 'tenants' could not have tenancy agreements because the estate was on requisitioned ground. They were officially addressed as 'licensees'. I have suggested that council house tenants are always influenced by feelings of insecurity. Licensees have an even less secure status. They could be summarily evicted and there was no local authority to whom they could appeal to deal with grievances. They had to go to a Minister of the Crown or have questions asked in Parliament.

The Minister of Supply was the next authority with whom the Residents' Association had to deal. He held sway from 1945 to 1950. However, by this time some of the factories were no longer in need of housing and the City Council let some to families on their waiting list. They were not quite quick enough, however, and, in 1946, thirty bungalows were taken over by 'squatters'. The Rural District Council refused to adopt the estate and, in 1950, the Ministry of Works took over from the Ministry of Supply. The day-to-day affairs of running the estate were transferred from the City Council to an independent agency. The Residents' Association and the agency came into sharp conflict, and the Residents' Association tried when it could to bypass the agency and deal with the Ministry direct.

In addition to the 'owners' of the estate, the Residents' Association dealt with public bodies responsible for such services as water, gas, electricity, education, and transport.

In 1946, Residents' Association candidates swept the board in parish council elections, unseating six villagers. They then magnanimously coopted the six villagers with full voting rights. In 1952 the estate became a ward electing its own councillor to the Rural District Council.

The right of the Residents' Association to represent the tenants was, by and large, recognized both within the estate and outside it. Over half the residents subscribe to the Association. This does not mean however, as we shall see, that they accept its second claim to organize social and recreational unity within the estate. In relation to the outside world, the licensees act as one and the Residents' Association represents them. Internally they are divided by views on their own status. There is a sense in which the Community Centre run by the Residents' Association unites the estate. But it does so only by providing a focus for their quarrels. Before demonstrating this further, it is worth briefly describing the Residents' Association as external representative in action.

In May 1950, when responsibility was being moved from

one Ministry to another, a meeting was held to discuss the effects of this transfer. All the people concerned with the estate were present, about thirty in all. These included representatives of the Ministries, the County Council, the City Council, and the Rural District Council, together with four committee members of the Association. The Chairman, on behalf of the delegation and indeed all the residents, asked to be rehoused in permanent houses. The authorities pointed out the difficulty involved in this and the Association conceded the problem. They did, however, counter with demands for improvements such as plastered walls, sound-proofing, pavements, gutters, and downspouts. Only the last two had been provided by the time the fieldwork ended, despite much subsequent agitation.

The failure of this meeting was therefore part of the atmosphere when in September 1951 the rates, and hence rents, in the estate were put up.

The agency sent formal notices to quit to each licensee, together with new agreements which involved the higher rents as well as various petty restrictions (on keeping dogs for example). The Association called a protest meeting attended by three hundred residents, elected a deputation to meet the Minister, appointed a defence committee to prevent evictions and decided to take the matter up with the local M.P. The committee of the Association met the Member of Parliament and later the Under-Secretary at the Ministry in London and obtained assurances about evictions and rent which they accepted as a reasonable compromise.

In this situation the Residents' Association attracted mass support on the estate and it continued to be seen as the people's representative against the agency and external authority. However, much of this work was carried out by a small committee. 'Meetings at which large numbers of members can participate in face-to-face relationships are only held at long intervals; these are formal occasions with their own established procedures' (Lupton and Mitchell, 1954).

The Residents' Association has tried to promote cohesion in face-to-face groups through the Community Centre and other recreational activities.

The Association had an entertainment sub-committee which organized social evenings, concerts, dances, and whist drives which were held in the Community Centre. A darts club also functioned there. Other attempts to start activities had been less permanently successful. A youth club, football team, and drama group came and went and came again.

'A gala held each summer until 1951 was one of the ventures which was organized by a committee of the Residents' Association, but it had to be discontinued owing to lack of support and financial difficulties. Its programme included a fancy dress parade, band, field sports and other traditional features of such occasions, and some of the leading figures in the community regard its discontinuance as a great loss as this was one of the few activities in which the people of the neighbouring village seemed to take an interest' (Lupton and Mitchell, p. 25).

There remained, apart from churches and political organizations, three independent voluntary associations in 1951, a poultry club, the British Legion, and a surviving drama group which had broken away from the Centre.

The main recreational institution on the estate still remained the Community Centre. There were about 660 members who paid the half-crown a year subscription. A central feature of the Centre was its licensed bar. The decision to apply for the licence was taken against strong opposition. The two arguments that won the day in its favour were that the nearest pub, apart from the inhospitable village, was two miles away on foot and that the revenue would be very useful. The licence was granted in 1949, the bar set up in the club room and a steward appointed to look after it.

'The bar has become very popular with some of the residents, but there are others who claim that but for its existence and the type of person frequenting it, they would use the Centre and help to extend its activities. As long as there is a bar there, they refuse to join' (p. 26).

The committee of the Centre and the committee of the Residents' Association were in fact the same people. They had a dual role, but it was in their capacity of community centre organizers that they formed an especially coherent corporate group. For they not only discussed, they also did.

Moreover, committee members are not only charged with the duty of directing general policy and making decisions about the action to be taken in specific situations, but are also responsible for taking the steps necessary to ensure that their decisions are carried out. Indeed, unless they did so the continued existence of the organization would be doubtful, as very few ordinary members are willing to give assistance (p. 34).

I would add here that in my experience in Glynceiriog, and elsewhere, any attempt by ordinary members to usurp such functions would be regarded with suspicion and distrust. Officials and committee members were thus, as in Watling, kept busy. They had committee and sub-committee meetings. They had to go to the Centre to prepare for social functions, to attend the functions themselves, and to clear up afterwards. They collected subscriptions, distributed circulars, and did minor repairs to the building. 'These activities necessarily bring committee members in close and frequent contact with each other and, not surprisingly, they constitute a closely-knit group' (p. 34).

There were fourteen such committee members of which the most important were the chairman, vice-chairman, secretary, and treasurer. There was one ex-chairman who was also a key figure. The remaining five women and four men worked but did not decide.

The chairman was a man in his middle thirties. A founder-member of the Residents' Association, he was a former convenor of shop-stewards and President of the Union branch which met on the estate.

The secretary was a single woman skilled worker active in her trade union. The treasurer was a local government official and had also been active in his union. The deputy-chairman was a full-time trade union official. The ex-chairman was now a parish councillor and chairman of the local Labour Party. Three of the five women were house-wives, one was a nurse and one a supervisor in a factory. Two of the men were semi-skilled workers; one was a skilled worker and one a clerk.

Leadership in the Community Centre was in the hands of those who, while being themselves manual workers, were just a little different from the general run – craftsmen, clerical workers, and those with achieved leadership status elsewhere which they could carry over into the estate situation. The conclusions to *Neighbourhood and Community* argue that this is to be explained in terms of special skills. As I have argued earlier above, there are other and to me more convincing sociological factors involved (p. 97).

Looking at the situation on the estate showed that there were some estate dwellers who avoided using the Centre. Some of these openly said it was because of considerations of prestige. They described the Centre as nothing but a 'drinking school'. Those who went there were a 'rough crowd' and 'not the kind of people one likes to associate with' (Lupton and Mitchell, p. 42).

The authors did not, however, find a correlation between occupational status in terms of skilled, semi-skilled, and unskilled, and this rough and respectable status in the community. They distinguish between *conferred* status in an industrial hierarchy where management gives power and hence prestige to supervisors and foremen, and *assumed* status on the estate.

Those who assumed high status on the estate did so as a technique of adaptation. Uncertain how to behave and in an attempt to maintain their privacy, they did not join the Residents' Association, stayed away from the Community Centre and did not participate in other large scale activity, except significantly the Parent–Teacher Association off the estate. They did not merely not go to the Community Centre, they stayed away. They kept themselves to themselves.

Liverpool differs from Watling in that grievances continued and thus the Residents' Association continued to function. It is similar in so far as the recreational activities which continued had become segregated by status group. But whereas in Watling it was the low status who withdrew, in Liverpool it was the high. The next estate I shall consider is one in which the common recreational activities disappeared altogether.

SHEFFIELD 1951–2

The Sheffield estate is occupied by about 6,000 people in 1,666 houses. It was built between 1926 and 1936 as a slum-clearance estate. Whole streets of people were moved together from the old to the new and set down again still as neighbours but in a new environment. The estate is unusual in that it is both near the centre of the city and yet isolated. It is on a hillside in a triangle marked off by a railway line, an escarpment, and a stretch of waste ground. There are ten shops, a school, and a pub on the estate, and it is near to churches and a cinema.

The difficulties involved in the initial transfers were immense. Nearly two thirds of the new tenants had paid less than seven shillings a week for their old houses; whereas after the move, at a time of severe unemployment, they were expected to pay as much as nine shillings or ten and sixpence for two or three bedroomed houses. Much of their furniture was in such a bad condition that they were unable to take it with them, with the result that many got into serious debt by ordering new equipment on the hire-purchase system, or else they bought from junk shops old furniture which was often little better than their own had been. The windows, huge by comparison with those in the old houses, demanded curtaining, and many solved this problem with the help of newspaper hung across curtain rods (Hodges and Smith, 1954).

A fifth of those who moved in moved out again. There was no preponderant age-group as in Watling or the post-war estates, but in 1931 the proportion of children under ten was twice the national figure.

In 1930 forty per cent of the household heads were unem-

ployed and the authors suggest that unemployment 'was
certainly an important factor in the development of
community life, as it provided a common background of
experience and need which made the residents willing to
cooperate together in various kinds of social activities and
also provided the leisure which gave them the opportunity
to do so'.

Before 1939 there were only three voluntary associations
on the estate. None of these was operating in 1951. A
gardening club, a Tenants' Association, and a Community
Centre were formed and run by the latter. In 1940 a
Methodist Mission and a Roman Catholic School were set
up. The Anglican church near the estate ran a youth club in
the estate school. The Methodists ran an old people's club.
There were no local political party branches. The most
active surviving activities were the youth clubs and the
British Legion.

Out of a probable potential membership of a thousand
young people between fourteen and twenty years old about
two hundred actually participated. This compared with a
national average of 40 per cent and a Sheffield average of
55 per cent.

The pre-war gardening club lasted about ten years. It
provided a satisfying means of employing enforced leisure,
helped out economically by providing cheaper food,
through cheap seeds and shared implements, and increased
the social standing of some residents by enabling them to
have neat and well-cultivated gardens.

'But the first two functions largely disappeared with the
drop in unemployment before the war, and social pressures
do not seem to have been a strong incentive, as the state of
the gardens rapidly deteriorated after the passing of the
first enthusiasm. The club seems to have suffered from
difficulty in finding officers and from conflict between groups
within it. It disintegrated at the beginning of the war, leaving only a few rather vague memories behind it' (Hodges
and Smith, p. 82).

The Tenants' Association was even more short lived. It

was founded to agitate for the replacement of gas lighting by electricity. It was one of the leaders of this who was instrumental in establishing the Community Centre.

This started in 1933 as the result of a discussion in the dole queue at the local Labour Exchange. A public meeting of 250 people was held, a plot of land on the edge of the estate acquired from the council, and with the help of a builder's mortgage, a hut costing £250 was built.

The Centre opened in 1934 with 480 members each paying a subscription of a penny a week. Dances, whist drives, and boxing matches were organized by an elected committee of twelve to pay for its maintenance. Conflicts arose over the behaviour of young 'rowdies' at dances and on one occasion the secretary was beaten up. Nevertheless, the Centre was kept open all day and in the evening. Unemployment declined and so did membership until after about eighteen months only a hundred members were paying regular subscriptions. The dances and other social activities failed to compete with similar attractions in the city and the Centre ran into debt. After unsuccessful negotiations with the local Council of Social Service and two breweries, the City Council reluctantly took over. Down to sixty members by now, a paid secretary-warden was imported but failed to revive it. It struggled on until the war, became a civic restaurant, failed again, and was finally dismantled. Nothing similar has replaced it.

The information on the Sheffield Centre is necessarily scrappy, since ten years and a world war intervened between its disappearance and the appearance of the researchers. It is clear, however, that there is the same connexion between external opposition, an agitational body, and an attempt to unify recreation that we found in Watling and Liverpool. Its failure is at least partly explained by proximity to the city and the absence 'of potential leaders whose status was high enough to enable them to be recognized and accepted, but not so high as to make it impossible for them to associate informally with the members of the group' (Hodges and Smith, p. 140).

'GREENLEIGH' AND BARTON

No one supposes that housing estates are places where men work; it is evident from this chapter that it is only to a limited extent that men play there. Women, however, do work there and for some full-time housewives it is their main place of work.

Up to now I have been concerned mainly with life outside the council house and with men. Now I shall consider the theme that the Englishwoman's home is her factory. The housing estate very often cuts married women off from outside paid work and hence from their contact with the wider world. Thus, in the traditional housing area of St Ebbes in central Oxford (Mogey, 1956), thirty householders yielded twenty-two working wives and five retired from paid employment. In the new housing estate which Mogey compared with it there were only twelve working wives in thirty households. As we shall see, a move to a housing estate for a woman may mean being cut off from her kin, from her mother, and from her work. Each of these presents a narrowing of the scale of social relationships. The problems are most clearly seen and stated by Young and Willmott who followed forty-eight families from Bethnal Green (see Chapter 7) to the fictitiously named estate of Greenleigh.

Greenleigh is some twenty miles out of London on the Tube. Architecturally it is in sharp contrast to Bethnal Green. The variety of different types of dwelling interspersed with shops, pubs, and workshops which is Bethnal Green is replaced by drab rows of seemingly identical houses, two chrome and plush pubs, and a shopping centre. The flatness of Bethnal Green is replaced by hills. But if the housing is less picturesque it is more comfortable. As Young and Willmott say: 'The attraction is the home. Our couples left two or three damp rooms built in the last century for the "industrious classes", and were suddenly transported to a spacious modern home. Instead of the tap in the backyard, there was a bathroom with hot and cold water. Instead of the gas-stove on the landing, a real kitchen with a sink and a larder. Instead of the narrow living-room with stained wallpaper and shaky floorboards, a newly painted lounge heated by a modern solid fuel grate. And instead of the street for children to play in, fields and trees and open country.'

Mogey relates how one couple moving from St Ebbes to Barton found the lino from the old best bedroom just fitted the new bathroom.

Another feature which Bethnal Greeners moving to Greenleigh welcomed was the better environment for the children. To benefit their family at one level, the new generation, they had to break it at another, the old. This contradiction between loyalty to Mum and the wider family and duty to the children was perhaps a major reason for the high rate of removal back to the East End in the early days of the estate.

Those who moved and stayed, however, certainly saw less of their relatives, as one would expect. Young and Willmott give a case study of a family they call the Harpers:

Mrs Harper, a stout, red faced woman in her late thirties, had, like her husband, always lived in the same part of Bethnal Green before she went to Greenleigh in 1948. She came from a large family – six girls and two boys – and she grew up amidst brothers and sisters, uncles and aunts and cousins. When she married at eighteen, she went on living with her parents, and her first child was brought up more by her mother than by herself. As the family grew, they moved out to three rooms on the ground floor of a house in the next street. Their life was still that of the extended family. 'All my family lived round Denby Street,' said Mrs Harper, 'and we were always in and out of each other's houses.' When she went to the shops she called in on her mother 'to see if she wanted any errands'. Every day she dropped in on one sister or another and saw a niece or an aunt at the market or the corner shop. Her many longstanding acquaintanceships were constantly being renewed. People were always dropping in on Mrs Harper. 'I used to have them all in,' she told us, 'relations and friends as well.' At her confinements, 'all my sisters and the neighbours used to help. My sisters used to come in and make a cup of tea and that.' And every

Saturday and Sunday night there was a family party at Mrs Harper's mother's place: 'We all used to meet there weekends. We always took the kiddies along.'

That busy sociable life is now a memory. Shopping in the mornings amidst the chromium and tiles of the Parade is a lonely business compared with the familiar faces and sights of the old street market. The evenings are quieter too: 'It's the television most nights and the garden in the summer.' Mrs Harper knew no one when she arrived at Greenleigh, and her efforts to make friends have not been very successful: 'I tried getting friendly with the woman next door but one,' she explained, 'but it didn't work.' It is the loneliness she dislikes most – and the 'quietness' which she thinks will in time 'send people off their heads'.

Her husband is of a different mind. 'It's not bad here,' he says. 'Anyway, we've got a decent house with a garden, that's the main thing – and it's made all the difference to the children. I don't let other people here get me down.' He still works in Bethnal Green – there are no jobs for upholsterers at Greenleigh. This has its drawbacks, especially the fares and the time spent travelling, but it means he is able to look in on his parents once a week and call about once a month on his wife's father and eldest sister – Mrs Harper's mother having died, 'the old man lives with Fanny'.

Mrs Harper herself seldom sees her relatives any more. She goes to Bethnal Green only five or six times a year, when one of her elder sisters organizes a family party 'for Dad'. 'It costs so much to travel up there,' she said, 'that I don't recognize some of the children, they're growing so fast.' Tired of mooching around an empty house all day, waiting for her husband and children to return, with no one to talk to and with the neighbours 'snobbish' and 'spiteful', Mrs Harper has taken a part-time job. 'If I didn't go to work, I'd get melancholic.' Her verdict on Greenleigh – 'It's like being in a box to die out here.'

Mrs Harper's story shows how great can be the change for a woman who moves from a place where the family is linked to relatives, neighbours, and friends in a web of intimate relationships to a place where she may talk to no one, apart from the children, from the moment her husband leaves for work in the morning until he comes home again, tired out by the journey, at seven or eight at night. It is not just that she sees less of relatives than before; as a day-to-day affair, as something around which her domestic economy is organized, her life arranged, the extended family has ceased to exist. Other women remarked on their sense of loss.

'When I first came I felt I had done a crime,' said Mrs Prince, 'it was so bare. I felt terrible and I used to pop back to see Mum two or three times a week.' 'It's your family, that's what you miss. If you're with your family, you've always got someone to help you. I do miss my family.' 'We do miss the relatives out here,' 'I miss my Mum,' others told us in similar vein (Young and Willmott, pp. 132–3).

This experience is confirmed by the answers of others. For example, twenty-four out of forty-one wives in the sample saw one or more women relatives daily when they had lived in Bethnal Green. In Greenleigh only three of them still did. Their husbands often continued to work in London – the fare is expensive but having paid it in order to go to work the men use it also to visit relatives. And, in contrast to Bethnal Green, they may call also on their wife's kin. Some wives, also, were in the happy position of being able to work in London. For the rest, however, visiting London was prohibitively dear.

Visiting with kin and former neighbours changed its character. Kin came on a visit rather than called or dropped in. On a Sunday morning in summer the road from the station was 'like hospital on a visiting day', alive with people bringing fruit and flowers to visit their exiled kin (Young and Willmott, p. 137).

Mogey reports the same in Barton and St Ebbes and carries the argument further.

For many families, visiting the relatives in the former neighbour-hood becomes an affair for the weekend or for special occasions. Dressing up is required, everyone is on their best behaviour, stiff-ness and formality creep in, enjoyment escapes away, and the social contacts are subsequently broken. An important considera-tion in this break is the fact that estate families rapidly acquire a set of aspirations different from those of the older neighbourhood: wanting different things, they soon become estranged (Mogey, p. 83).

This situation breaks down the informal pattern of com-munity care for the ill or the temporarily hard up. Any prolonged illness of a wife makes calls on her husband to which in Bethnal Green he was unused. Depending on other factors, it may bring husband and wife closer together in cooperation or create unbearable strain.

Not only emergencies but everyday life, too, accentuates the dependence of husband and wife and immediate family upon each other and their isolation in the home. There is very often in housing estates (as in Greenleigh, Dagenham, Barton, and Coventry) nowhere else to go. In Bethnal Green there is one pub for every four hundred people and a shop for every fourteen households. In Greenleigh there is a pub for every five thousand and a shop for every three hundred people (Young and Willmott, p. 142). It is no wonder that the number of television sets per hundred households increased much more rapidly in Greenleigh than in Bethnal Green.

All this has a profound effect on the relationships of men and women. In Bethnal Green there was a community of women which was almost self-sufficient. Men, except the retired, were cut off from it by their daily exile at work. When they came home the women included them in the community by passing on gossip. In Greenleigh it is the women's work of raising children and keeping house which cuts them off. This activity which was a 'factory industry' in Bethnal Green has become a cottage industry in Greenleigh. Like all cottage industries child rearing and home building tend to encompass all the family. The man is drawn in as well. Here is the mechanism of changing networks, changing roles in action. Men spend more time doing jobs in the house and garden and watching telly than they do in the pub and at the football ground.

The 'home' and the family of marriage becomes the focus of a man's life, as of his wife's, far more completely than in the East End. 'You lose contact with parents and relations once you move out here,' said Mr Curtis. 'You seem to centre yourself more on the home. Everybody lives in a little world of their own' (Young and Willmott, p. 145).

How, if at all, do these little worlds relate? Why does there appear to be a war between the worlds?

Mogey interprets keeping themselves to themselves and unwillingness to be identified with any group 'almost amounting to an inability to enter into any obligation that looks like a contract' as a sign of social insecurity (p. 113).

It is interesting to take this phrase about contract and to explore it in comparison with the Irish countrymen described in Chapter 1. There we found the small farmer of Ireland willing and indeed compelled to enter into far reaching social obligations with his equals, reluctant and at pains to avoid commercial contracts with companies or suppliers other than those who represented in the town the same social stratum as he did in the country. The housing estate housewife represents an opposite pole; cautious in her dealings with neighbours, she is often an easy prey for the impersonal, commercial nexus with hire-purchase company or mail-order house (Wilson, 1963). Similarly, Mogey again points out that reluctance to join social clubs is not paralleled by reluctance to attend commercial social gatherings. 'Only in an audience where everyone is responding individually to a clear and distinct stimulus can newcomers be fitted in without any disturbance' (p. 113).

This discussion provides the key to the understanding of social relationships on housing estates.

It lies in uncertainty. The Irish countrymen know what to expect as the response of others to their particular behaviour. The estate housewife does not. She knows how the hire-purchase companies behave, she knows what to expect of her family, but her neighbours are a mystery. Hence she seeks privacy – she does not want others to know her relationships with the commercial outside world – and she wants her relationships within the family to be played out according to its internal expectation uncomplicated by the discordant expectations of the outside world. The problem is, she does not and cannot know whether the outside expectations are discordant or not. She cannot choose between discordance and conformity because there is no reference group to help her. Hence the appeal to the mass media and the status race.

How does this work out in Greenleigh?

Twenty-three of the Young and Willmott's forty-one couples interviewed thought Greenleigh unfriendly, ten friendly, and eight were undecided (Young and Willmott, p. 147). All denied their own unfriendliness and yet each behaved overtly in ways which in others they stigmatized as unfriendly. They kept themselves to themselves. They had myths to justify this – tales of what had happened to other people who had been friendly with their neighbours.

People do not treat others either as enemies or as friends. They are wary, though polite. They pass the time of day in the road. They have an occasional word over the fence or a chat at the garden gate. They nod to each other in the shops. Neighbours even borrow and lend little things to each other, and when this accommodation is refused, it is a sign that acquaintance has turned into enmity (Young and Willmott, p. 149).

One of the Greenleigh informants summed up the situation well by saying that he had not grown up with his neighbours, 'they come from different neighbourhoods, they were different sorts of people and they didn't mix'.

They had, in addition, the disadvantage of moving into a non-established district with low population density (a fifth of Bethnal Green) and few meeting-places outside the home. It is true that the immigrant to the traditional village is an outsider, but when he is accepted, even if only by being accorded hostility as a named intruder, rather than as one of a category, he is accepted by a group or at least a network. In Greenleigh it is a piece-meal acceptance and, as in other housing estates, it often does not extend beyond adjacent houses.

Although active interaction with neighbours is at a minimum, their presence is felt. They are perceived as watchful eyes looking for faults in the housewife's craftsmanship as wife, housekeeper, and mother. The husband's job, often far removed from the estate, is no longer the main criterion of status. A family is judged (or thought to be judged) by its mother and its mother is judged by the appearance and affluence of her home and her children's appearance. The standards to which the neighbours are thought to impel one are paradoxically not local but national – the standards of the women's magazines, newspapers, and television commercials.

Consumer goods are acquired because they are useful and because others have them. Some, like cars and telephones, are a means of retaining contact with the old way of life in the context of the new. Visiting sisters on other housing estates may only be possible by car. Urban public transport tends to go from periphery to centre rather than linking places on the periphery.

I have suggested in earlier chapters that conflict within consensus is an essential part of community. In Bethnal Green I described the friendly rivalry between streets and sub-districts. In Greenleigh the only possible basis for such unity creating conflict are the nuclear families in their 'little boxes'. As Young and Willmott suggest, relationships are often window-to-window rather than face-to-face (p. 163). The neighbours are ubiquitous but anonymous.

Though people stay in their houses, they do in a sense belong to a strong and compelling group. They do not know their judge personally but her influence is continuously felt. One might even suggest, to generalize, that the less the personal respect received in small group relationships, the greater is the striving for the kind of impersonal respect embodied in a status judgement. The lonely man, fearing he is looked down on, becomes the acquisitive man: possession the balm of anxiety; anxiety the spur to unfriendliness (Young and Willmott, p. 164).

I would have wished the authors to write woman in their last sentence, because it would emphasize that they are illustrating what has been called the alienation of man's life from his productive activity at the same time as they discuss what is essentially the industrial sociology of the housewife and the effect of urbanization on her conditions of work.

They pose the major problem not only of town planners and applied sociologists, but of 'successful' capitalist society. Must life become poorer as it becomes richer?

As I said at the beginning of this chapter, in writing about housing estates I have been highly selective. I have not, for example, considered Kuper's study of intimate relations on a Coventry housing estate (Kuper, 1953), Willmott's of long settled Dagenham (Willmott, 1963), or the later work on Bristol (Spencer, 1964 and Wilson, 1963). I do not think that they would affect my argument. I have followed through some of the themes of previous chapters and shown how voluntary associations play their part in forming housing estate social networks, and how the tendency towards segregation of men's and women's roles outside the home and integration within seems to work in such estates. In the final chapters of the book I shall try to show to what extent the partial societies I have described form a progression culminating in what many may think is a depressing picture of housing estate life. This value judgement may be misleading, as we shall see. The positive aspects of life on the fringes of the conurbation have to be evaluated within a different framework. Such a framework would start from the characteristics and latent relationships of the town. The retreat from community may in fact, at another level, be an advance.

A MORPHOLOGICAL CONTINUUM

CHAPTER 9

Societies as they are

In this second part of the book I want to redeem my promise in the introduction by trying to construct a morphological continuum along which the communities described in Part One could be ranged. It is morphological because although each stage is structurally more complicated than the one before, and each has a more diversified economy and technology, there is no necessary implication that the village of Glynceiriog in North Wales used to be like the mid-Wales parish, Llanfihangel, and will become successively like the coal-mining town of Ashton, the Derbyshire manufacturing town Glossop, or Banbury, Bethnal Green, Watling and Sheffield.

Nevertheless, at each level of organization there are linked changes. Twenty towns of 18,000 inhabitants scattered about the British Isles will have individual characters arising out of differences in history, situation, products (wood, cotton, coal). They will also have similarities in social structure and social behaviour. Mining villages in Yorkshire, South Wales, and Scotland are very different in terms of the feel of their social life and in their culture. The kind of social relations underlying the cultural difference – their structure – may be very similar. I do not visualize the continuum as a neat Euclidean straight line – the shortest distance between two points – but as a rather messy squiggle, blurred here and sharp there. Sometimes it may be pulled off course and then back on to it by the vagaries of, for example, economic change and immigration. Nevertheless, I think the tendency of direction of change is clear. To clarify it I shall need to discuss in order some key general concepts. These are mainly already familiar to sociologists: community, role, network, class and status-group, social conflict. I introduce one new concept, which I have borrowed and adapted from the theory of communication: social redundancy.

I shall also mention some of the principal theoretical exponents of these various key concepts in order to show the wide possibilities of application in each case and to illuminate the study of society in general.

Communities

All communities are societies, but not all societies are communities. Communities are peculiar in several ways. The first problem is one of scale. The societies which I have described in the first part of this book are all comparatively small in number. Rees's Llanfihangel has 500 inhabitants. Banbury has a population of 19,000. However, Margaret Stacey queries whether Banbury is in fact a community and answers that it is not.

Size, however, on its own, is not a distinguishing criterion. Willmott and Young find a community in some respects in Bethnal Green, despite a population of 54,000. They are perhaps really describing a congeries of communities. A group of two or three hundred people living together on an urban housing estate may or may not form a community. Size is not the only key.

Community implies having something in common. In the early use of the word it meant having goods in common. Those who live in a community have overriding economic interests which are the same or complementary. They work together and also play and pray together. Their common interest in things gives them a common interest in each other. They quarrel with each other but are never indifferent to each other. They form a group of people who meet frequently face-to-face, although this may mean they end up back-to-back. That people in such an area of social life turn their backs on each other is not a matter of chance. In a community even conflict may be a form of cooperation. I return to this point below.

The community cannot be described as a simple form of society. Its economy is simple, but this itself engenders a complexity in social life.

For example, when I lived in Glynceiriog, doing research,

and visited the University at Manchester, some of my colleagues would comment on how quiet it must be in the country and how much reading I must get done in the evenings. This town dwellers' stereotype of country life equals in inaccuracy the country view that city life is necessarily a gay social whirl. Participation in city recreations is for most of its inhabitants voluntary. Plays, films, dances, concerts, may be available, but they may be taken or left alone. If there was a play or concert in Glynceiriog Hall, villagers often felt obliged to go – 'to put in an appearance'. The organizer of the play was not an impersonal businessman in an office elsewhere whom one had never met. He was a cousin, a fellow church or chapel member, a friend, or just a fellow villager. His efforts had to be supported because it was the norm, because one wished him well or had to appear to wish him well (or at least not to wish him ill). The following week one might oneself be organizing a function or wanting to borrow some tools. One good turn deserves another. The economy was relatively simple and 'theatrical producer' was not a specialized role. The producer fills other social positions simultaneously and this creates complexity in social relationships. As we shall see, it is seldom possible for the community dweller to play one role at a time. The dilemma of Gilbert's shipwrecked 'elderly naval man' who ate his mates is a familiar one, for less horrific reasons, in face-to-face groups that have existed over a period of time. He was compelled, as a sad joke, to sing,

> 'Oh, I am a cook and a captain bold,
> And the mate of the *Nancy* brig,
> And a bos'un tight, and a midshipmite,
> And the crew of the captain's gig.'*

He remained to play all their roles because to survive he had to absorb them physiologically. Communities similarly suffer a shortage of actors to perform all available roles.

* For a full analysis of his plight, see *Comic and Curious Verse*, Penguin Books, 1952, pp. 88–91.

Roles

Society assigns a certain part to each individual and this is his social position. When he acts according to his part he is performing a role. The concept of a role as used in sociology always implies the existence of people playing other roles even if they are not actually physically present. They may, as in the origin of the metaphor, be merely an audience. They may interact directly with the role performer. Thus a man can only behave as a father if there are others who behave as children. To every role there are such relevant audiences. A man's total role may be made up of many roles – husband, father, son, uncle, worker, worshipper, game-player. This has been called multiple role, and conflict may arise if there is an overlap and the behaviour expected of him as a son, for example, conflicts with that expected of him as a father. This is a situation which may lead to dispute between a wife and her mother-in-law. Another situation producing conflict arises because of what Merton has called the role-set (Merton, 1957b). Merton points out that the incumbent of each social position has not one role expected of him but many. A schoolteacher as a schoolteacher relates to pupils, to the governors of the school, the headmaster, the school-caretaker, and several others. Each has slightly different, and not necessarily mutually consistent, expectations of him. This seems to me to be a special refined case of multiple roles that leads to built-in conflict which is structural and unavoidable. This does not mean that such conflict will lead to disputes. It is a characteristic of rural society that the performers of other roles in an individual's many role-sets are likely to be the same people. This is a point to which I shall return and then restate in a different form. Merton discusses a number of ways in which this structural conflict is resolved. Since social positions are not all equal in importance, the individual will behave to meet the expectations of the incumbent of the most important other role in his role-set. The rest of the role-set (assuming they share his appreciation of which *is* the most important) will accept this. The power of another role incumbent in the set may be greater than the others for structural or personal reasons. In the case of the teacher he may do what the headmaster or a colleague of forceful character expects. Some colleagues may be powerful in some situations and not in others. For example the head, although powerful in school, may not know what the teacher does in his spare time.

The generalized form of this factor, called by Merton 'insulation of role-activities from observability by members of the role-set', is of the greatest importance because its operation differs not only from social position to social position but also from society to society. In rural small-scale societies it is less true that 'people do not engage in continuous interaction with all those in their role-sets'. Since role-sets overlap in terms of their actual incumbents, all roles tend to be played in the public eye. The head knows what his teachers are up to all the time (and vice versa). Similarly, if there are conflicting expectations of a role this is more likely to become apparent. In such societies conflict lies nearer to the surface and special mechanisms exist which at once minimize the outbreak of disputes and may even turn conflict into a cohesive force. Knowing what behaviour is expected and fulfilling expectations correctly is difficult when each person has a multiplicity of roles to choose from. This is the familiar problem of whether Mr Jones should refer to his wife in the presence of the doctor as 'Mary', 'my wife', or 'Mrs Jones'.

When I buy a bus ticket in a city, the role relationships involved present little difficulty. If I quarrel with the conductor, this may possibly affect me the next time I go by bus, but there are so many conductors I may never see that one again. He may change shifts or jobs. The economy of the city is diversified and complicated. Each man in a day plays many parts, but to many different audiences. In a community there is not only a smaller number of roles but there are also an even smaller number of audiences. The bus conductor may also conduct the choir, be a chapel deacon, and be related by blood or marriage to most of his passengers. I call this the complexity of community life as against the complication of the city. I see complexity changing to complication as technological diversity causes and results from division of labour.

It is in the nature of society that its members are *committed* to certain roles. It does not follow that they like performing these roles. This led Erving Goffman to distinguish between role-commitment and role-attachment: 'Adoption agencies, for example, deal with two kinds of couples, the too fertile and the insufficiently fertile, the first being committed to the parent-role without being attached to it, and the second being attached to the role without being committed to it' (Goffman, 1961, p. 90).

We have seen that this is an especially relevant distinction in the study of social class. In Banbury those members of the wage-earning population which I have called 'locally oriented' are both committed and attached to their subordinate social roles. The cosmopolitan are also committed but not attached to the role. They direct conscious efforts towards reducing their commitment to it. Some are born to positions which determine future roles, some achieve roles, and some have roles thrust upon them late in life. I suggest that in communities people are committed to roles by birth – ascribed roles, and are more likely to become attached to them. In urban societies, individuals still have ascribed roles but add to them achieved roles. They are committed to both but are more likely to be attached to the latter.

Networks

The analogy of role is derived from drama. The role-performer in a community, like the stage original, is not usually interacting with one other but with many. The role-set is the first step in trying to deal with this added complexity. Another helpful analogy which I believe marks the first *major* advance in the language of sociology since role is that of 'network', which I have already mentioned in the introduction (see p. 18). It was introduced into community studies by Professor Barnes (Barnes, 1954). In 1952 and 1953, while Dennis, Henriques, and Slaughter were in Ashton, Williams in Gosforth, and I was in Glynceiriog, Barnes was in Bremnes, a fishing parish in Western Norway. This fieldwork gave him the opportunity to ponder on a drift-net piled up in a corner of a fishing-boat.

Barnes distinguishes three social fields: the first is territorially based and consists of the locality in which people live and carry on their day-to-day existence, the enduring unit of parish, hamlet, or village in which membership is slow to change. The second field he describes is based on occupation (in this case the fishing industry), the membership of which is not permanent but where each independent unit is temporarily linked in order to carry out its function to the full. The third field has neither unit nor boundary nor coordinating organization but consists of all the friends which a person builds up for himself throughout his life, whether such ties are formed through work or at leisure, through kin or by accident. Each person sees himself at the centre of his own particular network of friends, and each friend will himself overlap into someone else's network.

This way of looking at a social system was, of course, by no means invented by Barnes, although as far as I know, he was the first to make it fully explicit. It opens up existing possibilities for further development in sociology and especially in the study of rural societies. Barnes himself shows one way:

We may note that one of the principal formal differences between simple, primitive, rural or small scale societies as against modern, civilized, urban or mass societies is that in the former the mesh of the social network is small, in the latter, it is large. By mesh, I mean simply the distance round a hole in the network. In modern society, I think we may say that in general people do not have as many friends in common as they do in small scale societies. When two people meet for the first time, it is rare in modern society for them to discover that they have a large number of common friends, and when this does happen it is regarded as something exceptional and memorable. In small scale societies I think this happens more frequently and strangers sometimes find that they have kinsmen in common. In terms of our network analogy, in primitive society many of the possible paths leading away from any A lead back again to A after a few links; in modern society a smaller proportion lead back to A. In other words, suppose that A interacts with B and that B interacts with C. Then in a primitive society the chances are high that C interacts with A, in modern society the chances are small. The fact is of considerable practical importance for the study of societies by the traditional techniques of social anthropology, when we try to become acquainted with a limited number of persons whom we observe interacting one with another in a variety of roles. In a modern society, each individual tends to have a different audience for each of the roles he plays.

The communities of this book are intermediate in this sense. Nevertheless, as we moved through the book we found a progression. Thus the Irish countryside, studied by Arensberg, approximates to Barnes's 'primitive' model, but the urban societies at the end are similar to his model of modern society.

In the last sentence in the passage I quoted from Barnes above, the two analogies – dramatic-role and structural-network – are linked. Paradoxically this link, with its great relevance to life in *rural* communities, has been explored in a study of twenty *London* families by Elizabeth Bott (Bott, 1953 and 1957).

She in fact set herself the problem of explaining why husband and wife in some urban families had role relationships different from those of spouses in other urban families. She distinguished three kinds of family organization. The first she called *complementary*. In this case the activities of husband and wife are different and separate, but they fit together to form a whole. This is the case I have described in Part One as typical of the Irish and Welsh farm families.

The second case she calls *independent*. In this, activities are carried out separately by husband and wife without reference to each other in so far as this is possible. Glynceiriog men and women and the miners of Ashton and their wives are examples of this. This seems an appropriate point to say that the description of the Ashton family (see pp. 125–31 above) and its independent organization is considered to be overdrawn by some writers (see Young and Willmott, 1957, p. 19).

Finally she describes *joint* organization in which activities are carried out by husband and wife together, or the same activity is carried out by either partner at different times. Although there is no description in these terms in Banbury or Glossop, I feel sure that there are many families approximating to this pattern of organization at least among the 'cosmopolitans'.

Where complementary and independent organization predominates, Bott speaks of segregated role relationships. It is then possible to arrange families on a continuum ranging from those having highly segregated role relationships to those having joint role relationships.

Families in towns exist, she argues, not as part of an organized social group but as nodes in a network of relationships. This differs from the orthodox view of an organized group because in a network 'only some, not all, of the component individuals have social relationships with each other. For example, supposing that a family, X, maintains relationships with friends, neighbours, and relatives who may be designated as A, B, C, D, E, F, . . . N, one will find that some but not all of these external persons know one another. B might know A and C, but none of the others; D might know F without knowing A, B, or E. Furthermore, all of these persons will have friends, neighbours, and relatives of their own who are not known by Family X' (Bott, 1957, p. 58).

In fact, when she looked at the nature of the networks of her twenty research families, Bott found they varied in the degree of *connectedness*. She uses this term to describe the extent to which the people known by a family know and meet one another independently of that family. If they all know and meet one another she called this *close-knit* and if there were few such relationships she called it *loose-knit*. She is at pains to emphasize that these terms are limited. They only describe the networks of her research families and her comparisons of one with another. Nevertheless, we can see that the concepts can be used to differentiate types of society.

In rural Ireland close-knit networks will predominate, in Banbury and Glossop close-knit and loose-knit networks intermingle. In a new housing estate in a conurbation we would expect a predominance of loose-knit networks, unless of course it was a slum-clearance estate to which a community had been moved *en masse*. In fact, as Bott points out, if a network is sufficiently 'close-knit', as in the case of tribal societies, it is more useful to think of it as a social group.

Not only do Bott's categories of connectedness fit the societies we are considering but, with some modifications, her hypothesis also seems to hold good.

Bott shows for the town what is true of the country; the stage reached in the family cycle has an effect on the network connectedness and the role-differentiation in the family. Young children sharpen the division of labour between husband and wife at the same time as, in most of our communities, they increase the dependence of the wife on her kin and her own mother. The husband, his wife's attention absorbed elsewhere, may be drawn back to the peer group companions he forsook at courtship and marriage.* At the other end of the scale, the isolated couple may be forced into more joint role relationships by their dependence on each other's aid in child rearing.

Secondly, the change in the pattern of men's lives from rural–agricultural to industrial–urban is much greater than that in women's. Only in the most industrialized and urbanized groups are women even partially liberated from the chores of home and baby. Women, because of the nature of their work, remain enmeshed in a network of kin.

Despite the variations of the life cycle and between the sexes, it remains the case that the elementary family in urban society has a different position from its equivalent in the countryside, let alone in tribal society.

---

* Sociologists use the term 'peer-group' to refer to a group of people of the same age and status who meet and interact together continually. It is used especially of the groupings of men in urban neighbourhoods which begin as play groups at school and persist in varying forms throughout life.

Bott sees this as a process of *individuation*. She uses this term in preference to isolation which has only to be considered to be seen to be misleading.

Individuation means that 'the elementary family is separated off, differentiated out as a distinct, and to some extent autonomous, social group'. In all the societies I have considered this process is advanced, but a relative lack of informal pressure from gossip and public opinion leaves the elementary family of Banbury and Glossop more autonomy than it enjoys in rural Ireland, Wales, or Cumberland.

When Bott comes to consider the factors which influence the connectedness of social networks within the town, we see immediately the same mechanisms that are associated with the tendency towards the progressive loosening of networks as we proceed from country to town.

Firstly, even links between kin are greatly strengthened by the existence of common economic interests. This is clear in the relationships of the Irish peasant to his kin whether they remain in the countryside, move to town, or emigrate to Shanghai or America. In Banbury, the extended family remained (exceptionally) important in the case of the locally-oriented owners of traditional businesses – the burgesses. The socially and geographically mobile group I call the spiralists, who depend most on economic advance through examination qualifications, depend least on relationships with kin.

Secondly, the type of neighbourhood characterized for the urban setting by Bott as the 'long established working-class areas in which there is a dominant local industry or a relatively small number of traditional occupations' (p. 102) also describes many villages.

Thirdly, there is in a community little opportunity to make relationships outside the existing network. There is a lack of physical and social mobility. Here again peasant-farmer, miner, or even ex-quarryman stand in sharp contrast to the spiralists or the mobile wage-earning cosmopolitans of Glossop and especially Banbury. Once again, even in these categories, men are more likely to develop a loose-knit network than are relatively home-tied women. Bott finishes her discussion of the factors concerned in shaping networks by referring to personality factors. Whether in fact there is a rural or urban personality that can be compared is beyond the scope of this book.

Thus, using concepts developed for a purely urban study of husband–wife relationships, we can illuminate a linked pattern of development between certain roles and networks as we move from truly rural to thoroughly urban society. Professor Aidan Southall has attempted to unite role and network to produce a sociologically based rural–urban continuum of development in a more sophisticated way. If we follow his argument we find a contradiction between his view and Bott's the resolution of which will lead us naturally into the next chapters on class and status, social conflict and change (Southall, 1959).

He distinguishes between role and role relationships, for a person may play the same role towards several people. If an individual has many roles he has a wide range of recognized social activity. Whether these formal activities involve many other people or not is measured by the number of role relationships involved. Thus a teacher in a classroom of forty pupils has one role, that of teacher–pupil, and forty role relationships. A husband, with his wife in a monogamous society, has one role and one role relationship. The father who has his son as a partner in a firm of solicitors has two roles, namely, father–son, partner–partner, but only one role relationship.

In any given area it is theoretically possible even if it is not practicable to count the number of roles available to each individual and the number of role relationships associated with each role.

In principle, therefore, the distinctive sociological characteristics of different societies, or distinguishable segments of them, can be measured by a formula that expresses the relationship between the number of persons occupying a given geographical area, the number of role relationships played by them, the narrowness and specificity of role definition, the proportion of latent role relationships, the degree of inequality in distribution, and the comparative duration over time of role relationships. Although all these factors require exposition for the sake of intelligibility they would not all necessarily have to appear as separate terms in the formula (Southall, 1959).

He calls the combination of them all, the *density of role texture*. He then postulates that urban communities may be defined in terms of 'the marked rise in the density of the role texture which occurs in the passage from rural to urban'.

Stated baldly in this way this sounds rather forbidding. It will become less so as each term of the formula is explored in turn. Role relationships we have already explained.

We consider interactions in any society in terms of five major type categories of roles. These are: (i) kinship and ethnic, (ii) economic, (iii) political, (iv) ritual or religious, and (v) recreational. These divisions do not require great sophistication to make. If we set out to analyse the compartments of our own lives without any theory of role at all we would produce something very similar.

In rural society (and still more in tribal society) any role is likely to splay across all five of these areas of activity.

This is what is meant by broadness of role definition. Thus the father–son role in the Irish countryside exists at once in the first four of the areas. In Banbury it is less likely to do so. In no society have these five areas watertight boundaries. In rural societies they are more likely to be blurred than in urban. In fact it is possible to see the process of social development as a process of role differentiation. Father/employer/ritual leader/teacher, etc. (which we could perhaps in German put as one word) become, in more developed society, father, and employer, and ritual leader, and teacher. There are exceptional cases in which differentiated roles become regeneralized to which I shall return below.

At the same time as roles become more narrow in their application to different sectors of social life, they become less diffuse and more specific in their definition. Thus, within the economic sphere in the peasant countryside, there are few specialists – one must plough *and* sow *and* reap *and* mow to be a farmer's boy. In a town the preparation of raw materials is carried out by one group of specialists, the processing by another, their packing by a third, transport by a fourth, and so on. One diffuse role has been replaced by many specific ones.

The way in which local magistrates and councillors in Glynceiriog, Glossop, and Banbury, and local trade union officials in Ashton have lost their power to various other agencies outside is an indication of the same process in the political sphere.

The development from overt role relationships to latent role relationships is a particularly interesting one. This marks the difficulty in studying urban society by the simple participant observation methods used for rural communities.

In the rural area role relationships are overt: that is they are mediated by direct face-to-face interaction. Latent role relationships exist in town situations. For example, the role of fellow member in a voluntary association may be a role relationship which never brings its incumbents face-to-face (see Laslett, 1956, p. 177). In the study of communities, one becomes, as the reader has discovered, more and more concerned with voluntary associations, voting patterns, and political and religious allegiances and prejudices. These are in fact indications of latent role relationships in this sense.

The final terms in Southall's formula are the degree of inequality of distribution of role relationships and their comparative duration over time.

Theoretically, at least, at the extreme rural end of the continuum, everyone in society has an equal opportunity to interact with everyone else. Even in rural Ireland, however, the nature of women's work has already cut them off from full interaction. In all the communities discussed in this book there are some members the scale of whose life is wider than that of others and the number of whose role relationships is therefore potentially greater. This factor is of course closely associated with social class and status as well as with sex.

Finally, there is a contrast between the blossoming of ephemeral roles at the urban end of the scale compared with the relative continuity of roles in rural society. 'The King is dead, long live the King' is equivalent in ideology to the arrangements for ensuring succession in Ireland. It differs from the 'he used to be a friend of mine', or 'yes, he did work here once' remarks that are the commonplace of urban life.

Of course, not all urban areas are like the classical description of Watling – 'not much more than a huge hotel without a roof; the constant turnover of its population is the greatest single handicap to its developing into a community' (Durant, 1939, p. 119). In some areas, like Bethnal Green, there is a settled population which has endured over several generations. Here individuals become incorporated into a community through their children and grandchildren and the affinal links that they create.

We can summarize the two ends of Southall's continuum in a table. We must remember that the communities of this book all lie on the continuum at points nearer to the urban end. Although not all are towns all are integrally tied into and influenced by an industrial civilization.

Southall's Continuum

Low population density	High population density
Broad roles (cutting across 5 areas)	Narrow roles
Diffuse role definition	Specific role definition
Overt role development	Latent role development
Equality in role distribution	Inequality in role distribution
Long-standing role relationships	Ephemeral role relationships
Low density role texture	High density role texture

This continuum will be partly included in and partly supplementary to my own (see page 285).

In each case the direction of development is towards

increasing role differentiation. Even though a man's political and economic life may not be greatly changed, once his various roles have become more specialized and cut and dried his recreation and leisure activities are similarly affected, which in turn increases the number of exclusive parts he has to play. The effect is cumulative.

There are, however, exceptions to this general rule. The first is the unspecialized town, like the great accumulation of the traditional West African city which although densely populated is still based economically on agriculture and socially on kinship. That does not concern us here. The second is the highly specialized, mechanized, and industrialized agricultural areas – the 'high farming areas of North America' and the capitalist organized business farming areas of Britain. Unfortunately no account of social life in such an area of Britain yet exists. This is one of the most glaring gaps in the literature.

The characteristic of such an area is in the first place an economic base which *is* agricultural, but this is agriculture with a difference. Transport and communications, trading, service industries, and food processing plants are all highly specialized and differentiated. The agricultural contractor who hires out machinery by the day is the key to the economy and much social life is centred on the town. But these areas still differ from the town in one important respect – the sparseness of their population. Usually population density increases with specialization, but in a highly mechanized agricultural community this may not be so. Here the general role structure will be similar to that of the dominant society of which it forms a part, which will be highly diversified; but as there are fewer people in these pure farming areas and in the small towns dotted around them, each person will have to take over many roles. Then people whose roles in a highly specialized community do not usually coincide will find themselves on intimate terms. This is an example of role generalization.

It is also possible that at the top levels of western society – among the elite – roles have always been to some extent generalized. In Britain the roles of old Etonian, company director, cabinet minister, prime minister's affinal relative may all be linked to Cecil and Cavendish, Salisbury and Devonshire, and to the distribution of many powerful roles among few people. In the United States the diachronic distribution of Rockefellers and Roosevelts and the diachronic and synchronic distribution of Kennedys suggests a similar state of affairs. The 'old boy network' is not a misnomer and it is of the close-knit variety. Elites in small towns like Banbury and Glossop, and even in some milieus of cities like Manchester, reflect the same multiplicity of roles.

There is a parallel development in industry. Thus the early craftsman made the whole complex commodity – let us say a vehicle – himself. As, through technical advance, the division of labour progressed, the individual craftsman made less and less until finally each simple operation was carried out by one man and one machine. No one man could make one vehicle, but hundreds in cooperation could make thousands. Each machine has its specialized attendant. The coming of automation regeneralizes the craftsman's role but at a higher level. One man and one, albeit vast, machine now make a thousand.

But the most striking example of all is that which arises from Bott's hypothesis, for given that networks lose some of their close-knit character as towns develop, it follows also that the clear definition of sex roles becomes blurred in the joint role relationships of some modern urban marriages. This only becomes possible when the roles involved in child care and housework have become differentiated and separated out. Teachers, doctors, health workers and laundries now perform some of the housewife's tasks. The role residue leaves time for women to do other work not limited by the demands of housework.

Secondly, a man's work and travelling to work tends to absorb less time and as a husband he is left with time in which he can help his wife to cope with the chores that otherwise bind her to the home. She may thus gain time she can devote to other roles.

In this chapter we have discussed the changes that take place in face-to-face relationships, in roles and networks, as we move from one end of the continuum to another. We have found a situation more complicated than we might have expected. The next chapter adds further complications at a higher and broader level. There we shall have to discuss the major divisions of society used by sociologists; social class and status; social conflict and the contrast between what social actors intend and what in fact occurs. We have tried to show what our studies of community can illuminate of the histology of society – now we move to anatomy and physiology.

Class and Status, Latent and Manifest Function, and Social Conflict

Class, Status, and Conflict

CLASS, status, and conflict are perhaps the most discussed and most variedly defined terms in the vocabulary of sociology. They are, that is, those about which there seems to be the least agreement. Each writer has his own definition. Nor are these definitions merely, in Wright Mills's terms, invitations from each author to others to agree to use words as he uses them so that the discussion about real issues can begin. Definitions of class often have implicit in them whole theories of social organization. The use of the word 'class' in many empirical studies has implicit in it an unconcern with explicit theory. Again, one looks in vain in such monumental works on class and conflict as Dahrendorf's (1959) for any references to the sort of detailed community studies that I have been considering.

My view of class relations is essentially based on differing relationships to the means of production, that is to property, and in this I am following Marx. I am particularly interested in Marx's views on class for it was he who saw that the struggle between the classes created social change, and he was particularly concerned with the increasing divergence of rural and urban societies. His ideas and analysis are therefore helpful and relevant to my argument.

The concept of class has been with us since the Roman census of tax groups, but its present use derives from the nineteenth-century classical political economists and especially from the arguments of Marx and Engels. However, it is not easy to understand what Marx did mean by class for he died before completing Chapter 52 of Volume III of *Capital* in which he was to define the concept. Several people have since completed the fragment of the chapter for him, a task from which Engels wisely abstained, but the most interesting and recent attempt is that made by Ralf Dahrendorf.

Ralf Dahrendorf ingeniously sets about completing Marx's chapter with a series of quotations from Marx linked together by a commentary. One may object to it, however, by pointing out that the way in which the quotations are arranged makes no allowance for development in Marx's thought. What is clear however is that Marx uses 'class' always in the same general sense, but that he sees it as a concept which changes its meaning in different social situations.

The passage in which this becomes most evident is in *The Eighteenth Brumaire of Louis Bonaparte*, in which French peasants are described as being at once a class and not a class.

In so far as millions of families live under economic conditions of existence that separate their mode of life, their interests and their culture from those of other classes and put them in hostile opposition to the latter, they form a class.

In so far as there is merely a local interconnexion among these small-holding peasants, and the identity of their interests begets no community, no national bond and political organization among them, they do not form a class (Marx, 1954, pp. 171–2).

Marx did not introduce the idea of class for the sake of describing society neatly. He regarded the dynamic driving force of social change as struggle between classes. This does not mean that he thought that classes in this sense are at all times engaged in the sharpest forms of struggle for their opposing interests. This is an erroneous view which has been shared by some of his most fervent supporters and his most vehement critics. Were it true, society could not continue nor would any production take place. In relatively stable periods of history class differences may become blurred by status, or routinized into institutions which assume a conservative function. Conflict which arises out of structural opposition is not confined to relations between classes, as we have already seen. Class conflict does not necessarily show as revolution, any more than all role conflicts become open disputes.

In Chapter 1, on rural Ireland, we found class relations between two categories with different relations to the means of production – large farmers who hire labour, and peasant near-subsistence farmers. Conflict between classes in the Irish countryside was not so long ago civil war; it now seems to be parliamentary debate. It takes place off-stage but affects the behaviour of our players.

It does this in two ways. First, it appears directly in terms of political behaviour; second, indirectly it creates a status group. In Llanfihangel again, class conflict takes place off-stage and is complicated by differences in 'style of life'. In Gosforth, in my view, Williams's seven-fold division into 'classes' is better described as a division into 'status groups'. There are only three economic 'classes' there in my use of the word: those who live on rent or capital, those who farm on their own account, and those who work for wages. Once again class conflict is played out mainly off-stage.*

In Glynceiriog, most of my discussion is concerned with wage-earners only. While this is also true of the Leeds University report on Ashton, there we follow miners to work and are able to see the working of class struggle more directly. In Glossop, and especially Banbury, classes are reported to confront each other and clash in the political field, and express their consciousness of conflict by avoiding informal contact outside work and local government.

It is apparent that my view of class relations, following Marx, is essentially based on differing relationships to the means of production – that is to property. I must specialize my use of 'class' (or some other word) in this way to proceed with my analysis. Dahrendorf and others regard this use as unacceptable; he writes: 'Control over the means of production is but a special case of authority . . . Whoever tries, therefore, to define authority by property defines the general by the particular – an obvious logical fallacy' (p. 136–7).

* Williams discusses his terminology in an appendix.

He derives this view partly from the formal argument that wherever there is property there is also authority; but it is possible to find authority without property legitimizing it. His view seems to me to confuse levels of argument. Thus it is true that in considering a sub-system like a modern state school, teachers have authority not based on property. But considering the development of society as a whole, one most significant kind of authority relation, in the sense of power to control others, is based ultimately on property.

Dahrendorf does not, however, rest his case there. He also presents empirical arguments to support his contention. One is the separation of the ownership and control of industry associated with what Burnham has described as 'the managerial revolution', and hence the emergence of a post-capitalist society. Secondly, he cites the analysis of socialist society by Djilas in *The New Class*. This does not concern us here. Thirdly, he argues that there is no general law linking control of industry (where authority and property relations admittedly do go hand in hand) with control of the state – 'Should this law nevertheless be advanced as a hypothesis, then it was refuted by the first government of a labour party in an industrial country.'

These statements seem to me so naïve about the realities of class, status, and political power as to defy answer by less than a treatise (cf. Jenkins, 1959).

I have laboured this defence of my use of the concept of class because I want now to put forward another concept based on it and derived from Marx – namely 'proletarianization'. By this I mean the tendency towards polarization of classes so that eventually capitalists as a class face workers as a class nakedly, with their conflicts stripped of the cloaking effect of cross-cutting ties.

At the same time as ties between the workers and capitalists are reduced to the cash nexus, so the ties between the workers themselves undergo a transformation. While the workers live in small settlements and work in small workshops a multiplicity of ties strengthens the solidarity of regional or local groups. The growth of giant factories and urban centres rescues the workers from the 'idiocy of rural life'. This growth first of all breaks down the links between them and then forces them to recognize their common interests. They form trade unions, political parties, and other associations which once more forge new ties between them. These are reinforced by their common residential and recreational experience which differs from that of their employers. So the small-scale solidarities of the worker are broken down by the development of capitalist industry only to re-emerge on a wider stage and in a new form capable of developing into a conscious class antagonism towards other classes.

Status Groups

Marx used class in a way that was at once precise in its reference to ownership of property, and imprecise in delimiting the spheres of action in which class operated. Max Weber in an often quoted essay, 'Class Status and Party', seems to me to enable us to refine our view of the interrelations of class and status (Gerth and Mills, 1948, p. 180).

He describes three 'orders' of social activity. Firstly, the economic, concerned with the market and with *class*. 'The way in which social honour is distributed in a community between typical groups participating in this distribution (of power) we may call the "social order".' Secondly, the group acting within the social order – the *status* group. Finally, in the legal order, parties may be formed often on the basis of status groups or sections of classes consciously seeking power.

What characterizes a status group for Weber is a particular concept of status honour and the adoption of a particular style of life. Further, he writes: 'Class distinctions are linked in the most varied ways with status distinctions. Property as such is not always recognized as a status qualification, but in the long run it is, and with extraordinary regularity.

'With some oversimplification, one might thus say that "classes" are stratified according to their relations to the production and acquisition of goods; whereas status groups are stratified according to the principles of their consumption of goods represented by special styles of life.'

Armed with these concepts we can elaborate a scheme to deal with and explain the empirical difficulties we have met with in studying small communities.

Since we have not found revolutionary situations, we have not found the sort of class or status hierarchy which Watson has described as Neapolitan ice-cream. The gentry and the county we had little difficulty in defining. The problem came in dealing with the so-called 'middle class'. In my use of terms they are middle status groups or strata. To deal with this, Watson, as a result of his study of a small mining town in Scotland and his knowledge of Glossop invented the term 'spiralist' and applied the term 'burgess'. I have borrowed these.

There is much literature in sociology on what is sometimes called the new middle class, Burnham's managers or Dahrendorf's 'functionaries without capital' (as opposed to the old middle class now become 'owners without function') (p. 44). The term *spiralists* overlaps with these.

'The progressive ascent of specialists of different kinds through a series of positions in one or more hierarchical structures, and the concomitant residential mobility through a number of communities at one or more steps in this ascent, forms a characteristic combination of social or spatial mobility which I propose to call spiralism' (Watson, 1964).

(It is interesting to note that Bacon, in the first great period of capitalist expansion, in his essay 'On Great Place' wrote, 'All rising to great place is by a winding stair'.)

In each of the communities I have considered in this book we may find such people – civil servants, schoolteachers, and technologists in local factories. They may be young and still mobile or they may have reached their highest and farthest point, that is, they may be 'blocked spiralists'. But they do not of course form a class in the sense I have adopted. They do not form a potentially independent political group in Britain. They do not have specific economic and social aims in opposition to other groups within our society. They may act together because they feel they are a group but they do not act to change their basic position in society. They can in fact develop communal but not societal action.

The whole process of training of spiralists is one of selection and adaptation to a conservative pattern. Spiralists do not own the means of production but are given a share in control by those who do as long as they stick to the rules. Really successful spiralists become capitalists (as Watson himself implies when he points out that they are given shares in their companies). Top spiralists who rebel within the framework of the system may be tolerated and encouraged. Top spiralists who rebel against the system are, in revolutionary situations, sent back to the propertyless class where they belong. In more stable situations they too may remain tolerated but they do not get into control. We have not found them participating in the social life of our small communities.

The way in which the intelligentsia, like doctors and lawyers, have ceased to be self-employed and become wage-earners is common ground to economists and sociologists. The fact that company lawyers are paid monthly and general practitioners on a modified piece-work basis does not affect their class position. If they are slow to translate this into societal terms this is because sharp conflict between classes has not arisen in Britain since this transformation took place. To say this is not to deny the importance of status differences between the various sections of that large population who earn their living by selling their ability to work.

One of the essential features of a class is the political aims that its members pursue in common. The voting behaviour of Glossop and Banbury is also interesting evidence of the distinction already mentioned between the communal and societal aims of the spiralists.

'The disparity of attitude and interest, for example, between the small scale traditional proprietor and the large scale non-traditional manager ... is obscured by a common opposition to the Labour Party and its policies ... In terms of their party allegiance the common social and economic interests and values of the owner and manager are paramount' (Stacey, 1960, p. 40).

Another important section of the middle stratum are 'burgesses', local businessmen, brought up in the area and looking to it for their social interests and their prestige.

While all burgesses are locally-oriented, not all spiralists are cosmopolitan. Those who are still mobile will tend to be, those who are blocked are likely also to become *local*. Examination of the town councils of Glossop and Banbury revealed how important locally-oriented blocked spiralists can be in filling leadership-roles in small towns.

Just how internally stratified the working class is in the communities I am describing it is difficult to say. Stacey, in Banbury, classifies them as rough, ordinary, and respectable. She recognizes five status divisions in the 'top' 2·1 per cent of the population and three among the remaining 97·9 per cent. This may be because manual workers are the section which sociologists study most but mix with least.

On the other hand, some might hail this as evidence against the decomposition of labour into the hierarchy of prestige, seen by Dahrendorf and others as empirical indication of Marx's mistake about proletarianization (see Dahrendorf, p. 51).

Once again, this apparent contradiction may be solved by looking at studies of communities. It may be true that there is a hierarchy of industrial jobs in modern factories in contrast to the 'proletarian, the impoverished slave of industry who is indistinguishable from his peers in terms of work, his skill, his wage and his prestige' (Dahrendorf, p. 51). This status at work, however, does not necessarily carry over unchanged into the life of the communities. In Stacey's terms there is not a simple one to one correspondence – skilled = respectable, semi-skilled = ordinary, and unskilled = rough.

Status in rural society is total, in urban society it is not.

This may be because status in towns is ascribed to categories who share clusters of characteristics but with whose component members one does not necessarily interact. In rural areas status may arise out of daily face-to-face interaction. Simplifying the issue, one could say that in the town considerations of status determine with whom interaction takes place – status decides whether. Banbury illustrates this strikingly. In the countryside status determines how people meeting behave towards one another – status decides how.

For our purposes a significant division in the industrial working class of both Banbury and Glossop is that between what Stacey calls traditional and non-traditional, and what I am calling local and cosmopolitan. This, as I have suggested above, is a division between those workers who are committed and attached to their subordinate role and those who are merely committed. Those who are not attached may seek to escape either by individual social mobility or by political activity designed to change the content of the role.

I would expect that workers would tend to *embrace* their role in rural society and to *reject* it in urban. In other words, *all* the working class who remain in rural areas are locally oriented. Status and class do not coincide exactly in any society. Nor are they the only categories which align individuals and divide them. In rural society the lines of division for different purposes are less likely to coincide.

The relative ease of social mobility between status groups, characteristic of urban society, does not necessarily weaken class solidarity and conflict. T. H. Marshall has pointed out a change from the ideology of 'that education to which your status entitles you' to 'that status to which your education entitles you'. This, however, is an educational train which has to be caught early or not at all. As he writes:

The ticket obtained on leaving school or college is for a life ourney. The man with a third class ticket who later feels entitled to claim a seat in a first class carriage will not be admitted even if he is prepared to pay the difference. That would not be fair to the others (Marshall, 1950, p. 65).

Some social mobility between classes serves not to weaken, but to strengthen the class system as a whole. In a way structurally analogous to the revolt against the bad king which strengthens the kingship, so the social mobility of individuals emphasizes the rigidity of the class system through which they move. Individual rebellion against class, especially if successful, may serve merely to reassert class values (Gluckman, 1954).

These last considerations about class and status mobility must lead to a more general discussion about the function of social conflict. The view that conflict is always disruptive of the social order must be firmly repudiated. I argued its cohesive function in the chapter on Glynceiriog, and Margaret Stacey hints that election campaigns in Banbury enable the parties to live together amicably the rest of the year. What theoretical considerations cause us to distinguish between rebellion and revolution or division and cleavage? This discussion brings us to the root of the aims of sociology and the discussion of manifest and latent functions (cf. Merton, 1957a).

Manifest and Latent Functions

W. S. Gilbert can again provide us with a text in the words of Little Buttercup in *H.M.S. Pinafore*:

> Things are seldom what they seem;
> Skim milk masquerades as cream,
> Highlows pass as patent leathers,
> Jackdaws strut in peacocks' feathers.

The Captain's comment on her song is also an awful warning: 'Incomprehensible as her utterances are, I nevertheless feel that they are dictated by a sincere regard for me.'

The study of manifest or obvious and anticipated actions and that of concealed or unintended behaviour is extremely important and one of the most rewarding aspects of sociology. I would also like to argue that latent functions are likely to be more numerous in rural than in urban society.

Of the writers whose work I have used in writing this

book, I think that only Arensberg and Kimball and myself *centre* their analysis on the search for latent functions. Rees and Williams look for explanation in historical terms, asking the question, 'How did this come about?' They nevertheless show themselves aware of latent functions although they do not analyse them fully. Dennis, Henriques, and Slaughter, Birch, and Margaret Stacey are faced with the difficulty of treating much larger, more 'complicated' but less 'complex' areas of social life. The studies of Ashton and Banbury, however, contain occasional passages which are analysed in a functional way. The description of the weekend concert in Ashton which I quoted verbatim above is one example (see p. 136).

The search for latent functions has a profound effect not only on the theoretical analysis of material once collected, but on what sort of material is actually looked for by the authors of these studies.

Firstly, it enables the observer to explain or at least to clarify behaviour which otherwise seems totally mysterious or even irrational. There are many examples of this in the chapter on Glynceiriog. If we consider cock-fighting in Gosforth and other parts of Cumberland, it must be admitted first of all that people like and enjoy cock fights. Secondly, that there is a long tradition of holding them. I would argue, however, that the immense trouble and risk involved in defying the law means that this is not the whole story. In fact, the holding of cock fights is an expression of Cumberland solidarity against outsiders at a time when power over the lives of Cumberland folk moves farther and farther away from the doorstep. (An argument that has been explicitly used, by Isabel Emmett, to explain poaching in North Wales, Emmett, 1964.)

Another advantage of this approach is that it directs attention to fields of inquiry which have the greatest potential interest for the development of a sociological theory. The theme of jocular behaviour is a problem area of this kind.

Alwyn D. Rees gives an example when he describes the boys

of Llan ridiculing a middle-aged widow for enticing a young lad and, as I pointed out at the time (page 62–4 above), this tallied with the findings of Professor Radcliffe-Brown that such a relationship involves both attachment and separation, social conjunction and social disjunction. 'Social disjunction implies divergence of interests and therefore the possibility of conflict and hostility, while conjunction requires the avoidance of strife.' He goes on to suggest that such a situation can only be given stability in two ways; either by extreme respect carried to the point of avoidance, or by licensed disrespect – a joking relationship. We see in political and social relations between classes and status groups in Banbury precisely that combination.

Situations in which mutual avoidance is impossible, and mutual disagreement is inevitable, are especially likely to occur in small-scale rural society. Furthermore, people whose conflicts arise from one situation are especially likely to have to be friendly in another. For these reasons we expect the joking-relationship and extreme respect situations to arise in such societies. This will add another term to our continuum. In urban society, relations of conjunction and disjunction are most often found where people of disparate interests and income must cooperate – that is in the factory and at the negotiating table between employers and employed.

'But by far the greatest change has been brought about by the segregation of people of different social classes into large homogeneous residential areas, particularly in the suburbs. Physical distance has replaced social distance.

'. . . But within the work-place segregation cannot be practised. The educational and occupational basis of the contemporary class structure is presented in unmistakable and significant terms. Marks of rank are insisted upon, and often deliberately elaborated and multiplied; we have found wide agreement among industrial managers with suggestion that the floor space of offices, the appearance, comfort and cost of furnishings, the size of desks, the number and colour of telephones, height of partitions, the appearance of one's name in the internal telephone list or on the door of one's office, are all matters which have become more and more closely associated with rank, more and more used as expressions of one's position in the hierarchy of status' (Burns and Stalker, 1961, p. 149).*

The search for latent as well as manifest functions also helps to avoid replacing sociological analysis with naïve moral judgements or even the mere expression of surprise. The interpretation of cock-fighting in Cumberland which I have emphasized takes us a good deal farther than saying it is wicked and cruel. It does not of course preclude us from adding the value judgement that it *is* wicked and cruel if we should want to.

It does, however, indicate that inveighing against it in a London or Manchester newspaper is more likely to confirm 'ordinary Gosfer folk', if they hear about it, in their liking for it than to stop it. This conclusion has a general validity for those interested in engineering social change.

The functional approach is not unique to sociology, but when dealing with people in a society it is difficult to carry out procedures to their logical conclusion and to assemble data systematically. In this book, in which I am trying to combine a functional with a morphologically evolutionary approach, we have constantly come up against these problems. Furthermore, since it may stimulate its readers to look critically at their own towns or villages or even the voluntary associations to which they belong, I think it is worth looking at the problems of the technical equipment used in a functionalist study, together with a description of the practical operations necessary for its use.

One must first of all be clear to what items of behaviour functions are being imputed. Quaint customs may have some function but they may just be quaint customs. Or they may have the function of bringing in the tourists and photographers and providing cover illustrations for the publications of the British Travel and Holidays Association. It is important to know what consequences actors think are

* See also Bradney, 1957; Freud, 1960; Barnes, 1959; Girling, 1957.

going to follow from their actions as well as knowing what does actually happen. A distinction is made therefore between subjective dispositions and objective consequences.

No society is totally homogeneous, made up of people whose interests, life experience, and life chances are identical. All the communities we have described are divided by class and status, internally and externally. It does not follow therefore that a pattern of behaviour which is functional in one situation is functional in another. Nor can we take for granted that what is functional for one group is functional for all. The burgesses of Banbury looked on the tennis club as a place to meet their equals. This was its manifest function for them. Its latent function for them was a part of the web of interaction which preserved their togetherness as a group and their *local* orientation. Some of them may have been aware of this and some not. To the spiralist, and especially the young and still socially mobile spiralist, the manifest function was somewhere to play tennis. Its latent function *could* have been to unite the middle class across the cosmopolitan/local division. In fact, the differences in function could not be contained within the one organization, and conflict became dispute and dispute led to split. A parallel situation was the division of men and women in the organization of Glynceiriog football.

At a more fundamental level, some discussion is necessary of the functional prerequisites of society. Each account in Part One begins with a description of how men and women get their means of livelihood, although sometimes they do this outside the residential community. Each community also has to have some means of socialization – integrating newcomers by birth or immigration into the social pattern. 'Mechanisms', through which such functions are mediated, and possible alternatives within the same total framework have to be considered.

It does not always happen that there is only one social institution to achieve each function. Nor of course can one assume that each institution has only one function. There is an element of *uncertainty* in social life which in some ways is greater in rural than in urban situations. This will be considered in more detail in Chapter 11. There are more ways than one of killing a pig. To some extent, however, the number of ways is limited by the structure of the pig as well as by social custom and the purposes to which the carcase is to be put. In other words, concepts of structural constraint or context are relevant.

As Marx said: 'Men make their own history, but they do not make it just as they please; they do not make it under circumstances chosen by themselves, but under circumstances directly encountered, given and transmitted from the past' (1954, p. 15).

It is only in fantasy that villagers like those of Gosforth or Glynceiriog can solve the problem of their relationship to the rest of Britain by proclaiming their independence, as the people of a London borough did in the Ealing Studios comedy, *Passport to Pimlico*.

Nor is the external or internal structure necessarily stable; it is subject like everything else to change. What is functional today may have a different function tomorrow or even be dysfunctional. It is a paradox of this study (as of many others) that in the attempt to illustrate and illuminate a theory of change it has to deal with societies as if they did not change. This is a device of method which does not imply a belief in eternal stability.

Finally, there remain two vital problems in all functional analysis of which I can only indicate awareness. How does one know that the latent functions suggested are valid and how does one eliminate the personal and ideological bias of the observer? To these questions there are no simple answers. The validation has often to be left to the test of time and practice. We have, I think, found that personal bias does not so much affect the validity of the matter put into the books I am considering as determine what is left out.

It may be, for example, that the Ashton study underemphasizes the social life of women, and Glynceiriog the social life of men. *Small Town Politics* may overemphasize the vertical religious divisions of Glossop in the nineteenth century and under-emphasize the divisions of social class. The status divisions of Gosforth may be overstated. A critical reader may suspect all this and more, but except where there are inconsistencies, or data enabling me to make a new analysis, I have had to assume (heuristically) that all the field workers including myself were competent and unbiased.

The two topics of conflict and latent functions are related ones since it is especially in the field of conflict that latent functions are to be found. Although at first sight this sounds paradoxical the principle is consciously used in attempts to create social cohesion. Thus, the authorities of large comprehensive schools set up 'houses' and tutorial groups to cut across forms in the hopes of aligning and opposing sets of overlapping groups of children. 'Enemies' in one context are 'allies' in another and the unity of the whole should be strengthened.

Thus the contradiction between manifest and latent functions becomes most apparent in the discussion of social conflict and it is to this I will now return.

Conflict and Cohesion

It is in the sphere of conflict that things are most impressively not what they seem. It is true that conflict within a social grouping may be disruptive, but it may also be exactly the opposite. The conditions which determine whether it is the one or the other are very relevant to our theme (see Gluckman, 1955).

Conflicts about particular issues may be functional for some groups and disruptive for others. In one society some issues may lead to disruptive conflict and others may not. It will depend on the type of issue over which conflict is joined as well as on the type of social structure in which it occurs.

I am suggesting that in rural societies conflict is more omnipresent and more likely to be disruptive if it breaks into open dispute. At the same time, the nature of such society enables, if it does not demand, the channeling and institutionalizing of conflict in such a way that the occasion of dispute becomes the occasion of coherence. The contrast can be expressed in the terms that in rural communities there are divisions but no fundamental cleavages; there are rebellions but not revolutions. The end-point of such rebellions is an immediate reassertion of the values and unity of the group. In some circumstances, however, the long-term effect may be to bring the era of cleavage and perhaps revolution nearer.

Thus, I suggest that there is a series of quarrels around different activities in Glynceiriog which enables villagers to go on living together by blaming past activities and present strangers for their discontents. Nevertheless, the death of each activity leaves a residue of unresolved conflict. This may lead to the withdrawal of an individual from social participation until a group is built up which is driven outwards by village quarrels at the same time as it is drawn away by the attractions of a larger society. Less interaction will lead to fewer sources of dispute, but also to less sentiment and fewer cross-linking ties. Ambivalence becomes indifference. A community becomes linked groups of neighbours, and linked groups of neighbours become collections of households which just happen to be near each other.

This process does not mean (to quote Durkheim), 'that the territorial divisions are destined to disappear entirely, but only that they will become of less importance. The old institutions never vanish before the new without leaving any traces of themselves. They persist not only through sheer force of survival, but because there still persists something of the needs they once answered. The material neighbourhood will always constitute a bond between men; consequently, political and social organization with a territorial base will certainly exist. Only, they will not have their present predominance, precisely because this bond has lost its force' (Durkheim, 1960, pp. 28-9).

Bethnal Green, as described by Willmott and Young, stands as a monument to Durkheim's accuracy.

In general and formal terms:

Internal social conflicts which concern goals, values or interests that do not contradict the basic assumptions upon which the relationship is founded tend to be positively functional for the social structure . . . Internal conflicts in which the contending parties no longer share the basic values upon which the legitimacy of the social system rests threaten to disrupt the structure (Coser, 1956, pp. 151–2).

In small closely-knit communities of the type with which we are mainly concerned the participants tend to be deeply involved in every aspect of local social life. As we have seen there are few actors and many roles. Conflict arises not only out of the clash of individuals who may interact in several of their different roles, but also in the clash of role expectations affecting each individual. But these are societies in which status is total; thus it is not possible for the individual to escape the contradictions by putting on one face to one audience and a different to another (cf. Littlejohn, 1964). Villagers may avoid the disputes to which this gives rise by pretending to an ignorance which they do not in reality possess.

It has often been noticed of country people, as I remarked in Glynceiriog, that they rarely give the lie direct to statements made in public, or even those made in private by people whom they do not know well. They rarely refuse a request, but delay indefinitely fulfilling one of which they disapprove. Village committees, like Cabinets before Lloyd George, do not keep detailed minutes when there are no leaders with ascribed or charismatic status; they try to maintain an appearance of impersonal, unanimous, leaderless unity (Frankenberg, 1957 and Barnes, 1954).

Without the concept of latent function we might easily interpret such behaviour as do many English residents in North Wales and townsmen resident in English villages: 'The scenery here is beautiful but the people are such hypocrites', 'Every prospect pleases but only man is vile'.

It is interesting that the countryman faced with the

townsman who behaves in different ways in different situations also cries hypocrisy.

In the last analysis, village unity may only be maintained by adopting an enemy, real or imagined, outside. Thus 'foreign' football teams, gamekeepers, and policemen are taken seriously by such societies. If they can find nothing else in common they may microcosmically imitate the nation or the wartime allies and become united only by their common enemies.

Ruth Durant pointed out in her Watling housing estate study that community life flourished while new residents fought against external authority, but might perish when the battles for gardens, tarmacadam, and street lights had been won (Durant, 1939). Something, however, remained. Conflict with the local authority created bonds between the local authority and the local community. It also created bonds within the local community itself. It acted 'as a stimulus for establishing new rules, norms, and institutions, thus serving as an agent of socialization for both contending parties' (Coser, 1956, p. 128). It made 'the readjustment of relationships to changed conditions possible'.

Conflict then, both internal and external, does not necessarily disrupt the system: it may even strengthen it, if only temporarily.

This is at least partially true of societies like Gosforth, County Clare and Glynceiriog considered *in isolation*. Once they are put in their social environment, what is creativeness and progress at one level may appear to be death-throes at another. In Banbury, however, there are cleavages, not merely divisions, and the bridges across the divides are not over stable. But even here, in Weber's terms, there is not 'a formless sandheap of individuals, but rather a buzzing complex of strictly exclusive, yet voluntary associations' (Gerth and Mills, 1948, p. 310). The *local* system of Banbury remains governed by ascribed and total status. Conflict maintains the values within this system because the values themselves are not questioned. Liberals may be excluded from formal political life, but their social life marches with that of the Conservatives. In certain circumstances the common enemy is the *cosmopolitan* wage-earner who questions the very basis of local society. The other group of cosmopolitans – the spiralists, 'mobile individuals striving for station and status' denied the benefits of ascription, 'are thrown on their own resources'. Their organizations, even if nominally or manifestly aimed at playing golf or bridge, actually stand opposed (by those whom they welcome and those whom they reject) to both working-class and *local* burgess life. Their occupational and professional associations, when they are nationally organized, are disruptive both of local values and of local systems. Durant also believed that this was the case in Watling (Durant, p. 119).

At a national level, 'instrumental associations in modern society bring structure out of struggle, bring form into what otherwise would be chaos, and socialize individuals by teaching them, through conflict, the rules of social order' (Coser, 1956, p. 141).

In the case of cities Elizabeth Bott has written:

. . . an urban family exists in a network of many separate unconnected institutions, each with a specialized function. In a small-scale relatively closed society, the local group and the kin group mediate between the family and the total society; in an urban industrialized society there is no single encapsulating group or institution that mediates between the family and the total society (Bott, 1957, p. 100).

If she is right and if also there are many families which do not belong to any voluntary association, one could question whether a national society exists at all as a discrete unit which is more than a legal state or a common language category. This is one of the problems facing those who wish to integrate immigrants. What is there to integrate them with?

It was this conclusion also which led Durkheim to the view below which was as premature as that of Marx and Engels on the emergence of the proletariat:

. . . geographical divisions are, for the most part, artificial and no longer awaken in us profound sentiments. The provincial spirit has disappeared never to return; the patriotism of the parish has become an archaism that cannot be restored at will. The municipal or departmental affairs affect and agitate us in proportion to their coincidence with our occupational affairs. Our activity is extended quite beyond these groups which are too narrow for it, and moreover, a good deal of what happens there leaves us indifferent . . . A nation can be maintained only if, between the State and the individual, there is intercalated a whole series of secondary groups near enough to the individuals to attract them strongly in their sphere of action and drag them, in this way, into the general torrent of social life (Durkheim, 1960, p. 28).

In this chapter I have discussed the problem of class analysis and stratification, the difficulties inherent in studying the hierarchies and interrelation of classes in small communities, their diverse aims and interests, and the subtleties of status. But even more fascinating than what groups appear to do is the underlying meaning for their behaviour, which often explains how they solve problems of social conflict. External disagreement may strengthen basic unity and ultimately encourage cohesion, but destructive elements are also present and in the next chapter I shall go on to discuss alienation and anomie.

In discussing such key concepts of sociology as role, network, manifest and latent functions, class, status, and conflict, I have in each case been led by their classical exponents into a theory of social change, a progressive and historical development from rural to urban, mediated by industrialization, division of labour, and role differentiation.

In each case this is said to lead to an unsatisfactory state of life for the urban dweller. In terms of role theory he may be said to be role-confused; in terms of Durkheim's division of labour – anomic; in terms of Marxian proletarianization – alienated.

I shall first discuss these terms and then return to networks. I shall subsequently attempt to subsume all these ideas under the one concept of social redundancy.

CHAPTER II

Theories of Social Change: A Continuum

THE ties linking individuals in urban areas are, as we have seen, fewer than their rural counterparts. The mesh of the network in towns is larger, but the city dweller may make up for this loss by a larger number of more formal role relationships. There is always the possibility that the individual's links with other members of society may become tenuous. *Alienation*, in the strictest sense, means the situation that the wage-earner–producer finds himself in. The product of his labour does not belong to him but to the employer who pays his wages. His product has become a commodity separate from him – alienated or estranged. He no longer has control over its fate. Indeed the work he has done, and the social cooperation required in production, are no longer recognized. The commodity has become a thing in itself which seems to have a life of its own and even in some senses to stand opposed to its producer.

This alienation of the products of labour is already present to a great extent even in the Irish, Welsh, and English countryside, although the peasant producers maintain control over and themselves consume much of their product. It thus never becomes a commodity on the market. In cosmopolitan Banbury alienation in this sense is complete. The products of the aluminium works in no sense belong to the workers who work there, nor will they ever. If the concept of alienation ended there it would be of little interest to this study, but the concept can be carried further.

In the same way as economic change moves first economic and then social life outside the village, so economic alienation leads on to alienation from the cultural goals of society at large.

This point is made in *Coal is our Life*:

Obviously enough, the channels of real transformation, such as the treble chance coupon, will carry only the exceptional and fortunate few, and the rest will in the main produce only short-lived or modest improvements. It is a fact that wage-workers remain wage-workers until they are sixty-five. The ideals of behaviour, the good things of life, in short the cultural ends of the society in which they live, remain for most men a vision only, in the glossy magazines, the newspapers, on the cinema and the television screen, and in the lives of a few people they will never encounter. These 'cultural goals', to borrow expressions from Merton, are not equally available to all participants in the culture because of the inequality of the 'institutionalized means' placed at their disposal (Dennis *et al.*, 1956, p. 37, and Merton, 1949).

It is not only true that the values of society in the sphere of the arts and sciences are set by minority groups outside the village and outside the ordinary social life of the towns; but also the goals and aims of society are set in a way that makes them incapable of achievement by the majority of the population. There is in Merton's sense of *anomie* 'a dissociation between culturally prescribed aspirations and socially structured avenues for realizing these aspirations' (Merton, 1957, p, 134).

Thus alienation from products of labour has become alienation from cultural goals. Such a situation may lead to deviance and delinquency. In other words, it leads to an *alienation from norms*. This I think is a more precise formulation of the nature of anomie than 'normlessness' or the 'state of de-regulation'.

This does not mean that I am advocating the simple answer of returning to the village community – since this has gone through the same sequence already. In Trotsky's words:

The present-day city is transient. But it will not be dissolved back again into the old village. On the contrary, the village will rise in fundamentals to the plane of the city. Here lies the principal task. The city is transient, but it points to the future, and indicates the road. The present village is entirely of the past. That is why its aesthetics seem archaic, as if they were taken from a museum of folk art (Trotsky, 1957).

Both Durkheim and Marx suggested answers to this state of affairs. Durkheim in *The Division of Labour* denied that it was a natural end-point of the division of labour and saw the solution in the encouragement of *spontaneity*. This would make sure that everyone did the job for which he was best fitted and lived the life his social contribution justified. Marx considered the proletariat would become increasingly aware of the deprived nature of their lives, both economically and culturally, and would 'take arms against a sea of troubles, and by opposing end them' (Durkheim, 1960, pp. 353 ff. and Marx, 1957, p. 156).

Both saw the conflicts arising out of alienation and anomie as destructive conflicts which, far from maintaining social cohesion, were the instruments of social change. Thus at the same time as the consensus of norms which fosters cohesive conflict disappears, destructive conflicts are engendered. The number of ties linking individual to individual across lines of division are reduced.

There are those who have argued that the problems of modern society are only a matter of communication difficulty arising out of size. Once free communication is restored, the conflicts will appear to be unreal. There is indeed a sense in which communication may be relevant, but it involves a more sophisticated view of the nature of communication. To explore this I must return to the theme of networks. Barnes spoke of people as being 'in touch' with a number of others. Thus the sociologist shows himself aware, through metaphor, of social interaction as a form of communication. That being so modern communication theory can be applied profitably to the study of our suggested series of social changes leading from rural *community* to urban *alienation* and *anomie*.

To do this we must consider the concepts of *uncertainty* and *redundancy*.

All language and all concepts are metaphorical and our concepts have been no exception. Some metaphors are, however, more metaphorical than others. 'Role' is a straightforward analogy, the term itself borrowed from drama which reflects life. Together with 'class' and 'status' it forms a group of concepts which *denote* areas of behaviour or membership of categories with common characteristics. 'Community' and 'conflict' are less precise. They are operational concepts which *delimit* fields of interest rather than denote specific phenomena. 'Function', 'alienation', and 'anomie' are in the way I have used them *interpretative* concepts. The field having been delimited, and the entities within it denoted, these terms are used to explain relationships between the denoted parts. The reason that *function* can be a particularly confusing term is that it has *analogues* in both mathematics and biology. It is not always clear whether sociologists are using it in either, in both, or in neither of these senses. In this section I want to argue in frankly analogical concepts derived from communication theory in general and cybernetics in particular.

Analogies are always dangerous and often arbitrary (see Bell, 1962, p. 55). Some analogy is really a form of shorthand and cannot be extended by logic or argument. Thus, if we compare the nation to the body, the government to the head, the workers to the arms and legs, and so on, it is not profitable to seek a liver, spleen, or kidney in the body politic.

Seeking *analogues*, however, is a different matter. The oscillations of a pendulum and of an electrical oscillatory circuit can be expressed in the same mathematical formula. The results of empirical study of one of these systems can be translated into formulae applicable to the other.

Adapting Bell, I am distinguishing between analogy and analogue in this way: analogy is the 'process of reasoning from parallel cases'.

'Since the operative word is parallel, which is here used metaphorically, there can be no rigorous physical or mathematical control of the process of analogy' (Bell, 1962).

An analogue is a physical model which has the same mathematical model as the reality we are trying to analyse. We are left with a 'which comes first, chicken or egg?' type of dilemma on the relationship between analogues and analogies.

Redundancy is used by students of language and communication in two distinct but related senses. Cherry defines it as 'a property of languages, codes and sign systems which arises from a superfluity of rules, and which facilitates communication in spite of all the factors of uncertainty acting against it' (Cherry, 1957, p. 18).

He sees language as being the resultant of the opposing forces. The one, the desire to be understood, promotes redundancy. The other, the desire to be brief, tends to eliminate it.

Stripped of the teleology involved in using 'desire' in this context, we can apply this to rural and urban society. The contradiction is seen at its sharpest in Banbury. Here we are told the new technical men at the aluminium works quarrelled with the traditional middle class over the activities of the tennis club. On the one hand social interaction was to be promoted in a whole series of ways including tennis. The uncertainty as to whether tennis would provide exercise and company was to be overcome by providing redundant activities. On the other hand all redundancy was to be stripped away and the tennis club seen as an organization which arranged tennis as efficiently as possible. The dispute between women and men over football in Glynceiriog can be seen in similar terms.

On a wider historical time scale the relations of employer to employee can be regarded as going through a similar change from redundancy to less redundancy. The slave is clothed, fed and protected for his whole life by his owner. The serf feeds and clothes himself most of the time, but receives protection. The wage-earner can require from his employer only wages – the wherewithal to obtain clothing, food, and protection – for the period he works. The relationship is stripped of redundancy – the language of behaviour between classes has become a code.

Every role relationship at the rural end of our continuum is, so to speak, redundantly contaminated by the content of other role relationships. In urban society this is quantitatively less true. I would emphasize that this is a matter of degree. A role relationship with no redundancy is as rarely found in sociology as natural codes are in linguistics.

The other sense of redundancy in communications concerns networks. The idea of a network as a *topological* graph is a key one both to communication theorists and telecommunication engineers. Cherry, using the same image that inspired Barnes, introduces it when he writes:

> Roughly speaking a topological graph is the mathematical name given to a set of lines connected together into any kind of network. We may imagine a number of wires, having hooks at each end, which can be hooked together into different network patterns; the hooks, or ends of the wires where they are united, are called nodes. The distinction between networks and true geometrical figures is that the former consist of lines which have no specified shapes or lengths but are merely connected by their ends; magnitudes are not involved but only number and connexion. A fishing-net is a topological graph; so are the various flow charts or *sociograms* to which we have referred (Cherry, 1957, pp. 26-7).

If it is wished to send an electrical impulse from point A to point B, it is only necessary to connect them by a single channel. If the channel is in good order the signal will arrive, if not it will not. A negative result at B therefore may mean that no signal has been sent or it may mean the channel is out of order. The would-be receiver cannot judge which is the case. A way out of this difficulty is to provide alternative pathways, and this is in fact what telecommunication engineers do. These extra, in one sense, unnecessary additional channels create *redundancy* in the network. The reliability of the components now becomes less important than the number. There is considerable mathematical literature on this kind of redundancy, which fortunately does not concern us here.

The two kinds of redundancy are linked in Cherry's other definition:

> Redundancy may be said to be due to an additional set of rules, whereby it becomes increasingly difficult to make an undetectable

mistake. The term therefore is rather a misnomer, for it may be a valuable property of a source of information. If a source has zero redundancy, then any errors in transmission and reception, owing to disturbances or noise, will cause the receiver to make an uncorrectable and unidentifiable mistake (p. 185).

We can look at Barnes's and Bott's networks in this light. Another way of expressing the situation which Barnes describes as a small mesh network is to say that Person A is linked to B not only directly but also through a number of other individuals. These links operate in a number of different situations. There is redundancy. The same is true for Bott's highly connected network; in the arrangement of nodes and links it is like the Hammock network in Figure 10.

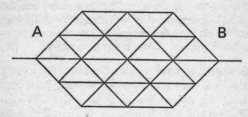

Fig. 10. Redundancy in communication network between A and B.

On this argument we can say that in both senses rural societies show greater redundancy. As we move towards the urban end of the continuum redundancy in social relations decreases, social relationships become less complex, processes are formalized and bureaucratic forms introduced. Elements of behaviour are stripped of latent and not so latent side-functions.

This argument is, I think, basically sound but needs modifying. Social redundancy does not disappear altogether but merely changes its form. A similar change is observed in language in the distinction between writing and conversation.

Conversation is rarely correct in grammar or syntax, sentences may remain uncompleted, words may be repeated, or phrases uttered several times in different ways. With writing it is another matter; the writer cannot observe his readers and can only make prior judgement of their difficulties. His writing is therefore premeditated and usually conforms more closely to the rules.

... *Conversation is built out of a relatively small vocabulary ... but the words may be arranged with great fluidity into varied patterns with repetitions, stressings, gestures and a wealth of reinforcing 'redundancy'. Writing must make up for the lack of gesture or stress, if it is to combat ambiguity, by introducing redundancy through a wider vocabulary and a closer adherence to grammatical structure* (Cherry, p. 120, my italics).

The parallel with the ends of the rural–urban continuum seems close. Rural social life is built up out of a relatively small number of role relationships – which are arranged with great fluidity into varied patterns. Urban life makes up for the loss of these by a large number of role relationships and their formalization.

This is all, of course, analogy building, but nevertheless potentially useful, since it shows an area in which the concepts, mathematical and otherwise, used to analyse other systems regarded as networks might be applied in sociology. Something of this kind has already been attempted both for industrial organization and economics (Beer, 1959 and Tustin, 1953). Bavelas and his successors have explored small group behaviour by artificially constructing communication networks to simulate patterns which occur in society. A star pattern is similar to a dictatorship, a chain to a bureaucracy and so on. While one does not want to carry these analogies too far, they have already stimulated interpretation in industrial sociology and could perhaps fertilize thought in the study of communities (Burns, 1961 and 1962).

Electrical networks involve two sorts of factors – topological, which we have been discussing – and *energetic*. In considering social networks we need to make a similar division. For Bott's purposes it was enough to know with what other people the families studied interacted. The affective content of the relationship could be left aside. She is very conscious of this and writes:

> Before the analysis can become at all precise it will be necessary to define degrees of intimacy and obligation of the various relationships. . . . If possible it would be advisable to interview several members of a network, following the links of interaction from one person to another, instead of relying on what each couple say about their network as I have done. Precise definition of connectedness would require quantitative analysis of the total network, of the independent networks of husband and wife, of their joint network (the people with whom they have joint relationships), and of that part of the total network composed of kin, that composed of friends, and that composed of neighbours (Bott, 1957, p. 61; see also Laing, 1960, 1961 and 1962).

The study of social networks is relatively new and there are as yet no studies of such differential networks as Bott suggests.

Merton, however, in making the distinction between locals and cosmopolitans which I made great use of in the chapter on Banbury, distinguishes between the sorts of networks which locals and cosmopolitans have a desire to have (Merton, 1957a, pp. 398–400).

'Locals [he writes] seek to enter into manifold networks of personal relations, whereas the cosmopolitans *on the same status level* limit the range of these relations.' He goes on to argue that the political success of locally-oriented politicians derives from their large networks. Locals are concerned to know a lot of people. They seek a quantitatively determined network. Cosmopolitans want to know only the 'right' people – they put quality before quantity.

In a formula which at once simplifies and highlights the essential fact, we can say: *the influence of local influentials rests not so much on what they know but on whom they know.*

We can use this distinction to add another dimension to the continuum I am trying to build up. It is now time to summarize the other dimensions of this continuum.

THE CONTINUUM

Nearly everybody is part of at least one small group. Most people belong to several, some to many. There are very few who are total social isolates. This means that some, if not all, of the characteristics that are typical of the rural end of the continuum remain as a part of town life.

In the move from countryside to town, the nature of society, of the group outside the primary face-to-face group, changes. This may cause some people to suffer unwanted intimacy or loneliness, although not everyone likes the sense of being perpetually under observation which living in a village may create. I am not arguing that village life is 'better' than that of the town. To do so would be to condemn all those people who flowed into the towns from the beginning of the nineteenth century onwards as irrational (see Saville, 1957 and Sprott, 1958, p. 89). Nor, however, do I personally believe that the life of modern English towns or cities is perfect and cannot be improved. I do not think there is any possibility of returning to village life even if we wanted to. In my view the gains of urban life, actual and potential, are infinitely greater than the losses. I would rather enough cubic feet of housing space and an efficient milkman than three acres of land and a cow.

My object has been to illuminate the differences between truly rural and less rural areas of Britain that happen to have been studied by sociologists. I think this is interesting in itself. Together with other facts and interpretations, this knowledge helps to shape my views and the views of other people on what Britain in particular is like. I set out also to illuminate what society in general is like and the processes of social change.

One way of doing this is to set up a model and then compare realities with it. More strictly I have set up two models and placed the communities I am describing in what I consider is the correct place between the two. Incidentally, this is a comparatively painless way of introducing the layman to some of the concepts which professional sociologists use.

Models, however, are not theories. The difference has been succinctly stated by Wright Mills:

> A model is a more or less systematic inventory of the elements to which we must pay attention if we are to understand something. It is not true or false; it is useful and adequate to varying degrees. A theory, in contrast, is a statement which can be proved true or false, about the causal weight and the relations of the elements of a model (Wright Mills, 1962, p. 36).

Once again I must repeat the warning that I am not an historian, nor do I accept the irreverent view that a sociologist is a historian without dates. George Homans, sociologist and historian, states the difference clearly, although even in his own opinion perhaps too sharply:

> ... there are now two main methods of studying social behaviour, one specializing, upon the whole, on types of institution, concerned with time-series, and mainly non-comparative; another specializing on the contemporary, concerned with the interrelations of institutions and often comparative in its emphasis. The former is history, the latter, sociology (Homans, 1953, p. 33 and 1962, p. 146).

This book then must be regarded as the work of a realistic, model-building sociologist, not a romantic, theorizing historian. This chapter summarizes, and hence distorts, by simplifying what has gone before.

For convenience, I call my models 'rural' and 'urban', aware that this begs many questions about the nature of towns and cities. 'Urban' might more accurately be called 'less rural'.

(A) RURAL	'URBAN' (less rural)
Community	*Association*
Rural societies have a community nature; people are related in diverse ways and interact frequently. They have – or feel as if they have – interests in common.	Urbanized societies have an associative nature. Although there may be a greater number of possible relationships, they do not overlap. There is often comparative infrequency of interaction. People tend to feel they have needs, rather than interests, in common.

RURAL	'URBAN' (less rural)
(B)	
Social fields involving few	*Social fields involving many*
In rural society a small number of people make up the total social field of an individual.	The number of people met by an individual in urban society may be large.
(C)	
Multiple role relationships	*Overlapping role relationships*
People in rural society tend to play different roles to the same person, i.e. they have more numerous multiple role relationships.	People in urban society tend to play different roles to different people, i.e. they tend to have less numerous multiple role relationships.
(D)	
Role conflict within a role set	*Role conflict in different role sets*
The major, but not the only, source of role conflict in rural society arises out of the transparency of the conflicting expectations within a role set. This gives some of its characteristic redundant form to social activity in the countryside, where cohesive ritual and ceremonial develop which 'socialize' this conflict.	In urban society the major source of conflict arises out of multiple roles in different role sets. A commonly cited extreme example is the Italian catholic communist.

(see Chapter 9, page 240)

(E)	
Simple economy	*Diverse economy*
Most inhabitants in the ideal type of rural society tend to be engaged in one common activity – agriculture.	In urban society the population is engaged in many different productive activities.

Nevertheless, even in towns people have much of their leisure activity in common. Here, of course, the model proves too simple. Further questions arise: What are the differences between a mining town like Ashton and a manufacturing and market town like Banbury? Does a town which combines coal and cotton, for instance, differ from both? Obviously a straight-line continuum is not sufficient. The presence or absence of paid work for women within or outside the home is another set of variables which prevents the continuum from being a single straight line.

RURAL   'URBAN' (less rural)

(F)

Little division of labour   *Extreme differentiation and specialization*

In rural society there is a high percentage of overlapping jobs (generalization), though this applies less to mechanized agricultural areas.

In urban industrial society few jobs overlap, though with automation regeneralization is occurring.

(see Chapter 9, pages 241 and 252–3)

(G)

Mechanical solidarity   *Organic solidarity*

In rural society social solidarity tends to be based on uniformity of individuals.

In urban society social solidarity stems from the diversity and complementarity which has developed with the division of labour.

Durkheim suggested these terms to describe the changes wrought in social life by the development of the division of labour. This development makes the individual dependent on society as the cell is on the body – hence the analogy of the organism. Durkheim's use of it in this way reflects the biology of his but not our time.

(H)

Complexity   *Complication*

Owing to the simplicity of the economy and the comparative lack of the division of labour, together with the multiplicity of role relationships, life in small-scale societies tends to be governed by links between individuals which cut across and reinforce each other.

In larger scale societies, the intricacy of the economy and the division of labour plus the diversity of role relationships results in links between individuals cutting into and even running counter to each other.

This aspect might be, perhaps over-imaginatively, described by saying that for the individual growing into adulthood involvement grows by geometrical progression in rural and arithmetical in urban societies. For the rural individual new social ties are multiplied; the same people, new relationships with them: the urban dweller's are additive; new relationships, new people.

RURAL	'URBAN' (less rural)

(I)

Ascribed status

For the individual in rural society his family origin is the first factor fixing him in a social position, and every action in every sphere modifies his social standing. Status depends on *who* he is and determines how he is treated.

Achieved status

This is also true in urban society, but later in life his occupational role tends to be the primary factor in fixing him in a social position. Status depends on *what* he is and determines with whom he associates.

This is a gross oversimplification for in both models there is considerable interaction between the *who* and the *what*. This is an alternative version of attributional and interactive status.

(J)

Status

Another way of stating (I) above is to say that people in a rural society are treated and expected to behave appropriately to their status, which is outside their control.

Contract

People in an urban society are expected to do what they have agreed to do in a social position they are supposed to have chosen and worked to attain.

If the genealogy of these ideas is traced back we arrive at Sir Henry Maine and his classical statement:

'The word Status may be usefully employed to construct a formula expressing the law of progress thus indicated, which, whatever be its value, seems to me to be sufficiently ascertained. All the forms of Status taken notice of in the Law of Persons were derived from, and to some extent are still coloured by, the powers and privileges anciently residing in the Family. If then we employ Status, agreeably with the usage of the best writers, to signify these personal conditions only, and avoid applying the term to such conditions as are the immediate or remote result of agreement, we may say that the movement of the progressive societies has hitherto been a movement *from Status to Contract*' (Maine, 1946, p. 141) (1861).

(K)

Total status

In rural societies status spreads from situation to situation. A man's status is the same whatever activity he is engaged in.

Partial status

A man's status may be high in some activities and low in others.

RURAL   'URBAN' (less rural)

(L)
Education from status   *Status from education*
Again, in rural society a person's   In urban society a person's social
educational possibilities tend to be   status tends to depend on his edu-
dependent on his social status.   cation.

The point is made by Marshall (see Chapter 10, page 263)

(M)
Role embracement   *Role commitment*
People with an ascribed status in a   People in an urban community
stable rural community tend to   may be merely attached or just
accept their roles unquestioningly   committed to roles. They may
and indeed enthusiastically.   show this by discordant displays
                                   of role distance (see below).

If it is argued that anyone in a given situation is committed by
that situation to playing a particular role, it does not follow
that everyone does it with equal enthusiasm.

Goffman introduces his concept of *role distance* by describing
the behaviour of small boys who are no longer enchanted by
the role of merry-go-round horse rider:

'The image of him that is generated for him by the routine
entailed in his mere participation – his virtual self in the context – is an image from which he apparently withdraws by
actively *manipulating* the situation. Whether this skittish behaviour is intentional or unintentional, sincere or affected, correctly appreciated by the others present or not, it does not
constitute a wedge between the individual and the role,
between doing and being. This "effectively" expressed
pointed separateness between the individual and his putative
role I shall call *role distance*. A shorthand is involved here: the
individual is actually denying not the role but the virtual self
that is implied in the role for all accepting performers. . . . *role
distance* was introduced to refer to actions which effectively con-
vey some disdainful detachment of the performer from a role
he is performing' (Goffman, 1961, pp. 109–10).

Performers may go beyond role distance to rebellion and to
attempts to escape from commitment – individually or collec-
tively; this is role rejection.

(N)
Small mesh, or close-knit, networks   *Large mesh, or loose-knit, networks*
Multiple roles in rural societies   Particular roles in urban societies
result in a dense texture of rela-   result in loose texture of relation-
tionships.   ships.

(see Chapter 9, pages 245–8)

RURAL   'URBAN' (less rural)

(O)
Locals

Rural society may be dominated by influentials who seek to exercise local power in terms of local values.

Cosmopolitans

Locals are still present but in urbanized society another, overlapping, set of influentials is oriented towards the power and values of wider, large-scale, society.

(see Merton's distinction between quantitative and qualitative networks on page 284 above, and also Chapter 6, page 155)

(P)
Low density role texture   *High density role texture*

(see Southall's continuum, Chapter 9, page 248)

(Q)
Economic class – one division among many

In rural society the difference in economic class is one among many differences.

Economic class – dominating social life through the cash nexus

In urban society economic class tends to determine all other differences.

(see the discussion of proletarianization, Chapter 10, page 258)

(R)
Latent function

In rural society social actions tend more often to have unintended consequences, unforeseen by the actors.

Manifest function

In urbanized society things are more often (but by no means always) what they seem. Social action is often aimed at what it appears to be aimed.

(see pages 264–7)

(S)
Relations of conjunction and disjunction

In rural society conflicting groups remain in physical proximity. Conflicts have somehow to be resolved, and open disputes avoided.

Segregation of conflicting groups

In urban society conflicting groups can avoid contact, or, if disputes occur, it is possible either to break contact or not to remake it.

This leads to the relative importance of joking relationships in rural society. In urban society they are both rarer and largely confined to work situations when segregation of conflicting groups is not possible.

RURAL   'URBAN' (less rural)

(T)
Organization by general unanimity   *Organization by voting system*

> This is a rider of (R) since it arises out of the same difficulty in segregating hostile and friendly relationships (cf. Bailey, 1965).

(U)
Conflict and rebellion   *Cleavage and revolution*

> This arises out of (P) and appears at this point only because it is incomprehensible without an understanding of latent function. Manifestly all conflict may seem destructive in whatever situation it occurs.

(V)
Regional focus of life   *Occupational focus of life*

> This change is one of the themes of Durkheim's *Division of Labour* and is at the basis of Watson's discussion of spiralism and the growing interest in the study of the sociology of professions.

(see pages 274–5)

(W)
Integration   *Alienation and estrangement*
In rural society produce from   In urban society the worker meets
labour tends to remain in direct   the produce of his labour as a
relation to the worker.   commodity – estranged from him.

> An interpretation of Marx discussed at the beginning of the chapter, page 276.

(X)
Acceptance of norms and conflict within   *Normlessness, alienation from norms,*
consensus   *or anomie*

(see pages 276–8)

(Y)
The changing pattern of social redundancy

(see pages 278–83)

These twenty-five themes are not exhaustive. To mention only two glaring omissions, I have not discussed in any formal way religious changes or Weber's pattern of traditional/charismatic/rational/bureaucratic leadership. Nor have I tried to apply Parsonian pattern variables.

I hope that these models deepen the understanding of the societies described in Part One. As far as possible the communities were arranged in order from most rural to least rural. Each chapter began with a general description of the area and its economy. It continued to describe ascribed and achieved roles, social class and social status, the sources of conflict and of change and, where possible, 'dramatic' incidents. Each monograph that I have used was of course written for other purposes than this analysis. This means the information needed to describe the community in terms of my problems was not always there. This was as true, alas, of my own *Village on the Border* as of the others.

The analysis of dramatic incident has played a smaller part in the book than I would have liked. We can distinguish two biases – geographical and social anthropological. The geographical has a beautifully set stage but the players never appear; the social anthropological, a well-rehearsed cast and a good play, but the scenery is sometimes sketchy. It will not be difficult for the reader to judge the bias of the original monographs from my chapters.

The analysis of a cycle of dramatic incidents within their historical and geographical setting seems to me to be the way forward for British community studies (for this see Turner, 1957; Goffman, 1959; Stein, 1960, pp. 313 f.; and Frankenberg, 1965).

When this is done we can learn from the descriptive protocol Merton has abstracted from the practice of existing 'functionalist' sociologists (Merton, 1957a, p. 60).

For any incident that we wish to analyse we need to know at least five kinds of factors:

Firstly, from which categories of the total population which could take part are the actual participants drawn? Are they, for example, men or women, high status or low status? How are they related to each other and to others not participating?

Secondly, what are they not doing as a result of this particular activity? Are there other members of the same population otherwise engaged? One might summarize these two points by stressing the importance not only of observing who does what but also who does not do it, and what it is they do not do. Sherlock Holmes's analysis of the case of Silver Blaze is relevant here:

Colonel Ross still wore an expression which showed the poor opinion which he had formed of my companion's ability, but I saw by the Inspector's face that his attention had been keenly aroused.
'You consider that to be important?' he asked.
'Exceedingly so.'
'Is there any other point to which you would wish to draw my attention?'
'To the curious incident of the dog in the night-time.'
'The dog did nothing in the night-time.'
'That was the curious incident,' remarked Sherlock Holmes.

Thirdly, what do those who take part think and feel about their actions?

Fourthly, how is their behaviour expressly related to their reasons for taking part?

Finally, are there any patterns of behaviour involved of which the participants are partially or even not aware but which nevertheless an outside observer can see are essential to the continuation of the activity?

If we apply this scheme briefly to one of the various aspects of behaviour surrounding the Football Club in Glynceiriog, we see that, firstly, the participants in a football committee are drawn from among the men. Not all the men could be involved; there is a class dimension imposed by the nature of the task. They become involved partly out of an interest in football, but also because of relationships of kin and friendship engendered in other situations. Secondly, they chose football at a particular time as against other activities which have existed or will exist again. The reasons for this are analysed in the chapter on Glynceiriog. Thirdly, they aim to promote by their meeting the holding of football matches. They become emotionally committed to this aim and to the aim of keeping the Football Club going as an end in itself. Fourthly, the different motivations, leading to the contradiction between football as fun for local lads, and football to win and gain prestige for club and village, lead also to different and mutually inconsistent actions. Finally, their actions are a resultant of their expressed aims and consequences flowing from their social positions, as men and as workers in an economically declining village economy.

This brief account indicates the social areas from which relevant material is collected. It is not an analysis (for this see, for example, Gluckman, 1958). It indicates the sort of approach to field data that I would like to make in order to test the adequacy or usefulness of my continuum. In practice we do not often have the material to analyse in this way. Failing a description of a series of similar incidents in diverse cultural settings, one is forced to attempt some picture of the totality of each community and to compare these pictures.

As a method of learning about modern Britain this is supplementary and by no means antagonistic to the more orthodox sociological approach of choosing measurements of such things as birth rates, marriage rates, death rates, and the number of houses with piped water and using them as indices.

This latter approach is equivalent to the 'Black Box' method of the engineer who 'gets a lot of information about a transmission unit simply by comparing the signals that go in with the signals that come out. He often calls the unknown unit a "Black Box", and undertakes to determine its performance, by measurements at its input and output terminals, without looking inside' (Walter, 1961, p. 142).

By using models we attempt to see what goes on inside the 'Black Boxes'. But not only is our model inadequate, we also have not got enough Boxes to look in. It is partly in the hope of stimulating people to open more lids that this book has been written. We now have our model. We can make it

... serve as a kind of template, which we hold up against the real thing in order that any discrepancies may stand out more clearly, and guide us towards the making of a better one. We judge a model to be useful, therefore, not merely by its predictive successes, but also by the clarity with which its failures can be interpreted, and lead to its refinement. Only the unexpected yields fresh information; and even this is informative only when we know what to make of it – hence the crucial importance of disciplining our models as far as possible by the structural realities of the system we want to understand. The so called 'Black Box' approach may serve well enough in 'human engineering'; but, especially if we want our models to account for pathological as well as normal conditions, our progress in science is soon halted, if not totally misdirected, unless we work hand in hand with those who lift the lids and peer inside (Mackay, 1962, p. 16).

BIBLIOGRAPHY

ALDERSON, S. (1962). *Britain in the Sixties: Housing*, Penguin Books, Harmondsworth.

ALLCORN, D. H. (1954). *Social Life of Young Men in a London Borough*, Unpublished, Manchester Ph.D.

ARENSBERG, C. M. (1939). *The Irish Countryman. An Anthropological Study*, Macmillan, New York.

ARENSBERG, C. M., and KIMBALL, S. T. (1940). *Family and Community in Ireland*, Peter Smith, London.

BAILEY, F. G. (1965). 'Consensus as a procedure for taking decisions', in *Political Systems and the Distribution of Power*, Monograph 2 of Association of Social Anthropologists, Tavistock Publications, London.

BARNES, J. A. (1954). 'Class and Committees in a Norwegian Island Parish', in *Human Relations*, vol. vii, no. 1, London.

BARNES, J. A. (1959). 'Anthropology after Freud', in *Australian Journal of Philosophy*, vol. xxxvii, pp. 13–27, Sydney.

BARNES, J. A. (1957). 'Land Rights and Kinship in Two Bremnes Hamlets', in *Journal of the Royal Anthropological Institute*, vol. lxxxvii, pt 1, London.

BEER, STAFFORD (1959). *Cybernetics and Management*, English Universities Press, London.

BELL, D. A. (1962). *Intelligent Machines*, Pitman, London.

BENNEY, M. (1947). 'Storm over Stevenage', in *The Changing Nation*, Contact Books Publications, London.

BENNEY, M., and GEISS, P. (1950). 'Social Class and Politics in Greenwich', in *British Journal of Sociology*, vol. i, London.

BIRCH, A. H. (1959). *Small Town Politics*, Oxford University Press, Oxford.

BOTT, ELIZABETH (1955). 'Urban Families: Conjugal Roles and Social Networks', in *Human Relations*, vol. viii, no. 4, London.

BOTT, ELIZABETH (1957). *Family and Social Network*, Tavistock Publications, London.

BRADNEY, P. (1957). 'The Joking Relationship in Industry', in *Human Relations*, vol. x, London.

BRENNAN, T., COONEY, E. W., and POLLINS, H. (1954). *Social Change in South-West Wales*, Watts (The New Thinker's Library), London.

BURNHAM, J. (1945). *The Managerial Revolution*, Penguin Books, Harmondsworth.

BURNS, T. (1961). 'Social Norms and Social Evolution', in *Darwinism and the Study of Society: A Centenary Symposium* (M. Banton, ed.), Tavistock Publications, London.

BURNS, T. (1962). 'The Sociology of Industry', in *Society*, Routledge and Kegan Paul, London.

BURNS, T., and STALKER, G. M. (1961). *The Management of Innovation*, Tavistock Publications, London.

CHERRY, COLIN (1957). *On Human Communication*, M.I.T., New York; Chapman & Hall, London.

COLLISON, P. (1963). *The Cutteslowe Walls*, Faber and Faber, London.

COSER, LEWIS (1956). *The Functions of Social Conflict*, Routledge and Kegan Paul, London.

DAHRENDORF, RALF (1959). *Class and Class Conflict in Industrial Society*, Routledge and Kegan Paul, London.

DAVIES, ELWYN, and REES, ALWYN D. (1960). *Welsh Rural Communities*, University of Wales Press, Cardiff.

DENNIS, N., HENRIQUES, F. M., and SLAUGHTER, C. (1957). *Coal is our Life*, Eyre and Spottiswoode, London.

DENNIS, NORMAN (1961). 'Changes in Function and Leadership Renewal', in *Sociological Review* (N.S.), vol. iv, no. 1, London.

DJILAS, M. (1959). *The New Class*, Thames and Hudson, London.

DOHERTY, LEN (1955). *A Miner's Sons*. Lawrence & Wishart, London.

DONNISON, D. V., and PLOWMAN, D. E. G. (1954). 'The Functions of Local Labour Parties', in *Political Studies, II*, Oxford.

DURANT, RUTH (1959). *Watling: A Survey of Social Life on a New Housing Estate*, P. S. King, London. (See also GLASS)

DURKHEIM, EMILE (1960). *The Division of Labour*, Free Press of Glencoe, Illinois.

EMMETT, ISABEL (1964). *A North Wales Parish*, Routledge and Kegan Paul, London.

ENGELS, F. (1845). *Condition of Working Class in England in 1844*.

FIRTH, R., and DJAMOUR, JUDITH (1956). 'Kinship in South Borough', in *Two Studies of Kinship in London*, Athlone Press, London.

FRANKENBERG, RONALD (1957). *Village on the Border*, Cohen and West, London.

FRANKENBERG, RONALD (1965). 'British Communities: Problems of Synthesis', in *The Social Anthropology of Complex Societies*, Monograph 4 of Association of Social Anthropologists, Tavistock Publications, London.

FREUD, SIGMUND (1960). *Jokes and their Relation to the Unconscious*, Routledge and Kegan Paul, London.

GERTH, H. H., and MILLS, C. W. (Ed.) (1948). *From Max Weber: Essays in Sociology*, Routledge and Kegan Paul, London.

GIRLING, F. K. (1957). 'Joking Relationships in a Scottish Town', in *Man*, 57, July article no. 120, p. 102.

GLASS, RUTH, and FRENKEL, MAUREEN (1946). 'How they Live at Bethnal Green', in *Britain between East and West*, Contact Books, London.

GLASS, RUTH (1955). 'Urban Sociology', in *Current Sociology*, vol. iv, no. 4, UNESCO, Paris. (See also DURANT)

GLUCKMAN, MAX (1954). *Rituals of Rebellion in South-East Africa*, The Frazer Lecture, 1952, Manchester University Press, Manchester.

GLUCKMAN, MAX (1955). *Custom and Conflict in Africa*, Basil Blackwell, Oxford.

GLUCKMAN, MAX, (1958). 'Analysis of a Social Situation in Modern Zululand', in *Rhodes Livingstone Paper*, no. 28, Manchester University Press, Manchester.

GLUCKMAN, MAX, and DEVONS, ELY (1963). *Open Minds and Closed Systems*, Oliver and Boyd, Edinburgh.

GOFFMAN, ERVING (1959). *The Presentation of Self in Everyday Life*, Doubleday (Anchor Books), New York.

GOFFMAN, E. (1961). *Encounters: Two Studies in the Sociology of Interaction*, Charles E. Merrill Books, Ohio.

HENRIQUES, F. M. *See* DENNIS, N., HENRIQUES, F. M., and SLAUGHTER, C.

HODGES, M. W., and SMITH, C. S. (1954). 'The Sheffield Estate', in *Neighbourhood and Community*, Liverpool University Press, Liverpool.

HOMANS, G. C. (1953). 'The Rural Sociology of Mediaeval England', in *Past and Present*, no. 4, London.

HOMANS, G. C. (1962). *Sentiments and Activities*, Routledge and Kegan Paul, London.

JACOBS, JANE (1962). *The Death and Life of Great American Cities*, Jonathan Cape, London; Penguin Books, Harmondsworth, 1965.

JEPHCOTT, PEARL, SEAR, NANCY, and SMITH, JOHN H. (1962). *Married Women Working*, Allen and Unwin, London.

JEFFERYS, MARGOT (1964). 'Londoners in Hertfordshire', in *London: Aspects of Change*, Centre for Urban Studies, Report no. 3, London.

JENKINS, CLIVE (1959). *Power at the Top*, MacGibbon and Kee, London.

KLEIN, J. (1965). *Samples from English Cultures*, Routledge and Kegan Paul, London.

KUPER, LEO (1953). *Living in Towns*, Cresset Press, London.

LAING, R. D. (1960). *The Divided Self*, Tavistock Press, London; Penguin Books, Harmondsworth, 1965.

LAING, R. D. (1961). *The Self and Others*, Tavistock Press, London.

LAING, R. D. (1962). 'Series and Nexus' in *New Left Review*, no. 15, London.

LANCASTER, LORRAINE (1961). 'Some Conceptual Problems in the Study of Family and Kin Ties in the British Isles', in *British Journal of Sociology*, vol. xii, no. 4, London.

LASLETT, P. (1956). *Philosophy, Politics and Society*, Basil Blackwell, Oxford.

LITTLEJOHN, J. (1964). *Westrigg: The Sociology of a Cheviot Parish*, Routledge and Kegan Paul, London.

LLOYD, A. L. (1952). *Come All ye Bold Miners*, Lawrence and Wishart, London.

LOUDON, J. B. (1961). 'Kinship and Crisis in South Wales', in *British Journal of Sociology*, vol. xii, no. 4, London.

LUPTON, T., and MITCHELL, D. (1954). 'The Liverpool Estate', in *Neighbourhood and Community*, Liverpool University Press, Liverpool.

MAINE, SIR HENRY (1946). *Ancient Law*, Oxford University Press (World Classics), London.

MARRIS, PETER (1958). *Widows and their Families*, Routledge and Kegan Paul, London.

MARSHALL, T. H. (1950). *Citizenship and Social Class*, Cambridge University Press, Cambridge.

MARX, K. (1954). *The Eighteenth Brumaire of Louis Bonaparte (1852)*, Foreign Publishing House, Moscow.

MARX, K., and ENGELS, F. (1957). *The Holy Family*, Lawrence and Wishart, London.

MACIVER, R. M., and PAGE, C. H. (1961). *Society: An Introductory Analysis*, Macmillan (Papermac), London.

MACKAY, D. (1962). 'What is Cybernetics?', in *Discovery*, vol. xxiii, no. 10, London.

MERTON, R. K. (1957a). *Social Theory and Social Structure*, Free Press of Glencoe, Illinois.

MERTON, R. K. (1957b). 'The Role-set: Problems in Sociological Theory', in *British Journal of Sociology*, vol. vii, no. 2, London.

M'GONIGLE, G. C. M., and KIRBY, J. (1936). *Poverty and Public Health*, Gollancz, London.

MILLS, C. WRIGHT (1962). *The Marxists*, Dell, New York; Penguin Books, Harmondsworth, 1963.

MITCHELL, C. DUNCAN, LUPTON, THOMAS, HODGES, M. W., and SMITH, CYRIL S. (1954). *Neighbourhood and Community*, Liverpool University Press, Liverpool.

MOGEY, J. M. (1956). *Family and Neighbourhood: two studies in Oxford*, Oxford University Press, Oxford.

MORRIS, WILLIAM (1963). *News from Nowhere*, in *William Morris: Selected Writings and Designs* (ed. Asa Briggs), Penguin Books, Harmondsworth.

NADEL, S. F. (1957). *The Theory of Social Structure*, Cohen and West, London.

PLANNING (1947). 'Watling Revisited', *Planning*, XIV, p. 270.

PLOWMAN, D. E. G., MINCHINGTON, W. E., and STACEY, M. (1962). 'Local Social Status in England and Wales', in *Sociological Review*, vol. X, no. 2, London.

RADCLIFFE-BROWN, A. R. (1952). *Structure and Function in Primitive Society*, Cohen and West, London.

REES, ALWYN D. (1950). *Life in a Welsh Countryside*, University of Wales Press, Cardiff.

ROBB, J. H. (1954). *Working-Class Anti-Semite*, Tavistock Publications, London.

ROSSER, K., and HARRIS, C. C. (1961). 'Relationships through Marriage in a Welsh Urban Area', in *Sociological Review* (N.S.), vol. X, p. 243, London.

SAVILLE, JOHN (1957). *Rural Depopulation in England and Wales, 1851–1951*, Routledge and Kegan Paul, London.

SIGAL, CLANCY (1962). *Weekend in Dinlock*, Penguin Books, Harmondsworth.

SLAUGHTER, C. *See* DENNIS, N., HENRIQUES, F. M., and SLAUGHTER, C.

SOUTHALL, AIDAN (1959). 'An Operational Theory of Role', in *Human Relations*, vol.XII, no. 1, London.

SPENCER, J. (1964). *Stress and Release in an Urban Estate*, Tavistock Publications, London.

SPROTT, W. J. H. (1958). *Human Groups*, Penguin Books, Harmondsworth.

STACEY, MARGARET (1960). *Tradition and Change: A Study of Banbury*, Oxford University Press, Oxford.

STEIN, MAURICE R. (1960). *The Eclipse of Community*, Princeton University Press, Princeton.

TOWNSEND, PETER (1957). *The Family Life of Old People*, Routledge and Kegan Paul, London; Penguin Books, Harmondsworth, 1963.

TROTSKY, L. (1957). *Literature and Revolution*, Doubleday (Anchor Books), New York.

TURNER, V. W. (1957). *Schism and Continuity in an African Society*, Manchester University Press, Manchester.

TUSTIN, ARNOLD (1953). *The Mechanism of Economic Systems*, Heinemann, London.

WALTER, W. GREY (1961). *The Living Brain*, Penguin Books, Harmondsworth.

WATSON, W. (1964). 'Social Mobility and Social Class in Industrial Communities', in *Closed Systems and Open Minds*, Oliver and Boyd, Edinburgh.

WILLIAMS, W. M. (1956). *The Sociology of an English Village: Gosforth*, Routledge and Kegan Paul, London.

WILLIAMS, W. M. (1958). *The Country Craftsman*, Routledge and Kegan Paul, London.

WILLIAMS, W. M. (1963). *A West Country Village: Ashworthy*, Routledge and Kegan Paul, London.

WILLMOTT, P. (1963). *The Evolution of a Community: a Study of Dagenham after Forty Years*, Routledge and Kegan Paul, London.

WILLMOTT, P., and YOUNG, M. (1960). *Family and Class in a London Suburb*, Routledge and Kegan Paul, London.

WILSON, R. (1963). *Difficult Housing Estates*, Tavistock Publications, London.

YOUNG, M., and WILLMOTT, P. (1957). *Family and Kinship in East London*, Routledge and Kegan Paul, London; Penguin Books, Harmondsworth, 1962.

INDEX

INDEX

ABERYSTWYTH, University College, 65, 71
affines, 188
agricultural areas, 252
agricultural contractors, 252
Alderson, S., 197
alienation, 118–19, 232, 276 ff., 292
Allcorn, D., 126
analogue and analogy distinguished, 279 ff.
Anglicanism, association of Conservatism with, 151, 153, 165
anglicized gentry in Wales, 58–9
anomie, 200, 277 ff., 292
Arensberg, C., 10, 12, 25–44, 244, 265
Arsenal Football Club, 102, 144
ascription, 49
Ashton, 14, 114–39, 158, 237, 243, 250, 257, 265, 269, 287; description of family criticized, 244 ff.
aspirants: in Gosforth, 74; in Banbury, 160
association, 286 *see also* voluntary associations
associations, occupational and professional, 274
automation, 253
avoidance, 266; in Bethnal Green, 188

Bacon, Francis, 260
Bailey, F. G., 292
Banbury, 14, 72, 140–1, 154–73, 237–8, 242, 245–7, 249–50, 253, 261–6, 268, 273, 276, 280, 284, 287
Barnes, J. A., 10, 18–19, 53, 243–4, 267 n., 272, 278, 281–2
Barton, 225–33
Bavelas, A., 283

Benney, Mark, 153, 199
Beer, Stafford, 283
Bell, D. A., 279–80
Belloc, Hilaire, 11
Bethnal Green, 15, 141–2, 174–95, 198, 200, 225–33, 237–8, 251, 271
bingo, 136, 214
Birch, A. H., 10, 14, 140–54
'Black Box' method, 295–6
borough council, 147, 176
borough councillors, 147 ff.
Bott, Elizabeth, 19, 53, 92, 244–8, 274, 282, 284
Bott's hypothesis, 19, 92, 189, 245–8, 253
Bowen, E. G., 45
Bradney, P., 267 n.
Brennan, T., 124
Bremnes, 243
Bristol Social Project, 200, 233
burgesses, 73, 146, 161, 247, 260 ff., 268, 274
Burnham, J., 258, 260
Burns, T., 283; and Stalker, G. M., 267
bus service in Glynceiriog, 88

Cambridge University, 71, 75
Capital (Marx), 255
capitalists, 73, 261
carnival in Glynceiriog, 106 ff.
cash nexus, 154, 258, 291
category, 18
Cavendish, 253
Cecil, 253
Ceiriog, 89
Ceiriog Valley, 88
Celtic Football Club, 102
Cherry, C., 21, 280 ff.
Chesterton, G. K., 11
Chirk, 87
christenings, 191

MORE ABOUT PENGUINS
AND PELICANS

Penguinews, which appears every month, contains details of all the new books issued by Penguins as they are published. From time to time it is supplemented by *Penguins in Print* – a complete list of all our available titles. (There are well over three thousand of these.)

A specimen copy of *Penguinews* will be sent to you free on request, and you can become a subscriber for the price of the postage – 4s. for a year's issues (including the complete lists) if you live in the United Kingdom, or 8s. if you live elsewhere. Just write to Dept EP, Penguin Books Ltd, Harmondsworth, Middlesex, enclosing a cheque or postal order, and your name will be added to the mailing list.

Some other books published by Penguins are described on the following pages.

Note: *Penguinews* and *Penguins in Print* are not available in the U.S.A. or Canada

PATTERNS OF INFANT CARE IN AN URBAN COMMUNITY

John and Elizabeth Newson

Mother, doctor, health visitor, midwife – Spock, Gibbens, de Kok, Truby King . . . the amount of theory and advice, both professional and amateur, that showers on the young mother is equalled only by its astonishing contradictions. And indeed, as the authors quietly point out, 'very few theories of child rearing have been subjected to the inconvenience of being reconciled with the empirical evidence'.

What then is that evidence? Armed with common sense and a tape recorder, the authors interviewed in their Nottingham homes over 700 mothers of one-year-old children to find out, quite simply, how babies are brought up in England today. The result is a landmark in our knowledge of childhood. The answers parents gave on subjects ranging from breast- and bottle-feeding, sleeping, eating, and punishment, to father's place in the home and class differences in infant rearing make a fascinating and, on occasions, hilarious kaleidoscope of life with young children.

'Wonderfully human piece of sociological research' – *Yorkshire Post*

Also available

FOUR YEARS OLD IN AN
URBAN COMMUNITY

THE FAMILY AND MARRIAGE
IN BRITAIN

Ronald Fletcher

Pulpits, rostrums, and the more deeply entrenched batteries of press and radio still resound with lamentations about the decay of family life in Britain. Our modern society, it is said, is in a condition of moral decline. Immorality, divorce, delinquency stalk the land . . . or so we are told.

Is there any truth in this murky picture? Or, on the contrary, do the facts quietly pronounce that the family is more stable and more secure today than ever before in our history? For history, when we survey all classes impartially, is largely a long tale of poverty, drudgery, desertion, and vagrancy.

In his systematic analysis of the subject, a sociologist discusses the extraordinary strength and resilience of the family group in the face of rapid and radical social changes and provides answers to questions which are often anxiously posed to us: Are married women working in industry neglecting their children? Has discipline within the family utterly disappeared, or is today's relationship between parents and children a new and fuller one? Have teenagers really so much money to spend? And, even if this is so, is it so deplorable?

The book arrives at encouraging conclusions and discusses the basis for further improvements.

'. . . deserves to be compulsory reading in all schools and theological colleges' – *Times Literary Supplement*

'. . . the fullest outline there has yet been of the social history of the family in Britain' – Michael Young, *New Statesman*

THE FAMILY LIFE OF OLD PEOPLE

Peter Townsend

How do old people spend their declining years? Whom do they see and how often? How many of them are miserable or poverty-stricken?

Peter Townsend, one of the first members of the now famous Institute of Community Studies, gives here the first detailed answer to these questions by presenting, sympathetically and vividly, the results of his interviews with more than two hundred old people in Bethnal Green. He finds that the lot of the aged is perhaps less hard than it once was, and that family obligations are taken more seriously than before. But he also gives first-hand evidence of many shortcomings in the present social system, and these urgently call for attention.

'Superb study. . . . Here is a work of social science which is also, in its way, a work of art. . . . A novelist's eye for detail and power of description is nicely balanced by a passion for scientific analysis' – R. H. S. Crossman in the *New Statesman*

FAMILY AND KINSHIP IN
EAST LONDON

Peter Willmott and Michael Young

The two authors of this most human of surveys are sociologists.

They spent three years on 'field work' in Bethnal Green and on a new housing estate in Essex. The result is a fascinating study, made during a period of extensive rehousing, of family and community ties and the pull of the 'wider family' on working-class people.

'Probably not only the fullest, but virtually the only account of working-class family relationships in any country. The general reader will find it full of meat and free of jargon' – *New Statesman*

'This shrewd – and in places extremely amusing – book combines warmth of feeling with careful sociological method' – *Financial Times*

'Observant, tactful, sympathetic, humorous . . . I really feel that nobody who wants to know how our society is changing can afford not to read Young and Willmott' – Kingsley Amis in the *Spectator*

'No short account can do justice to this book, charmingly written, engaging, absorbing' – *British Medical Journal*

Obviously there have been changes in the two districts under survey during the last few years. This edition in Pelicans, with its fresh introduction and simplified appendix, is justified by the standing the report has achieved as a modern classic of sociology.